kamera
BOOKS

DISCARDED

kamerabooks.com

BY THE SAME AUTHOR

Hitchcock and the Making of Marnie, Revised Edition (2013)
Alfred Hitchcock's Movie Making Masterclass (2013)

TONY LEE MORAL

THE MAKING OF HITCHCOCK'S
THE BIRDS

kamera
BOOKS

First published in 2013 by Kamera Books
an imprint of Oldcastle Books,
PO Box 394, Harpenden, Herts, AL5 1XJ

Copyright © Tony Lee Moral 2013
Series Editor: Hannah Patterson

A CIP catalogue record for this book is available from the British Library.

ISBN
978-1-84243-954-8 (print)
978-1-84243-955-5 (epub)
978-1-84243-956-2 (kindle)
978-1-84344-155-7 (pdf)

2 4 6 8 10 9 7 5 3 1

Typeset in Univers by Elsa Mathern
Printed and bound in the Czech Republic

For Kitty

ACKNOWLEDGEMENTS

Thank you to Patricia Hitchcock O'Connell, Taylor & Faust and Steven Kravitz of the Alfred J Hitchcock Trust for giving me permission to quote and publish from the Hitchcock Collection at the Margaret Herrick Library in Beverly Hills, and also to the library staff, especially Barbara Hall and Kristine Krueger.

Letters, certain information regarding *The Birds* and *Marnie*, and other material from Evan Hunter's memoir *Me and Hitch* have been used with the kind permission of the author's estate ©1997. I also thank Anita Hunter and sons Richard and Mark for sharing memories of Evan, husband and father. Thank you to the Howard Gottlieb Archival Research Centre at Boston University and Dragica Hunter for giving me access to Evan's files.

Of the actors who worked on *The Birds*, I thank Rod Taylor, Tippi Hedren, Veronica Cartwright and Shari Lee Bernath for sharing their memories. From the Hitchcock crew I thank Robert Boyle, Jim Brown, John 'Bud' Cardos, Helen Colvig, Virginia Darcy, Hilton Green, Norman Lloyd, Marshall Schlom, Ted Parvin, Harold Michelson and Rita Riggs.

I owe a big debt of gratitude to Peter Bogdanovich who so generously allowed me to publish excerpts of his series of interviews with Alfred Hitchcock. Thanks also to Laura Truffaut for kindly allowing me to quote from her father François Truffaut's seminal book on Hitchcock. I am also very grateful to Bill Krohn for generously sharing his roundtable discussion on *The Birds* involving Bob Boyle, Albert Whitlock and Harold Michelson, originally published in *Cahiers du Cinéma* in 1982.

The Edith Head sketches were provided with the kind permission of the Motion Picture & Television Fund, and thank you to Valeri Furst for allowing me to publish from the Claudia Franck collection of letters at the Academy.

Permission to access and quote from *The Birds* files in the Penguin archives was granted by Penguin Books Ltd. Biographical information on Daphne du Maurier was provided by her son Kits Browning, biographer Richard Kelly and Ann Willmore. Thank you to Stephen Vagg who so generously shared his research on Rod Taylor. For those crew members who have long passed away, I have relied on interviews from Kyle Counts' excellent article on the making of the film, which appeared in *Cinefantastique* in 1980.

For the chapter on Remi Gassmann I thank the University of California, Irvine. I also thank MOMA and its past and present employees Eileen Bowser, Joanne Koch, Jo-Ann Ordano, Jim Watters, Charles Silver and Laurence Kardish, for help with Hitchcock's proposed screening of *The Birds*. Thanks to Universal Studios, both the marketing and legal departments, for their support in this project.

Other people I owe thanks to include Craig Barron, Emily Boyle, Nora Brown, Dave DeCaro, Syd Dutton, Irene Halsman, Steve Hare, Don Iwerks, Robert Kapsis, Daniel Raim, Bill Taylor, Lillian Michelson, Norma Shepherd, Steven C Smith, Marc Wanamaker and June Whitlock. Also the residents of Bodega Bay including John Bressie, Glenice Carpenter, Paul & Karen Bianchi, Leah Taylor and Michael Fahmie.

Permission to publish the photographs in the book was provided by the Chichester Partnership, Penguin, Richard Hunter, James O Mason, the Estate of Robert F Boyle, Deutsches Filminstitut, June Whitlock, Lillian Michelson, Norma Shepherd, the Alfred J Hitchcock Trust, Jerry Ohlinger Movie Materials Store, the Motion Picture & Television Fund, Universal Pictures/TCD and the Bison Archives/Marc Wanamaker. For the author's photo op with Brann the Raven, I thank Marie Mann Photography, Jo Sarsby Management and Lloyd & Rose Buck.

CONTENTS

INTRODUCTION

In his most ambitious, technically challenging and innovative film, *The Birds*, Alfred Hitchcock achieved what had never before been seen on screen. When the film was released in the spring of 1963, it proved to be his most avant-garde, modernist and experimental film, utilising pioneering special effects, audacious in its conception and execution. Hitchcock himself said, 'I suppose that *The Birds* is probably the most prodigious job ever done.'[1]

What are the birds supposed to signify? Hitchcock said that his film was about complacency, reflecting the fact that ordinary men and women go about their lives seemingly unaware that catastrophe may be imminent. The film was conceived during the period of the Cuban Missile Crisis, the Bel Air Fire, the Missouri Floods and the overshadowing threat of nuclear war. Hitchcock said he wanted to stir people out of their apathy and make them sit up and take notice of the danger all around them.

Today, on our volatile and disaster-prone planet, it's all too easy to identify with *The Birds*. Violence can erupt in our lives at any moment. We are threatened by hurricanes, earthquakes, tsunamis, storms and floods, yet the vast majority of us are oblivious to these dangers. Neither can man-made threats such as global warming and climate change be clearly divisible from natural dangers, and, in an age of international terrorism and worldwide terror networks, *The Birds* takes on a new significance. Most of us take nature for granted until we are faced with sudden loss and the eruption of chaos, as symbolised by the birds. The characters in Hitchcock's film represent those people who face up to disaster and reveal their inner strength, discovering in the process just how fragile and precious human relationships are.

2013 marks the 50th anniversary of *The Birds*. The film was made at the pinnacle of Hitchcock's career, following the monumental success of *Psycho* in 1960. Hitchcock felt he was entering his 'golden age'; he was brimming with ideas and was at his creative peak. *The Birds* would surely be his crowning achievement. It would take almost two years, from 1961 to 1963, to bring *The Birds* to the screen and its production exactly spanned the tumultuous background of JFK's presidency, which witnessed the Bay of Pigs invasion, the rise of Fidel Castro and Kennedy's own demise. Like *Psycho*, which prefigured the random murders and assassinations and unrest of the 1960s, *The Birds* was ahead of its time, triggering the cycle of horror, man-versus-nature, and disaster films.

With *The Birds*, Hitchcock achieved the dream of any director by assembling his repertory group, who were an expert group of professionals. They spent weeks working together on location in Bodega Bay and then back at Universal Studios in LA. This A-list production team was led by art designer Robert Boyle, who was able to bring together different special-effects departments in Hollywood to convey the impression of thousands of birds attacking mankind. Hitchcock was also inventive in other ways, experimenting with a pioneering electronic score with avant-garde German composers Oskar Sala and Remi Gassmann, as well as working with bird trainer Ray Berwick to orchestrate sequences that could only be achieved using trained birds and so was at the vanguard of an early form of natural history filmmaking. He also took on the demanding task of casting an untested model-actress, Tippi Hedren, in the lead role and in her first motion picture.

Hitchcock was audacious to make a film that was technologically ahead of its time. *The Birds* is an example of what can be achieved with real birds and live action using sodium travelling mattes. With 371 special-effects shots, *The Birds* at the time held the record for the complexity and number of special effects, and inspired future effects-driven films. In 1977, *Star Wars* would achieve a level of perfection using CGI and 350 effects shots, but those men who worked on the film knew in the backs of their minds that it had been done before on *The Birds*.[2] Such a revolutionary concept also led Hitchcock to improvise while he was filming, something not generally in his nature, which led to spontaneous results on screen, as well as the evolution of the film's ending while it was still being made.

The Making of Hitchcock's The Birds is the first book-length treatment on the production of this modernist masterpiece. The film has one of the most well-documented and fascinating histories of any Hitchcock production, which makes it ripe for analysis. As well as the memos and files held at the Margaret Herrick Library, there are numerous interviews with screenwriter Evan Hunter on record, including his own memoirs *Me and Hitch* (1997), as well as transcripts and oral histories recording the testimony of Hitchcock's art department, especially Bob Boyle, Albert Whitlock and Harold Michelson. Together they detail Hitchcock's creative process in shaping the screenplay and working with his design team to realise his vision. It shows the process by which ideas are created and executed on screen.

This book uses unpublished material from the Alfred Hitchcock Collection, Edith Head files, Peggy Robertson papers and production designer Robert Boyle's artwork, all held at the Margaret Herrick Library at the Academy of Motion Picture Arts and Sciences. This archival research is supplemented with interviews with the cast and crew, including Rod Taylor, Tippi Hedren, Veronica Cartwright, Shari Lee Bernath and the production team – Robert Boyle, Jim Brown, Albert Whitlock, Harold Michelson, Jim 'Bud' Cardos, Ted Parvin, Virginia Darcy and Rita Riggs. Some of the interviews were also conducted during my research for my two other books on Hitchcock, *Hitchcock and the Making of Marnie* and *Alfred Hitchcock's Movie Making Masterclass*.

I had the pleasure of speaking to Evan Hunter, the screenwriter, over a four-year period, and collected valuable information on *The Birds*. My work also enabled me to talk to Joseph Stefano and Jay Presson Allen, the writers working with Hitchcock immediately before and after the making of *The Birds*, which gave an insight into the screenwriting process. In addition, I interviewed Hitchcock's top-flight art directing team for *Marnie* and *The Birds* and, for the first time, excerpts from those rewarding conversations are published, with revelations about Hitchcock's creative process and thinking.

Chapters 1 and 2 deal with the genesis of the short story by the English author Daphne du Maurier, and how Hitchcock and his screenwriter, Evan

Hunter, deviated from the concept to come up with an original story. Chapter 3 focuses on biographies of the cast and crew, and Chapters 4–6 on the production and filming. Chapters 7 and 8 deal with the innovative electronic music and postproduction.

Hitchcock also felt that respectability eluded him, and Chapter 9 investigates the elaborate marketing campaign for *The Birds*, which, in the aftermath of *Psycho*, was the most expensive, prestigious and involved. His flirtations with the Museum of Modern Art in New York went astray, and this chapter uncovers the reasoning behind the cancelled premiere of *The Birds* at the museum and how Hitchcock had more luck with the French at the Cannes Film Festival.

2012 was deemed the year of Hitchcock. *Vertigo* was ranked the number-one film of all time in a poll of international critics for *Sight & Sound* magazine. But it was also the year that Alfred Hitchcock was accused in the popular media of sexual harassment and physical abuse, following a television dramatisation co-produced by the BBC and HBO. Many of Hitchcock's co-workers objected to this unflattering image portrayed of their director, friend and mentor during the production of *The Birds*, which they believed to be misleading and inaccurate. They were willing to be recorded on tape and, for the first time, share their views and memories in this book.

The Birds often ranks as one of the public's favourite Hitchcock films and, together with *Psycho*, is certainly one of the most memorable. In 2013, 50 years after the making of *The Birds*, the film has been lovingly restored and released in a Blu-ray version. Once again, the question is posed: what would happen if thousands of birds should mass overhead and suddenly swoop down to attack mankind?

NOTES

1   Alfred Hitchcock, 'It's a Bird, It's a Plane, It's *The Birds!*', *Hitchcock on Hitchcock*, University of California Press, 1997, p. 315
2   Bill Krohn, 'Roundtable on *The Birds*', *Cahiers du Cinéma*, 1982

DAPHNE DU MAURIER'S *THE BIRDS*

'Nat listened to the tearing sound of splintering wood, and wondered how many millions of years of memory were stored in those little brains, behind the stabbing beaks, the piercing eyes, now giving them the instinct to destroy mankind with all the daft precision of machines' – The Birds

DAPHNE DU MAURIER

The author of the short story *The Birds* was Daphne du Maurier. She was born in 1907 in London, the daughter of Sir Gerald du Maurier, an actor and theatre manager, and the granddaughter of George du Maurier, an artist for *Punch* magazine and author of the novel *Trilby*. After being educated at home with her sisters and then in Paris, Daphne began writing short stories and articles as a teenager. Her father's and grandfather's connections gave Daphne's literary career an initial boost, and an uncle published one of her short stories in his magazine *The Bystander* when she was still a teenager. In 1931, at the age of 24, her first novel *The Loving Spirit* was published, a family saga of four generations of Cornish ship builders and mariners.

By the summer of 1932, Daphne had married Major Frederick 'Boy' Browning, a military officer 11 years her senior who had sought her out after admiring her work. Daphne and Browning spent considerable time apart as he rose to the rank of Lieutenant-Colonel in 1936 and commanded the British First Airborne Division during World War II. When he eventually left the army he become comptroller and treasurer to the household of Princess Elizabeth and the Duke of Edinburgh, later becoming treasurer of the office of the Duke until his retirement.[1] During this time Daphne (Figure 1) continued to write. In 1936 she wrote *Jamaica Inn*, a story about pirates and smuggling on the Cornish coast which soon brought her critical acclaim and financial success. Daphne quickly became known as a creator of atmosphere and her novels and short stories often had a twist of the macabre. She hired a nanny to help take care of their son, Christian 'Kits' Browning, and two daughters, Tessa and Flavia.

In 1943 the Browning family moved to Cornwall, into a house named Menabilly, a seventeenth-century mansion. Daphne had seen the house with its ivy-clad walls on one of her earlier trips to Cornwall and had fallen in love with it. Owls hooted in the surrounding woods at night where a path led down to the coast. The owner leased the house to Daphne and she restored it from neglect, spending the next 25 years living there. Daphne's most successful novel was directly inspired by Menabilly, as the house became the model for Manderley, the setting for *Rebecca* (1938). Suddenly Daphne became one of the most popular authors of the day, as *Rebecca* was printed in 39 English impressions over the next 20 years and translated into more than 20 languages. Although Daphne went on to write 17 other books, including *Frenchman's Creek*, *The King's General*, *My Cousin Rachel*, *Mary Anne* and *The Scapegoat*, all republished by Penguin in 1962, *Rebecca* and *Jamaica Inn* remained her two most popular novels, inspired by her Cornish home and Cornwall. The surrounding landscape was also to be the inspiration for her next most popular work. However, it wasn't a novel, but a short story, and its genesis came about one late autumn morning.

INSPIRATION FOR *THE BIRDS*

Every day Daphne would walk from Menabilly down to Polridmouth beach along a well-worn country path (Figure 3). Over the coastline and rugged hills of Cornwall, birds wheel and dive, eking out an existence in the harsh landscape. Here nature is unforgiving, gale-force winds blow, coastal fog creeps in and temperatures plummet.

On her walk down to Polridmouth beach, Daphne would pass Menabilly Barton farm, where farmer Tommy Dunn often ploughed his fields in a tractor. One autumnal day, above Dunn's head, she saw a flock of seagulls. Daphne was immediately struck by the clamour of the gulls following the tractor. As it 'traced its path up and down the western hills, the figure of the farmer silhouetted on the driving-seat, the whole machine and the man upon it would be lost momentarily in the great cloud of wheeling, crying birds'.[2]

Tommy Dunn died at the age of 85 in 2010 and the farm was passed on to his son Richard. He described his father as 'a local character, a farmer who kept grass and corn which he ploughed. Winters are harsh and the farm is exposed to tremendous gales, wet thaws and coastal fogs. During these storms, the seagulls come in and land until they pass.'[3] A similar line was later used in Hitchcock's film when Melanie Daniels asks the pet-store owner in San Francisco what brings the seagulls in and the answer is a 'storm at sea'.

'Daphne saw my dad ploughing in the autumn and the birds were wheeling above him,' Richard remembers. 'If you do any cultivation work you get earthworms ploughed up – and the seagulls come from the sea looking for the worms. That's what Daphne saw, the seagulls dive-bombing for worms. She was watching and imagined them to be more aggressive than they really are – of course, they are a proper pain in the towns now, and more so than in the country.' So the gulls were in fact looking for earthworms that had been exposed by the plough, and they were circling above Dunn's head. But, from Daphne's perspective, they looked like they were attacking him.

An idea began to form in her mind. She always had a macabre imagination and began to think how awful it would be if the birds started attacking people and took over. Returning to Menabilly, she conceived the idea for *The Birds* and wrote the story quickly, in two months during the winter of 1951, on a typewriter in a hut at the end of her lawn. There was nothing inside the hut except a desk and chair and the window had a view of the sea.

Local farmer Tommy Dunn became the inspiration for Nat Hocken, the central character, and the story developed into his struggle to protect his family from the birds, set against a wild Cornish coastline where gales sweep across the stark hills, fields and isolated farmhouses. Because of the rural characters and the harsh landscape, the story has an elemental tone, where nature is omnipresent.

Daphne's story covers only a few days in the life of the family and examines what would happen if animals traditionally regarded as symbols of peace and freedom began to ruthlessly attack humans. There is an element of claustrophobia in the work, which is similar to other stories such as *Rebecca*, which features the heroine isolated at Manderley. The story opens with a cold bitter wind from the Arctic that has turned the autumnal English countryside into a place of winter cold. With the wind come the birds, restless, but strangely silent, different species flocking together in great numbers. More than usual this year, tenant farmer Nat remarks to his employer, who shrugs off the birds' numbers, as well as their increasing boldness. Nat awakens in the middle of the night to a tapping at the window, first by one bird, and then by half a dozen of them which attack him.

The tension and horror quickens as Nat's family suffers several vicious attacks by flocks of swarming birds, seemingly bent on destruction.[4] When writing, Daphne didn't have Hitchcock in mind, because she never had that sort of commercial mindset. She wrote what she wanted to write about and didn't think it was a project that would interest Hitchcock. She had been very disappointed with the film adaptation of *Jamaica Inn* (1939) but liked *Rebecca* (1940), mainly because of David O Selznick's involvement. And, at the end of filming, the original script for that film had been sent to her.

'My mother's and Hitchcock's paths never crossed because she lived in Cornwall, and he lived in California,' explains Daphne's son Kits Browning.[5] 'But he knew my grandfather from the London theatre.' Although Hitchcock and Daphne never met, Hitch did know her father, Gerald du Maurier, socially and had worked with him on a film called *Lord Camber's Ladies* in 1932.

Both Hitchcock and Daphne shared something else in common. They were both animal lovers and kept dogs. In Daphne's case she kept West Highland terriers and Hitchcock owned a pair of Sealyham terriers, a rare Welsh breed. He named them Geoffrey and Stanley and they made a cameo appearance at the beginning of *The Birds* when Hitchcock walks out of the pet shop. He loved his dogs and they would go everywhere with him. They would ride in the car, with Hitchcock's wife Alma driving, and Hitchcock also brought them to his office every day. As Alma drove, Geoffrey would bark at the back of the car. 'Quiet Geoffrey!' Alma would say. 'If you were driving you wouldn't bark so loud.'

For Daphne, her love of nature extended to birds, especially small birds. 'She had a great affection for all wild things,' remembers Kits. 'One time I discovered a seagull with a broken wing. I was only 14 at the time, and I went and told my mother and father. My father shot it to put it out of its misery – which was quite horrifying for me. It was the first time I saw a seagull in such a state and, after the shooting, all you see is a whole shower of white feathers everywhere.'

Daphne was very against animal cruelty, a sensibility she also shared with Hitchcock. There are a couple of sentences towards the end of *The Birds* that hint at the abuse man has inflicted over millennia and how nature would take its revenge: 'Nat listened to the tearing sound of splintering wood, and wondered how many millions of years of memory were stored in those little brains, behind the stabbing beaks, the piercing eyes, now giving them the instinct to destroy mankind with all the daft precision of machines.' The words suggest hidden and pent-up emotions stored in the brains of the birds over millions of years. Later, Hitchcock seized upon this analogy, and man's complacency, when writing his trailer for the film, which is expanded on in Chapter 9 of this book.

As well as nature taking revenge upon man, other readings of *The Birds* have been put forward. In the 1950s, the Cold War was at the forefront of people's minds and some reviewers have detected an undercurrent in Daphne's writing. The story presents an unrelenting portrait of terror and a compelling analogy of the atmosphere of fear generated in America and Europe during the Cold War. Asked about this, Kits Browning believes that his mother was more concerned with the psychology and physics of nature, such as the turning of the tides, than with anything political. Nat, for example, discovers that the birds time their attacks in conjunction with the tides, at six-hour intervals, and he uses this information to board the house up between attacks.

The story in *The Birds* has also been compared to the air raids that devastated Britain during World War II. Indeed, the du Maurier family did have direct experience of the air raids that bombed Plymouth where the family lived. Kits remembers going into the cellar when the raids began, and admits that his mother does draw analogies in the short story, such as battening down the hatches. 'He lights his last cigarette, switches on the silent wireless and waits' – so the story ends. Hitchcock may have picked up on these analogies when adapting it.

In his review of *The Birds*, Daphne du Maurier biographer Richard Kelly, writing for *Twayne's English Authors Series Online*, picks up on the claustrophobia of the air raid shelters: 'By limiting the focus of her story upon Nat Hocken and his family, du Maurier manages to convey the effect of a believable claustrophobic nightmare'. This sense of claustrophobia is heightened by the story's references to the bombing raids Britain endured during World War II and the paranoid atmosphere created by the threat of nuclear holocaust during the middle of the twentieth century.[6]

FIRST PUBLICATION OF *THE BIRDS*

The Birds was first published in cloth in a 1952 short story collection entitled *The Apple Tree* by Victor Gollancz publishers. Other stories in the compilation included *Monte Verita*, *The Apple Tree*, *The Little Photographer*, *Kiss Me Again Stranger* and *The Old Man*. There is a supernatural element in many of these stories, especially in *The Apple Tree*, *The Little Photographer* and *Kiss Me Again Stranger*. In addition, the long mystery story *Monte Verita* recalls the mood of *Rebecca*.

The Birds was printed in the US in the October 1952 issue of *Good Housekeeping*, and *The Apple Tree* was republished in the US as a collection entitled *Kiss Me Again Stranger* on 5 March 1953 by the publisher Doubleday & Company. Fortunately for Daphne, it was also selected as one of the short stories in an Alfred Hitchcock anthology, and this is how it caught Hitchcock's attention.

THE MASTER CALLS

In the summer of 1960, Alfred Hitchcock and his wife Alma were basking in the success of *Psycho*. This low-budget horror thriller, made for $800,000 and filmed with his TV crew, had quickly brought in $14 million. Hitchcock himself received $7 million in profits (Figure 5).

Never one prone to feelings of complacency, Hitchcock was looking for a suitable property for his next film, something to top *Psycho* and befitting of his reputation as the 'Master of Suspense'. Under consideration was an adaptation of the English author Winston Graham's novel *Marnie*, about a frigid kleptomaniac who is blackmailed into marriage by a man she robs.

Hitchcock hoped that it would be a suitable plot to lure Grace Kelly out of retirement, since she had abandoned Hollywood to become the Princess of Monaco.

While reading a copy of one of the short story collections published under the *Alfred Hitchcock Presents* banner, Hitchcock found what he was looking for. In 1957, publishers Simon & Schuster had approached him about compiling a book of short stories to be branded with the title of his popular television series *Alfred Hitchcock Presents*. Other publishers were keen to get involved, including Random House, Dell and Davis Publications, and more than 100 mystery books followed in the next 40 years.

It was a Dell paperback called *Alfred Hitchcock Presents Fourteen of My Favourites in Suspense*, published in 1959 by Random House New York, that caught Hitchcock's attention. The collection was promoted as, 'Here are 14 of the finest terror tales by the most diabolically effective writers who it has ever been Alfred Hitchcock's perverse pleasure to present.' Among the 14 short stories was Daphne du Maurier's *The Birds*.

Hitchcock, of course, was familiar with du Maurier's work. His adaptation of *Jamaica Inn* in 1939 had also been his last British film before moving to California, with a plot focusing on orphaned Mary (Maureen O'Hara), who goes to live with her aunt Patience on the coast where she and her husband Joss run the Jamaica Inn. But the inn is actually the headquarters of a band of smugglers who cause ships to wreck so that they can steal the cargo and kill the survivors. Mary saves the life of one of the gang members who is actually an undercover officer (Robert Newton). Together they fight to bring down the ring of smugglers and their protector, Sir Humphrey Pengallon, played by Charles Laughton.

Laughton co-produced the film and clashed with Hitchcock, changing his vision. Hitchcock would often say there were three things impossible to direct – children, animals and Charlie Laughton. Daphne du Maurier herself was not happy with the project and considered withholding the film rights to *Rebecca* when she heard that Hitchcock was involved. Critics, too, were not fans of the film, although it was a success at the box office.

As Daphne didn't like the adaptation of *Jamaica Inn*, it was Selznick's involvement that persuaded her to sell the film rights to *Rebecca*. Selznick is quoted as saying, 'I've paid a lot of money for this book and we are going to stick to the story.' And it was also Selznick who persuaded Hitchcock to adapt *Rebecca* as his first American movie, which prompted his move to

America. Daphne adored *Rebecca*, especially that they remained true to the original. She liked Joan Fontaine and Laurence Olivier and the fact that Hitchcock told George Sanders not to act. She loved the gossip behind the making of the film and of Olivier being so bored with Joan Fontaine and wanting Vivien Leigh for the part. Daphne's response was that 'Vivien Leigh would have sacked Mrs Danvers on day one'.

When Hitchcock read *The Birds* – and he confessed to having done so only once – he saw a film rich in cinematic possibilities, as well as both a creative and technical challenge. In the 1930s, he briefly considered filming H G Wells's *The War of the Worlds*. Marshall Schlom, Hitchcock's script supervisor on *Psycho*, recently remarked, 'After *Psycho*, Hitchcock didn't have the same ability to find material, and it was difficult to find material that he liked.'[7] Schlom took over Peggy Robertson's job as script supervisor when she was elevated to story editor in Hitchcock's office. A large, heavy woman, Peggy quickly became Hitch's right hand, was very loyal to him and was liked and respected by everyone.

'Hitchcock showed me the novella of *The Birds* when we were filming *Psycho*,' continues Schlom. 'And he indicated that he was looking for his next project. He felt that the story was the most important part of making films. If the script wasn't right, the story wasn't right. He'd say to actors, "I've written it, if it's in the script I'm going to shoot it, or if it's not in the script, I'm not going to shoot it."'

Patricia Hitchcock agrees. 'After my father made *Psycho*, which was such a big success, he was, as usual, having his major trouble, which was looking for a story. Everybody expected so much, you know. It was very hard to find stories, and he finally did find *The Birds*... And, at the same time, he wasn't sure if it would make a full-length movie.'[8]

Still unsure of the cinematic possibilities and story potential of the Daphne du Maurier novella, Hitchcock nonetheless set about acquiring the film rights at the beginning of 1961. Daphne had agents in both London and Los Angeles and it wasn't long before they picked up his interest in *The Birds*. A telegram from Dick Patterson, a Paramount rep in London, was sent to Hitchcock on 20 January 1961 at his home in Bellagio Road in Bel Air: 'Daphne represented Hollywood by Swanson who earlier this week smelled West Coast interest in Birds stop Agent here insists checking Swanie before negotiation stop Would appreciate it if your staff could feign abysmal stupidity for few days if Swanie contacts.'

Hitchcock replied in a cable to Patterson in London on 24 January: 'Notified that a TV producer Joseph Naar has made an offer for Birds stop Swanson who is local agent advised Ned Brown of this but added the offer did not approach the $75,000 he had been asking stop Do not know whether this offer has been transferred to London but anxious you make sure we do not lose this even if you have to go up to $50,000.'

So anxious was Hitchcock to secure the property, therefore, that he was prepared to go up to the sum of $50,000. But there was another stumbling block. An agreement already existed between CBS television and *Kiss Me Again Stranger*, the anthology of short stories printed in America in 1953, which included *The Birds*. In a memo about the agreement on 9 February, Hitchcock queried whether a film had ever been made based on the property, and, if not, whether the rights had reverted back to the author.

On 24 February, Samuel Taylor, Hitch's attorney from Taylor & Winokur, a law firm in San Francisco, wrote a letter advising him not to purchase *The Birds* because of a copyright existing between CBS television and the author.[9] But Hitch was persistent and further investigation revealed that CBS had not, as yet, produced any programme based on *The Birds*, as per the agreement made on 15 September 1958. That was good news for Hitchcock, because it meant that all rights which CBS had acquired under that agreement had automatically reverted back to Daphne. 'I was sitting in my office,' remembers producer Norman Lloyd, 'and Hitch came in and they had called him and told him that the deal had gone through for *The Birds* and he took the call in my office and he said, "Yes, buy it."' So Hitchcock instructed his agents to buy the story, and the sale was negotiated with Daphne's agent, Hettie Hilton at Curtis Brown. The story rights were sold for $25,000. What Daphne didn't know was that Hitchcock was so keen to secure *The Birds* that he would have been prepared to pay double that amount.

In addition, a cheque for $1,500 was made out to CBS, care of Charles Scott Television, for release regarding the 1959 agreement quit claim, which was then redrafted and signed. Shamley Productions, under the aegis of Alfred Hitchcock, finally acquired the film rights to *The Birds* in June of 1961.

And then something happened that meant Hitchcock's calendar for the next two years was about to become very full. He read of real-life bird attacks taking place across the US, and this timeliness created within him a sense of urgency as regards transferring *The Birds* to the screen.

THE REAL-LIFE BIRD INVASIONS

In the spring and summer of 1960 and 1961, while Hitchcock was busy acquiring the story rights to *The Birds*, a couple of real-life incidents occurred which helped him decide to adapt the story as his follow-up to *Psycho*. These reports of unusual bird behaviour in the media would help shape the final film.

In April 1960, in La Jolla, California, there was an unusual migration of Vaux swifts. These birds are a small type of swift native to North America and South America, which pass through southern California twice a year, migrating between a winter range in the tropics and a breeding range in the Pacific Northwest. Originally they used hollow trees for their communal roosting sites. However, with increased urbanisation, chimneys became a crucial habitat for these small birds along the West Coast, and it became quite common to see hundreds of them entering unused chimneys around dusk.

The spring of 1960 was particularly cold, with a windy April seeming to have concentrated them near the coast. On 26 April, following a great period of unsettled weather, vast numbers of Vaux swifts were seen in southwestern California. At the home of Mr and Mrs Mosher in La Jolla, without any warning, the swifts started to enter their chimney and an estimated total of 1,000 swifts caused pandemonium as they dashed from one side of the room to the other and entered every room or closet wherever a door or passageway was open. One of the birds became entangled in Mrs Mosher's hair. The great mass of the birds flew into the curtains and draperies, badly damaging them, knocking over delicate bric-a-brac, which crashed to the floor. The worst and most revolting damage was done by the pungent excrement the birds deposited on the carpets, furniture, bedspreads, pillows and books. Matters became so serious that, by 8pm, the police were called.

The details of this story were later used by Hitchcock and his screenwriter, Evan Hunter, as inspiration for the attack of the sparrows inside the Brenner house. In particular, the idea of birds becoming entangled in Mrs Mosher's hair was an image Hitchcock would replicate with Lydia Brenner. When hiring the actress Jessica Tandy, who was to play Lydia, Hitchcock instructed that a wig be made for her using mechanical birds. Other details gleaned from the La Jolla attacks were the broken china and other damage caused inside the house, and the idea of burning the bodies of the birds in a bonfire, in a scene that was later deleted.

But it was a bigger incident that prompted Hitchcock to move forward with *The Birds*, and this took place in Santa Cruz on Friday 18 August 1961. Santa Cruz is a seaside town in Monterey Bay, very near to where Hitchcock and Alma had a second home in Scotts Valley, where they would spend their weekends. A massive flight of sooty shearwaters, fresh from feeding on anchovies, collided with shoreside structures from Pleasure Point to Rio del Mar during the night.

Residents were awakened about 3am by the sound of birds slamming against their homes. Calls from alarmed residents jammed police and sheriff's office telephone switchboards as the birds, blinded by heavy night fog, flew into rooftops, poles and other obstructions. Many sooty shearwaters landed on highways and in streets, blocking traffic. This incident was also mentioned in the finished film when the residents of Bodega Bay are discussing why the birds are attacking and it's left to Mrs Bundy, the ornithologist, to tell the tale.

The *Santa Cruz Sentinel* ran a front-page headline, 'Seabird Invasion Hits Coastal Town'. So swift was Hitchcock to react to the news that the report ended, 'A phone call came to the *Sentinel* from mystery thriller producer Alfred Hitchcock from Hollywood, requesting that a *Sentinel* be sent to him. He has a home in the Santa Cruz mountains.'[10]

In other parts of America and in England, further reports of bird invasions also shaped the story. Barn swallows dive bombed newsboys on their paper rounds in a sleepy Midwestern town. In the port of Dover, England, thousands of gulls left their homes on the white cliffs and were invading the town, soiling cars and even hitting pedestrians. And during filming in Bodega, farmers visited Hitchcock and told how crows had attacked their newborn lambs and plucked their eyes out. This detail was later used for the attack on Dan Fawcett.

REPRINT OF *THE BIRDS*

With the film due to be released in 1963, Daphne's publishers were keen to capitalise on the marketing. As early as October 1961, after Hitchcock had acquired the rights to *The Birds* and was writing the screenplay, Victor Gollancz, publishers of the original hardback, began publicising the film tie-in. They approached Penguin Books, who were in the habit of celebrating the work of particular authors, usually those who had a history with Penguin, initially by a grand gesture known as the 'Penguin Million'. In 1946, Penguin did this for George Bernard Shaw, to celebrate his 90th birthday. Ten Shaw Penguins, mostly collections of plays, but also *The Black Girl in Search of God*, were issued in editions of 100,000 books – so a million Shaw books simultaneously flooded the market. It was reported that the entire million sold out in six and a half weeks, due to a combination of two irresistible brands: Shaw, an indestructible British national institution, and Penguin, an ubiquitous brand that was widely read during the Second World War.

Other Penguin Millions were also made for H G Wells, Evelyn Waugh, Agatha Christie and various crime writers. In 1962, the same was done for Daphne du Maurier, with the reprint of seven of her titles in smaller editions. So, with the release of the Hitchcock film, it was hoped that a tie-in with Daphne's short story collection, *The Birds*, would achieve the same success as had some of the previously feted authors.

Hilary Rubinstein at Victor Gollancz, the original publishers of *The Apple Tree*, wrote a letter on 27 October 1961 to Anthony Godwin of Penguin Books, publishers of all Daphne du Maurier's paperbacks:

Dear Tony,

You may have heard that Hitchcock is at present making a film from Daphne du Maurier's short story *The Birds*. It occurs to me that you might like to consider publishing the volume of stories in which *The Birds* appears – *The Apple Tree* – presumably calling the book *The Birds and Other Short Stories*. I know that you have quite a lot of Daphne's on your plate, but it does seem to me that the Hitchcock film tie-up is probably an opportunity not to be missed. And *The Birds* is, in my opinion, one of the great short stories of our time, and certainly among the best things that Daphne has done. Our file copy of *The Apple Tree* is enclosed.

Yours ever,
Hilary

By 11 December 1961, a contract for *The Apple Tree* was agreed, and by 27 December the contract had been signed and returned with only one slight alteration – the addition of a paperback. A deal memo dated 13 December shows that Daphne was given an advance of £750 for *The Apple Tree*, half of which was payable on 31 December 1961 and half on publication, with royalties of 7.5% for the Penguin edition.

On 10 April 1962, Patricia Siddall from the editorial department at Penguin wrote to Hilary Rubinstein at Victor Gollancz: 'The publication date of *The Birds and Other Stories* by Daphne du Maurier has been fixed for May, and I am sending you six copies for the author and your files. I should be grateful if you could ask the author if she would sign the seventh copy in the package and return it to Sir Allen Lane.' Lane was the man who had started Penguin, and du Maurier wrote on the cover, 'Sir Allen Lane with sincere good wishes Daphne du Maurier.'

Penguin were at this time coming to the end of a long and painful transition from typographic covers into more visually striking illustrated covers. Within a year, Alan Aldridge would be designing psychedelic and surrealist Penguin covers, winning over a whole new generation of readers and alienating whole generations of older authors.

A new, visually exciting cover was required for the reprint of *The Birds*, one which would resonate with the glossy image of Hitchcock's films. So Penguin employed the services of the American artist Virgil Burnett as the cover illustrator. One of his many jobs was providing cover art for those very recognisable Penguin paperbacks. He had designed the cover for the Penguin paperback of H G Wells' *War of the Worlds* and was part of the inspiration for the art design of the 1953 film adaptation. Burnett had created the previous du Mauriers, and he designed the cover of *The Birds* to keep the idea of the books as a 'set' – presumably to help boost the sales of the other titles. The cover picture (Figure 2) depicts the savagery of nature and the plumage of an eagle's head, which upon closer inspection is revealed to be a mosaic of hundreds of birds. The back cover blurb mentions and also capitalises on the forthcoming Hitchcock film.

Penguin tied it in after the film came out and, in accordance with Hilary Rubinstein's suggestion, decided to use the umbrella title of *The Birds and Other Stories* for the collection rather than *The Apple Tree*, which Gollancz had used for the hardback. According to Kits Browning, when the film *The Birds* was released, the publishers didn't do much of a publicity blitz as they weren't very commercially minded in 1962. The rights of the book were managed by Curtis Brown.

A Penguin Fiction press release dated February 1963 stated that 'Daphne du Maurier has a rare gift for dragging up those irrational fears that lurk just behind the smooth plaster of existence. In *The Birds* she somehow lends probability to an impossibility which is nearly too fearful to imagine. United by mad hatred, the birds – the gulls, finches, crows and tits – have combined to wipe out humanity. This strange haunting fantasy has been chosen by Alfred Hitchcock for the making of a horror film.'

When *The Birds* was reprinted, the following reviews appeared in the UK: 'Original and startling,' wrote *The Sunday Times*. 'Anyone starting this book under the impression that he may sleepily relax is in for a shock... continually provokes both pity and terror,' said the *Observer*. The *Times Literary Supplement* added that '*The Birds* would have pleased H G Wells... The title story... describes with skilful understatement the growth of an obsession.'

But there was to be one final twist to the tale. In 1936, a Cornish author called Frank Baker had written a novel called *The Birds*. After the film was released, he felt that his story had been plagiarised and wrote to Daphne du Maurier to say so, enclosing a copy of his work. Daphne was sympathetic to Baker and wrote a courteous letter back.

On 6 May 1963, Baker also wrote to Hitchcock's office, detailing that his novel was 'a long horror story, telling of the destruction of the human race by vast hordes of savage birds, who descended in malefic force upon London, and tore it to chaos'. But he found Hitchcock's office to be less sympathetic then Daphne. On 29 May, Joseph Dubin, head of the legal department at Universal Studios, wrote to Baker saying that an examination of Daphne du Maurier's work, as well as a viewing of the film, 'will clearly demonstrate to you that there is no actionable similarity between your work, the work of Miss du Maurier or the photoplay'. But Baker disagreed and on 4 June wrote back saying, 'The information which you give me does not clearly demonstrate, as you say, that there is no actionable similarity between my novel *The Birds* and Mr Hitchcock's photoplay.' He concluded by saying that his lawyers would be in contact but, in the end, was unable to file a suit for any claims of plagiarism.

A first-rate screenwriter was now needed to translate Daphne du Maurier's interior short story into a glossy two-hour thriller. In doing so, Hitchcock turned to a novelist to develop the sketchy characters, but the writing of the screenplay would turn out to be a lengthy process that would not be resolved well into the filming.

NOTES

1   Interview with Ann Willmore, Bookends of Fowey, 16 January 2013, Cornwall
2   Daphne du Maurier, *The Birds And Other Stories*, Penguin, 1963
3   Interview with Richard Dunn, 18 June 2012, Cornwall
4   Du Maurier's *The Birds*
5   Interview with Kits Browning, 16 June 2012, Cornwall
6   Interview with Richard Kelly, 26 October 2012, Nashville, Tennessee
7   Interview with Marshall Schlom, 30 November 2012, LA
8   Patricia Hitchcock in *All About the Birds*, Universal DVD, 2000
9   Margaret Herrick Library, *The Birds* folder
10 *Santa Cruz Sentinel*, 18 August 1961, p. 1

WRITING *THE BIRDS*

*'I think Hitch may have known when he hired me that he would need
something more than birds coming down a Cornish chimney for a
feature-length film. I guess I was hired to be the plot man'*
— Evan Hunter

Adapting *The Birds* into a film with all the trademarks of an exciting Hitchcock
thriller was to prove a monumental feat. Aside from the technical challenges
imposed by the screenplay, how do you, for example, show thousands of
birds attacking man? There was also the problem of the original characters
in Daphne du Maurier's short story. The Cornish farmer, Nat Hocken, and
his wife and two kids were hardly the glamorous types audiences were
accustomed to watching in a sophisticated Hitchcock thriller, far removed
from Cary Grant in *North by Northwest* or Grace Kelly in *To Catch A Thief*.

Hitchcock first approached Joseph Stefano, the screenwriter of
Psycho, to write a treatment. Joseph was a hip young writer from New
York who was in therapy at the time he wrote *Psycho*. '[Hitchcock] liked
things that were a little bit kinky,' Joseph would later recall. 'I told him
that I had problems with my own mother, and this fascinated Hitchcock.'[1]
Joseph ended up writing a superb screenplay for *Psycho*, managing to
generate great sympathy for the central character, Norman Bates, who

has a dual personality. But after *Psycho* came the huge expectations to top it. 'I think he felt that, in a strange way, he'd made a movie that trapped him inside his TV persona,' Joseph reflected. 'I don't know this to be a fact, but it's just how I see it. Audiences loved him on the TV show, and they wanted more *Psycho*. So he decided to make *The Birds*, but I felt that the birds themselves were not a good enough killer.'

Joseph still had a two-picture deal with Hitchcock, but when it came to writing *The Birds*, he had trouble mustering any enthusiasm for the subject matter. 'I told him that I wasn't interested in the story and wasn't interested in birds.' That upset Hitchcock more than a little and he must have taken those words to heart because Joseph didn't hear from Hitchcock again until it was time to adapt *Marnie*.

After Joseph turned down *The Birds*, Hitchcock looked for other writers to adapt Daphne du Maurier's short story. He approached James Kennaway who had written the novel *Tunes of Glory*. Kennaway said to him, 'Well, I see this film being done in one way, you should never see a bird.' That ruled out Kennaway straightaway. Hitchcock also asked Ray Bradbury to write the screenplay, but he was already working on a script for Hitchcock's own television series and Hitch didn't want to steal Bradbury away from his producer, Joan Harrison. He also interviewed Wendell Mayes, who had written Otto Preminger and Billy Wilder films, but he didn't feel right, either.

So Hitchcock turned to Joan Harrison and Norman Lloyd, the producers of his television series, for writer recommendations. The television series was being filmed at Revue Studios at 3900 Lankershim Blvd, Universal City. In 1958, the Music Corporation of America (MCA) had bought the Universal Studios film lot from Universal Pictures and renamed it, along with their television production company, Revue Studios. Here the television series *Alfred Hitchcock Presents* was filmed.

Harrison and Lloyd recommended New York novelist Evan Hunter who had already written one of the half-hour episodes from the series, 'Appointment at Eleven', which was based on a story by Robert Turner. Evan was a successful writer of short stories and novels, including *The Blackboard Jungle* and *Last Summer*. He also wrote under the pseudonym Ed McBain for the *87th Precinct* novels, a series about a police department in New York, which he had started in 1958. Evan first met Hitchcock when the director filmed *First Offense*, a story of Evan's featured on *Alfred Hitchcock Presents*.

'Evan was a good writer,' remembers Norman Lloyd, and Hitchcock was always a champion of good writing.[2] 'I came across those *87th Precinct* books of his and we tried to buy them. Manning O'Conner, who was vice president at MCA, wanted to come up with another series. I found Evan's books and I brought them to Manning. I remember him reading this story at lunch. He sat there and read it. We weren't able to buy it, I don't know why. But it was bought by another producer on the lot. Either we were too late or they wanted too much money. Hitch was very careful about money and Manning was more careful. I think Hubbell Robinson, an executive, bought it.' The *87th Precinct* series aired on ABC during the 1961–62 season.

'Appointment at Eleven' may have been on Hitchcock's mind when he asked Joan Harrison to call Scott Meredith, Evan's agent, for *The Birds*, because the Daphne du Maurier story involved just two main characters in a cottage. '"Appointment at Eleven" was a difficult thing to do because the story was just an internal monologue,' said Evan in retrospect. 'The kid thinking about the electrocution of his father at 11 o'clock. I transferred it to a bar where the kid's drunk and trying to get drunker and is obnoxious, and I put in all the bystanders in the bar to open it up.'[3]

When he got the call from his agent, Evan 'thought at first that Joan Harrison wanted me to adapt another story for Hitch's television show. But, no, it seemed Hitch had purchased motion-picture rights to a Daphne du Maurier novella entitled *The Birds*, and he wanted me to write the screenplay for the movie he planned to make from it. I told my agent I would have to read the story before I decided.' In truth, Evan would have done it even if it were about two pigeons in Central Park, so thrilled was he to be offered the chance to work with Hitchcock on a feature film.

Evan also asked his agent, 'Why me?' Later, he asked Hitchcock that same question. 'Actually, I think Hitch may have known when he hired me that he would need something more than birds coming down a Cornish chimney for a feature-length film. I guess I was hired to be the plot man.'[4] Hitchcock later confided to François Truffaut why he decided to hire Evan: 'The reason I chose to have Evan Hunter is because the average script writer (is) not strictly a creative person. He's a technician who shapes and orders material in the form. Now, when you have a short story and you need expansion, then it's necessary to get a creative writer who can write characters.'[5]

After telling his agent he'd like to have a shot at writing *The Birds*, the very next day Evan received a call from Hitchcock. 'The first thing he said was that he never wanted to work in Britain again, and certainly did not wish to use as his lead characters an inarticulate farmer and his dreary wife.' Matte artist and friend of Hitchcock Albert Whitlock later confirmed this, saying that Hitchcock disliked the rain, mudflats, and greyness of the Thames estuary in Kent, which he associated with filming in Britain, and had no real desire to do so again.[6]

Evan was also told to forget the story entirely; that the only elements they would retain would be the title and the idea of birds attacking humans. He discussed various plot ideas with Hitchcock over the phone before leaving his home in Pound Ridge, New York in mid September 1961 to meet with the director.

In those days, screenwriters were required to do their actual writing on the West Coast. Hitchcock remarked that he was contemptuous of New York writers who worked in the film medium for money, 'writers who come out from NY, they get a job at Metro for no special assignment, and they say, "What do you want me to write?" There are many writers from the theatre who come out in the winter for three months, and I know them to have a standard contract for that purpose... One of the problems I have is to find a writer to enjoy the fantasy that I enjoy – that's the hardest thing in America.' He was hoping that Evan would enjoy the fantasy along with him.

Today a writer can work wherever he wishes, so long as he delivers the script on time. But in the early 1960s the protocol of the studio system was still being honoured, and when a writer was hired he was handed a typewriter, a ream of paper, a secretary, and an office. 'I told him at once that I could not possibly write in a studio office,' said Evan. Hitchcock acquiesced, agreeing that he could do the screenwriting within LA, but that the pre-writing discussions would have to take place in his office at Paramount. It was agreed that Evan would fly out that weekend, get temporarily settled in a local hotel, and begin work on Monday 18 September. 'Bring some ideas,' Hitchcock said.[7]

EVAN ARRIVES IN LA

So, with ideas in hand, and excited to be working with the famed director, Evan flew from New York to LA on Saturday 16 September 1961. He was to start work at 9am on Monday morning and was first introduced to the two most important women in Hitchcock's office: Suzanne Gauthier, Hitch's personal secretary, and Peggy Robertson, story editor and all-round 'Girl Friday'. Evan signed a minimum-term, seven-week contract to write *The Birds*, for the sum of $5,000 a week, and was advised by Hitchcock that, as it might turn into a three-to-four-month assignment, he should plan on bringing his wife, Anita, and their three sons to California. In the end, Evan worked on the script for a period of 11 weeks from Monday 18 September until Friday 10 November 1961.

At that time, Hitchcock's Paramount offices were on Marathon Street, behind Melrose in Hollywood. As Evan recalled, Hitchcock felt he was entering his Golden Age and that *The Birds* would be his greatest achievement. 'I entered Hitch's creative life when he was looking for a respectability which he felt had eluded him,' said Evan. 'He told me he was at the peak of his career, and that he was brimming with ideas and thinking of future projects all the time.' Evan remembered being in his office on the first day and complimenting Hitchcock on the various awards lining the corridors. Hitch nodded and said, 'Always a bridesmaid never a bride.' He was referring to the fact that he had never received an Academy Award.[8]

It was a phrase he would use with many of his writers, as Jay Presson Allen would later testify, saying, 'How many times would I hear that a day?'[9] Hitchcock had been nominated five times as best director for *Rebecca* (1940), *Lifeboat* (1944), *Spellbound* (1945), *Rear Window* (1954) and *Psycho* (1960), but lost on every occasion. He later confided to Evan that he chose a famous novelist to write the screenplay for *The Birds* because he wanted to garner the critical respect and recognition that he felt had so far passed him by.

'Tell me the story so far' – this is what Hitchcock said to Evan every morning after they had drunk their coffee. During these discussions, Hitch would sit back in a black-leather wingback chair, dressed in a dark-blue suit, white shirt and black tie, hands folded over his belly. Hitchcock was very repetitive in his habits and would go over the story again and again. Evan would tell him the story to date, ending with wherever they had left off the afternoon before. In the beginning, of course, there was no story to tell.

In the first couple of days, Hitchcock dismissed two ideas that Evan had brought with him from New York. The first idea was to add a murder mystery to the basic premise of birds attacking humans, but Hitchcock felt this would detract from the real story he wanted to tell. The second revolved around a new school teacher who provokes the scorn of the locals when unexplained bird attacks start shortly after her arrival in town. Of the two ideas, what remained was the concept of a woman coming to a strange town, which is attacked by birds shortly after her arrival, but Hitchcock did not want an unglamorous school teacher for the lead. He wanted someone like... 'Well, Grace, of course. But she's in Monaco, isn't she? Being a princess.'

Both Hitchcock and Evan had no doubt in their minds that the lead character should be female, because they firmly believed that women fear birds psychologically more than men do. And it seemed to Evan that a society woman would be a good fit. 'And Cary for the man, of course, whoever or whatever the character may turn out to be,' continued Hitchcock. 'But why should I give Cary 50 per cent of the movie? The only stars in this movie are the birds and me... and you, of course, Evan.'

During that first week in mid September, Evan went for a stroll one lunchtime around the studio and suddenly came up with an idea. Why not start the film as a light screwball comedy that gradually turns into horror and terror? He mentioned the idea to Hitchcock who, always relishing contrast in his films – the autumnal beauty of New England disguising the scent of death in *The Trouble With Harry* (1955); the daylight opening of *Frenzy* (1972), with its light music, concealing a grotesque murder – immediately liked it.

'The opening of *The Birds* is an attempt to suggest the normal, complacent, everyday life in San Francisco,' explained Evan. 'The idea appealed to him at once. I think he saw in it a challenge equal to the one the birds themselves presented. I think, too, that he saw in it a way of combining his vaunted sense of humour with the calculated horror he had used to great effect in *Psycho*.' As Hitchcock later said, 'That was one of the things I made up my mind to avoid in *The Birds*. I deliberately started off with light, ordinary, inconsequential behaviour'. In other 'catastrophe' films, such as *On the Beach* (1959), he had noticed that the personal stories were never really part of the film.

That latter half of September and early part of October were spent just talking about the screenplay. Every day, from 9am to 5pm, Hitchcock and Evan just talked and talked. These discussions were often followed by dinner and brandies at Hitchcock's home in Bel Air. Hitchcock enjoyed Evan's company, as he was a very likeable and charming guy, bright, attractive and literate, and Hitchcock was an attentive and appreciative audience, as well as being an astute critic. This pattern was repeated with other writers that Hitchcock liked, notably Jay Presson Allen who followed Evan as the screenwriter on *Marnie*. As Hitchcock said, 'Certain writers one works with want to work every hour of the day, they are very facile. I'm not that way. Let's lay off for several hours, let's play. And then get down to it again, you see.'[10]

Hitchcock and Evan spent a great deal of time on the central romance. 'We spent a lot of time trying to figure out who "the girl" was going to be – that's Hollywood talk: "the girl"; it ain't my talk – and "the boy",' said Evan.[11] The "girl" came from Hitchcock's tendency to call the heroine that from the silent films. Evan was reminded of the old screwball comedies of the 1940s, at the centre of which was always a madcap society woman. And a lawyer is the very notion of solidity and stolidity, so it seemed that a lawyer would be a good type also.

The story wasn't entirely fictitious, though, and was often based on fact. 'I remember Hitch showing me a lot of newspaper articles about unexplained bird attacks as a reminder that these things do happen, so we weren't dealing entirely with fantasy,' said Evan, referring to the La Jolla and Santa Cruz articles, copies of which are in the Evan Hunter collection at Boston University.[12]

Hitchcock's idea to take nice, average people and put them in extraordinary situations was one he had been developing in his films ever since *Young and Innocent* (1935). '*The Birds* starts out like an average story, boy and girl meeting, she's on the make for him, very well to do,' said Hitch. 'Lighter but, out of the lightness, there are the two developments in *The Birds*, a light beginning and she walks into a very Oedipal situation, and the schoolteacher carrying the torch for him, but the mother beat her to it. This girl, who is a fly by night, a playgirl, comes up against reality. And the mother stiffens. So you have quite a situation and this is before the birds are gradually coming and taking over.'

Of the numerous special effects that would be needed, Hitchcock told Evan not to worry about them as the technical department would take care of the challenges. This gave Evan free rein to let his imagination run wild. 'Nothing would be too difficult to shoot, he assured me,' recalled Evan. 'Hence, scenes like the gull swooping down on the gas station attendant and the following fire and havoc, I never again gave a thought to the technical problems that might lie ahead. I understood there were plenty.'

MOVING THE FAMILY TO LA

After all the talking, the actual screenwriting began in October of that year after Evan decided to move his family out to the West Coast. At the time, Evan was married to Anita, an attractive, 29-year-old, russet-haired lady with green eyes, 'a welcome smile and a smart New York Jewish Girl sense of humour' as he described her in his memoirs.[13] Evan and Anita had met at Hunter College in New York where Evan majored in English and theatre studies and Anita in English and some psychology. They were married in 1949 and had three sons, Ted, who was 11, and twins Richard and Mark, who were 9 years old in 1961.

'Evan wanted me and the family to come with him to California,' remembers Anita (Figure 6). 'We had done other stints when he would commute to New York, and fly back from the coast, but that didn't work well for everyone.'[14] So they rented a house in the Brentwood neighbourhood of LA during the fall of 1961, and their sons enrolled in the local Bellagio Road elementary school.

'My father suddenly announced to us that we were going to live in California,' remembers Richard Hunter. 'Maybe because he was feeling the pressure to keep the family together or maybe it was to broaden our experiences.'[15] It was a difficult adjustment for the boys, who were used to walking to school from their Pound Ridge home in New York, to suddenly being driven everywhere in LA.

As mentioned above, Hitchcock had first met Anita and Evan a couple of years earlier, in 1959, when one of Evan's short stories, *First Offense*, was being filmed for *Alfred Hitchcock Presents*. He had taken an immediate liking to Anita, showing her around the set and introducing her to all the crew. That liking was rekindled when Anita moved to California in 1961. 'I think Hitchcock had a crush on my mother,' says Richard. 'She was attractive and intelligent and Hitch was very fond of her.'

When Evan left for the studio for work in the mornings, every day without fail Hitchcock would call Anita to find out how she was. 'He would talk for hours, I didn't know what to make of it,' remembers Anita. 'Somehow he knew the precise time that Evan left the house for the studio in the morning, and he would ring shortly after that. It was like having your dad call you. He would ask, "How are you, my dear? What are you going to do today?" I was a mom, and a wife, and I wondered why Hitchcock would show such interest in me. Maybe he was looking for another daughter.'

Anita was two years younger than Hitchcock's own daughter, Patricia, and, like her, had three children, though Anita had three boys as opposed to Pat's three girls. Hitchcock also invited the Hunters twice a week for dinner at his house, even showing them the wine cellar. Anita once touched one of the bottles to examine the label and disturbed the sediment, much to Hitchcock's dismay.

He also took them to Chasen's restaurant on a Friday night, where they sat at a conspicuous table. 'I learnt to adore English sole,' remembers Anita, which was specially flown in from Britain at Hitchcock's request. Anita recalls that Alma was 'a quiet woman, very devoted, very pleasant, kind of reserved and very interested in her family and daughter'.

Hitchcock's monopolisation of the Hunters was seemingly benign but it did take on an air of possessiveness, as Evan and Anita both remembered. 'We hardly had any time for our own lives,' said Evan. In amongst all the socialising, Evan still found time to write the script over the next 10 weeks, with little interference from Hitchcock. When he wasn't at the studio, Evan typed on a portable Smith-Corona typewriter in a small bedroom of his rented house. Hitchcock just let him get on with the task at hand, and never once did he ask Anita how the screenplay was coming along, or even talk about it to Evan when they were out socially.

By Thursday 12 October, almost a month after Evan had started work on *The Birds*, Hitchcock had written a 26-page story memo based on the screenplay. By 28 October, he had produced even more story notes. In an early draft, it is the character of Annie, not Melanie, who faces the wrath of the birds in the attic, on page 171, scene 758: 'We have to be very careful here to work out exactly why Annie goes into the room and closes the door to prevent the birds getting out. I would like to discuss this whole scene from 758 until 774.'

'Hitchcock was very good on suspense and very good on detail,' remembered Evan. 'He would say how long has [Melanie] been in Bodega Bay now? I would say, I don't know, two days? And he would say, "Has she called her father? No, don't you think she should call her father and tell him where she is?"'.

On 8 November, more story notes followed. An early scene where Melanie goes to her father's office at a San Francisco newspaper was discussed and later dropped. In scene 28, page 10, Daniels says 'Why do daughters have to grow up?' because he has lipstick on his face after Melanie kisses him. Hitchcock's comment was, 'Wouldn't he have been used to lipstick from the age of 14 or 15?' On page 52 of the script, Hitchcock wrote, 'When Annie says, "I mix a pretty good Tom Collins", please, don't think me carpy, but can a Tom Collins be good? I know a martini can, or perhaps a daiquiri, but wouldn't she perhaps offer her some alternative and then perhaps say, "If you'd like a long drink I mix a good Tom Collins"?' This critique recalls Evan asking for a Canadian Club whiskey on his first visit to Hitchcock's house. Hitchcock looked at him bemused, as his well-stocked bar didn't include Club whiskey. But the next time Evan came to visit, a bottle was waiting at the bar.

'He was wonderful, he was like the father every boy wishes he had,' said Evan. Hitchcock was approximately twice Evan's age and in good spirits and good health at the time. 'He was humorous, he was generous with his time and his patience. I was a new kid on the block out there in many respects, he took me under his wing.'

On Sunday 15 October, the Hunters celebrated Evan's 35th birthday. Their socialisation with Hitchcock continued. 'Most of the time, Hitchcock treated us with cordiality and respect,' says Anita, 'but there was one time we had made a date with some old college friends and were planning to go out in Beverly Hills. When Hitchcock rang and we told him we weren't available, he had a fit, an absolute fit. So we cancelled. He was very possessive.' Evan confirmed this story in his memoirs *Me and Hitch*.[16]

Maybe Hitchcock felt that the Hunters should be available to him exclusively at any time. 'I saw Hitchcock as someone who didn't like to be crossed,' says Anita. 'He was like "the iron hand in the velvet glove", seeming to be very gentle and pleasant on the surface, but someone who was very powerful and easily offended, so you had to be careful. He expected us to be always available to him socially.'

Claims of Hitchcock's possessiveness would later be made by Tippi Hedren, who said that Hitchcock often became angry and hurt whenever she made personal arrangements in the evening without consulting him.[17] Although Anita was never introduced to Tippi, she did see her from a distance on the set. Anita was of the opinion that Hitchcock's ego was at work in hiring an unknown. 'He was convinced that he could make anyone a star and that he didn't need Grace Kelly and Cary Grant, that he was the star. I thought it was an exercise in ego more than anything.'

According to Anita, it didn't occur to Evan, either, to question Hitchcock about the folly of using an untested actress as the lead in his film. 'Hitchcock was so dominating over Evan in terms of them working together, so we never talked about why he would cast an unknown actress,' says Anita. 'Tippi also had strong backup in the cast. Jessica Tandy and Suzanne Pleshette were good actresses.'

Privately, Evan was disappointed about the casting of Tippi in such a demanding part, saying, 'It was more of the master teaching the insecure and uncertain actress. Hitch enjoyed the role of playing Professor Higgins to her Eliza Doolittle.'[18] He would lament in his memoirs, *Me and Hitch*, that she was 'no Grace Kelly', calling her 'inexperienced' and 'bewildered'. When Evan was writing *The Birds* he had Grace Kelly and Cary Grant firmly in his mind as the leads.

THE BEL AIR FIRE

As Evan was nearing the completion of his time in LA writing the script, something catastrophic happened. On Tuesday 6 November, someone threw a cigarette butt from a car window, starting the Bel Air fire. Soon the whole area was ablaze, the fire fanned by 60mph winds that ignited the dry bush. Hitchcock rang the Hunters' house and suggested they check into a hotel. Hitch and Alma had already stored their art, silver and other valuables in the wine cellar and fled. Evan was typing the final scene of the film upstairs when birds gathered outside in his backyard, twittering noisily.

Anita, meanwhile, was working as a volunteer at the local hospital when she heard about the fire. 'I was driving on Sepulveda and I put on the radio and I heard the news. I went nuts and raced home. People were throwing their silver into the bottom of the pool and we were told to evacuate. Evan and Norman Katkov, a neighbour who was also a writer, went dashing up the street to rescue an old lady in her home. I was hysterical because I was sure they'd be killed.' In the near distance, fire engulfed houses and trees. Evan, Anita and Norman watched helpless, convinced that their own houses would go up in flames. Norman memorably remarked, 'Well, we may not be big on plot out here but we can sure do spectacle.'

'My twin brother Mark and I were evacuated from the school, while all around everything was burning,' Richard remembers. 'The principal was yelling, "Get these kids out of here!" Later, my brother Mark was interviewed by a local news crew and asked what he thought about the fire. His reply was, "I was so glad to be out of school."' The fire came dangerously close to their rented house at the time and there was a solid wall of smoke at the end of the street. After picking up their sons from school, Evan and Anita went over to one of the shelters for people who had been forced to flee their homes.

Maybe the fire was a signal for the Hunters to return home. Although the Hunters' rented place and Hitchcock's house had been spared, over 500 neighbourhood homes had been destroyed by the fire, causing $30 million in damages. Luckily, no one was killed, but 200 firefighters were injured. Like the eruption of the birds, the fire showed just how savage nature could be, how precarious human life, and how we often take it for granted. People came together in the face of tragedy and didn't panic, and this was a theme that Hitchcock ultimately believed in, one which was subtly developing in the screenplay of *The Birds*.

On Friday 10 November, four days after the Bel Air fire, Evan handed in his second draft. Peggy Robertson wrote to him saying that, in order to complete his services in connection with *The Birds*, he would be expected to put in an additional two weeks, probably in January 1962. Evan then returned to Pound Ridge, New York, with his family, and they were looking forward to spending Christmas at home.

Three weeks after submitting the screenplay, Evan received feedback from Hitchcock in a letter dated 30 November. The script had also been read by a number of other people in the technical department, more than nine people in total, including Bob Boyle, the production designer. The problem most frequently cited among them was that Melanie and Mitch seemed 'insufficiently characterised' in the script. The next problem, and this seemed of particular concern to Hitchcock, was that there were too many 'no-scene scenes' in the script.

'By this I mean that the little sequence might have narrative value but in itself is un-dramatic,' wrote Hitchcock. 'It very obviously lacks shape and it doesn't within itself have a climax as a scene on the stage might.'[19] Hitchcock went on to detail these scenes at great length: the scene between Melanie and her father in his newspaper office; two scenes in Bodega Bay where Melanie goes to buy some temporary overnight clothes and later tries to rent a room at a fully booked hotel; and, lastly, a scene inside the local church, where she runs into Mitch again, which was simply an excuse to get her to the birthday party. None of these survived the final draft or was ever filmed.

Evan, however, was asked to write one additional sequence. In a long and detailed paragraph, Hitchcock went on to suggest how they could begin foreshadowing the bird attacks from the very beginning of the film. 'For example: how would it be to open the picture on a San Francisco street with a series of cuts of upturned faces, some stationary, others moving slowly along, and what they are looking at is an unusual number of seagulls flying above the buildings of the city. We could continue the upturned faces until at last we came to Melanie also looking up and pan her right into the bird shop where she could make some comment to the woman inside who dismisses it with a remark to the effect that when the weather is bad at sea they often get driven inland.'

Hitchcock went on to suggest that another place in the script where they could foreshadow the bird attacks would be at the end of the night scene between Annie and Melanie. There could be the sound of a thump on the front door. When they open it they find a dead seagull and the scene could fade out on it. Annie says, 'Poor thing, it must have lost its way in the dark.' And Melanie's reply, 'But it isn't dark, Annie, there's a full moon.'

Lastly, he wondered whether they should start thinking about giving the script a stronger thematic structure, exploring exactly *why* the birds attack, and wrote, 'I'm sure we are going to be asked again and again, especially by the morons, "Why are they doing it?"'

The response to Hitchcock's script request came two weeks later, on 14 December. Evan sent Hitchcock 52 revised pages, among them a new scene between Mitch and Melanie, during which they try to understand why the birds are attacking. The scene takes place just after Lydia has gone to the Fawcett farm to investigate why the chickens aren't eating the feed bought from Brinkmeyer's.

Hitchcock's reply came a week later, in a four-page letter dated 21 December. 'Now, Evan, I'm still a little worried about the first meeting between Annie and Melanie. For instance, Annie sounds a little unreal when she repeats the amenities of Bodega Bay school and she should also realise that Melanie is not there to sell pencils, etc. Somehow, to me, Annie seems a little coy here. When one remembers that Melanie will appear quite *soignée*, it seems to me that Annie looks foolish making these remarks to a young sophisticated woman [such as] Melanie appears to be.'

Discussions also took place with Hitchcock's story editor, Peggy Robertson, in his office, and the conclusion was reached that Melanie ought not to be entirely a social butterfly. 'I think we ought to indicate a background of some accomplishments. I thought in the scene after dinner, where they are washing up and she is alone with Cathy, we could have her seated at a small upright piano (not very well tuned) and play some Debussy. She could do it with some style and talking to Cathy through it, and also pulling at her cigarette now and again... We only show Melanie describing her piddling work at the travellers' aid in San Francisco and, while this is intended to feel inadequate, I do think that we should indicate that her expensive education has born some fruit.'

With regard to the problem of the scene outside the church, designed merely to get Melanie to the birthday party, Hitchcock solved this by suggesting a phone call at Annie's after Melanie has returned from dinner at the Brenners. 'Now the only other thing in the script that concerns me is the scene in the Tides Restaurant after the blackbird episode at the school,' wrote Hitchcock. 'First of all, I still think it is way too long and so do most of the staff. Another thing that concerns me is the type of people that we have at the meeting. They seem to me to be types that you get in any movie involving a small town.' Hitchcock had had a similar thought many years before when working with Thornton Wilder on *Shadow of A Doubt*, which also deals with small town life.

'I'm a little worried about people like Brinkmeyer, Deke Carter and Sholes – that they all seem to be the same village types and speaking the same language,' Hitchcock continued. 'As you know, when we were up there, there were other elements such as the women who belonged to San Francisco and owned that big farm we looked at. In other words, it seems to be in Bodega Bay they weren't all small-town people but there was a mixture of sophisticates as well.' Hitchcock went on to say he would rather be in the position of having definite characters with distinctive attitudes so that he'd be forced to cast them exactly as they were written. The onus then was on Evan to create characters, not stereotypes, for the Tides restaurant scene. 'One final thought that has been bothering me for some time: have we really related the whole of the bird invasion to our central characters? Maybe it's not necessary to do so, but you know we are going to run into all kinds of critiques from the highbrows. Not that they sell us any tickets, but they do write their stuff in certain journals that may affect ticket buyers in metropolitan areas.' So Hitchcock was thinking about his audience all the time.

He ended with the words, 'Well, Evan, there it is – I pray I am not giving you too much to think about over the Christmas holidays. Perhaps it would be nicer if you took this letter and put it under the tree and then, on Christmas Eve, you could pull it out and say, "Oo look, a present from Hitch."' It was signed 'Love Hitch' with a PS – 'People are still asking, "Why did the birds do it?"'

Hitchcock and Alma then travelled to St Moritz in Switzerland where they traditionally spent their Christmas holidays. Hitchcock even asked Evan and Anita to join them, saying to Evan, 'You can afford it,' raising an eyebrow to indicate that, at $5,000 per week, Evan was being extravagantly paid. The Hunters graciously declined, and Evan started to address the Tides scene. 'The people involved are trying to understand what's happening so that we can proffer different things here,' he said. 'I don't know how we discovered where we would take them, the central characters, Melanie and Mitch, but once I knew it was a restaurant, the Tides, then I had the whole scene in place and it just wrote itself.'

WRITING THE SONG

A memorable part of *The Birds* is the song 'Risseldy Rosseldy', which the children chant in the school as the crows gather on the jungle gym. Hitchcock cleverly uses counterpoint to contrast the singing children and the horror of the crows. He asked his screenwriter to come up with a song, and Evan derived his inspiration from his three sons who were the same age as the Bodega Bay schoolchildren. Evan's boys sang the song 'Risseldy Rosseldy' at their Pound Ridge school in Westchester County, New York. When Evan heard them singing he called their teacher and she sent him the music. After looking it up, he found out that it was a song that was in the public domain. 'You know, it's an old folk tune that goes back forever. And I used it. And I gave them four or five stanzas, whatever, of the song, the actual song.'[20]

In a letter dated 27 December 1961, Evan wrote to Peggy: 'Concerning the song the children sing, the correct title is "Risseldy Rosseldy", and it is, as I suspected, an old folk song. It can be found in a book called *More Songs to Grow On*, which is a collection of songs compiled by Beatrice Langdeck and published by William Sloane Associates. I do not think there will be any copyright problem on the song as it seems to be public domain; at least many other songs in the book carry copyright notices and this does not.'

In the New Year, Evan received a call from Peggy requesting more lyrics for the song. When Evan asked why, she explained that it wouldn't cover the scene on the jungle gym. So Evan wrote two more stanzas, after the lyric about butter and cheese, enough to cover more crows arriving on the jungle gym to stretch out the suspense. He had to join the American Society of Composers and Publishers before they would allow him to use the lyrics in the film. 'And I still get royalties from ASCAP on *The Birds* for the lyrics I wrote for that scene.'

1962 AND THE CUBAN MISSILE CRISIS

With the turn of the New Year, filming was now only a couple of months away, and the script had still not been completed to Hitchcock's satisfaction. On his way back from St Moritz, on 4 January 1962, Hitchcock stopped off in New York to meet with Evan to discuss script development. They talked about deleting the scene outside the church, covered Lydia's reactions to the attack on Melanie in the attic, and took care of Cathy and Mitch's reactions to Annie's death. Hitchcock then returned to LA.

By 17 January, Evan had completed what he was calling the final version of *The Birds*, incorporating the changes that had been discussed in New York. The two biggest changes in the script were the scene between Annie and Melanie where they discuss the possibility of Oedipal problems involving Mitch and Lydia, and the meeting in the Tides restaurant. In his letter to Hitchcock, Evan went on to say that he had introduced a woman ornithologist, who took much of the burden from Sebastian Sholes, leaving him in the position of having an open mind. The scene now had Mrs Bundy (the ornithologist), an alarmist, a pacifist, and Mitch and Melanie, all debating what is causing the birds to attack. 'On the whole, I think it plays very well and serves our needs beautifully,' wrote Evan, who would later state that he felt that the Tides restaurant debate with the townspeople was the best-written scene in the film. 'I love that scene. That was like a one-act play.'

Evan also went carefully over each of the bird attacks in the story and the reactions of the principal characters following the attacks. 'I honestly do not feel we now have a simple reaction of terror. It seems to be that the characters now are changing throughout the entire length of the screenplay and that each change is a logical one following the change before it.'

On 22 January, Evan wrote another letter following changes discussed on the phone the previous night with Hitchcock about Melanie's character. 'I didn't want to come right out and say that Melanie had been sleeping around since there is an old theatrical rule of thumb that claims if a girl takes one drink on the stage she's socially acceptable, if she takes two she's a drunk, and if she takes three she's an outright alcoholic. I think the scene between Mitch and Melanie now implies that she wasn't exactly virtuous but, at the same time, leaves her "socially acceptable".'

While Evan was writing the script in the early spring of 1962, the Cuban Missile Crisis was front-page headlines across America. On 3 February, the US embargo against Cuba was announced by President Kennedy, prohibiting the importation of all Cuban goods. 'I remember us sitting around the dinner table and discussing Cuba,' says Richard Hunter. 'My fear was that we were going to have a nuclear fall out.'

On 28 February, three weeks after the declaration of the embargo, a group of 15 American Jupiter missiles, with nuclear warheads, became operational at Cigli in Turkey within striking range of the Soviet Union, which was 1,000 miles away. The presence of these American nuclear missiles in a nation bordering the Soviet Union became a key issue, especially when the Soviets in turn brought missiles to Cuba, within striking distance of the US.

It was against this backdrop of the Cuban Missile Crisis that Evan continued to write *The Birds*. The bird attacks would later be interpreted as an analogy of the crisis and Hitchcock himself likened the attack on the Brenner house to the London air raids. The Hunters, being an intellectual family, discussed everything relating to religion, politics and society at the dinner table in Pound Ridge. 'My father supported liberal political causes throughout his life,' remembers Richard. 'He was a supporter of the Kennedys, he was anti-religious and was in favour of progressive politics.' So Kennedy and his politics were part of the atmosphere of the Hunter household.

Some references to President Kennedy would even make it into the final script of *The Birds*. Evan wrote a Kennedy-style speech on the radio after the attack on the Brenner house, and Mitch is modelled after a young, active Kennedy, spending his weekends at his country home, proactive, wearing genteel clothes, and respected by his peers. The Brenner family, too, are depicted as bohemian gentry in Bodega Bay, rather like the Kennedys.

At the beginning of February, Peggy Robertson wrote to Evan saying that a bound final script of *The Birds* would be ready that week, and would he like 'to return the leather-bound copy Hitch gave you so we can have the book-binders insert the final version?' A leather-bound script was sent to Evan on 12 February 1962. But, bound or not, the script was far from finished.

HITCHCOCK SENDS THE SCRIPT TO OTHER WRITERS

Although Evan was not aware of it at the time, Hitchcock was less than satisfied with many facets of the storyline. He had already emphasised that he felt the link between the characters and the bird attacks was tenuous, and that the characters themselves were insufficiently developed, especially Melanie Daniels. Unbeknown to Evan, at the beginning of 1962, Hitchcock sent *The Birds* script to other writers for revisions and suggestions. Sending out the script to other writers for a second opinion wasn't an unusual move for Hitchcock; he had done the same thing on his previous films. He was very concerned with good writing and also with developing characters who were psychologically realistic, so it was a customary tactic for him to garner a variety of opinions. A copy of the script was sent to Hume Cronyn, a friend and actor who had received adaptation credit on *Rope* (1948) and *Under Capricorn* (1949). Cronyn was the husband of actress Jessica Tandy and the two of them were living in Rome at the time, as Cronyn was starring in the Roman epic *Cleopatra* (1963) with Elizabeth Taylor.

At the end of 1961, Hitchcock had sent a cable to Jessica asking if she'd be interested in playing the role of Lydia Brenner, the possessive mother of Mitch. Jessica replied on 15 December, 'I have always wanted to cast you as Svengali, provided of course that I can play Trilby.' She also went on to say that she didn't want to be separated from Cronyn as the two had only been together for three months in the past two years, but that she'd be interested to read a script.

When Cronyn received a copy of the screenplay, he wrote to Hitchcock from Rome, on 13 January 1962: 'First, I agree that there's room for improvement in the development and relationship of the principal characters, and these seem particularly important in view of the extreme and macabre nature of the events.' The character of Mitch was described as lacking in humour, 'a trifle smug, even priggish'. Also, 'the implied arrogance, silliness and selfishness of the early Melanie may need heightening' so that the maturity she evinces later on would be more marked and endearing. Substantial notes were made by Cronyn on the part of Lydia. 'Of all the characters, Lydia seems the most likely to be affected by the birds,' Cronyn observed, paying particular attention to the role that his wife would play in the movie.

Cronyn made a few additional suggestions, mainly concerning the development of Lydia, and also questioned the final attack on the house and the ability of the characters to sleep afterwards. 'I wonder if the sleeping business, scene 574, page 161, is not unreal, and the dialogue in scene 579 in danger of seeming ludicrous? Could they possibly sleep in the face of the noise and circumstance described? Also, might it not be better to keep the sleeping business for scene 589 alone – in the hiatus. Silence, exhausted sleep, and the gradual emergence of a new sound.' Jessica Tandy cabled Hitchcock on 17 February to say, 'Think script wonderfully improved.'

Hitchcock also sent the script of *The Birds* to an old friend of his who lived in Berkeley, V S Pritchett, a short-story writer who was a book-review editor for the *New Statesman*. Pritchett wrote back to Hitchcock on 16 March, agreeing with the majority of those who had already read the script. 'I do think that the link between the characters' love story and the terror is not very strong.' He went on to say that audiences of *The Birds* would 'get the impression that they are in two different stories – in this case a light comedy and a terror tale – that do not weld together.'

By this time, Hitchcock was a third of the way into filming and was still trying to give the central characters depth and meaning. He wrote back to Pritchett on 9 April: 'Confirming our phone conversation of this morning, if you would look at the script around pages 73 to 76. It is during this scene that I would like you to work it with a view to dropping in some reference to Melanie's mother having gone off with another man when she was 12 years of age.' The resulting dialogue on the sand dunes would cause great consternation during filming in the following months, particularly for Evan Hunter, who did not write the scene. When he discovered that Hitchcock had brought someone else in, he was far from pleased.

THE ENDING

While filming had started on location in March 1962, Hitchcock and Evan still had not decided on an ending that satisfied them both. Hitchcock wanted the scene to have more purpose and relate it to the journey arc of the central characters. 'He asked me to take another look at the final scene, with an eye toward giving it a deeper meaning and a stronger purpose,' said Evan. So they devised the idea of the birds attacking the Brenner family while they attempt to flee in Melanie's convertible. On 30 March, Evan wrote to Hitchcock, who was staying at the Fairmont Hotel in San Francisco during the location filming, 'The revision on that last scene in *The Birds* will be coming your way next week. I want to tell you that it's a little difficult to be poetic when the roof of an automobile is slowly being shredded to bits by attacking birds.' But he added that he thought he had given the ending more of a sense of the character resolution Hitchcock was looking for.

In the scene, Mitch leaves with Lydia, Cathy and the wounded Melanie in the convertible, which has a soft-cloth top. Evan wanted this final assault of the birds to show them attacking the car's top. Additionally, as the characters leave the Brenner house, he intended the audience to see the devastation that has been visited on the town itself. There is a clean stretch of road ahead. 'Here we go,' Mitch says, and rams his foot down on the accelerator. Instantly, thousands of birds take to the air after the car. The road is winding and twisting, the same road Melanie negotiated into town at the beginning of the film. As Evan said, 'There was a reason for that high shot at the beginning. We see at the end that the birds fly in a straight line, relentlessly attacking the car, slashing at it.' As the road straightens out and Mitch hits the gas pedal, the car moves off and the birds fall back. In the car they all catch their breath and Mitch's sister says, 'Mitch do you think they'll be in San Francisco when we get there?' and he replies, 'I don't know, honey.' And that's the last line of the movie.

Hitchcock relayed this final scene in a letter to V S Pritchett on 9 April. 'The suggestion is that, after the convertible roof has been torn off,

Melanie struggles out of Lydia's arms and cries, "Let me out, let me go back! Mother, I want you, I want you. Come back to me, please, please come back to me." At this point, Jessica (Tandy) can succeed in pulling her down and holding her in her arms to comfort her. After this we will go to the long shot with the car speeding down the straight road to safety.'

Well into filming, Hitchcock was still trying to infuse *The Birds*, and specifically the Melanie Daniels character, with psychological meaning. Hitch described Melanie's cry as 'the cry of a child who lost her mother. Lydia pulls her down and holds her tightly – becomes her mother.'

Pritchett was doubtful about what he thought was facile psychoanalysing. On 12 April, he wrote back to Hitchcock: 'The only line I was uncertain of in the little bit of dialogue for the end in your suggestions was "Come back to me, please. Please come back to me". The reason for my doubts is that she is calling for the mother to come back to her, whereas she, Melanie, is hysterically proposing to get out and to get back. She is rightly the most important and active figure at this moment. I would prefer her to end her sentence with some such words as "I want to find my mother". As you will see, on the enclosed sheet I've made even another suggestion; that she has the illusion her mother is actually there, back in the village. She could even say, "I want to save my mother." Perhaps this is adding what the audience might take for a loose end.'

Blithely unaware of this exchange of dialogue that was taking place between Hitchcock and Pritchett, Evan wrote on 2 April: 'Here are the final pages for *The Birds*. I have taken the liberty of transposing several of your outlined shots in order to present the menace as a growing and cumulative one. For example, I didn't feel the shot showing "only a few gulls" in the road would cause the consternation it did in your outline. Considering the number of birds they have already seen, their reaction to these few seemed a bit excessive. Two, I feel it necessary to provide a trapped feeling when they approach the hundreds of gulls sitting in the middle of the road. In other words, there is no choice: they are literally surrounded and must go through the centre of the waiting birds.'

In the end, Hitchcock decided to drop the scene referencing Melanie's mother in the car and ignored Pritchett's suggestion. In August 1962, he confided in Truffaut about his uneasy feelings with regard to the script and the last-minute improvisation its problems entailed. 'Something happened that was altogether new in my experience. I began to study the scenario as we went along, and I saw that there were weaknesses in it. This emotional siege I went through served to bring out an additional creative sense in me. I began to improvise.'[21]

So *The Birds* went into production with an unresolved ending and a feeling of dissatisfaction about the inconclusive central characters. Melanie Daniels was for Hitchcock 'a fly by night, a nothing character' whom he tried to inject with some depth. Very unusually for Hitchcock, he would be rewriting the screenplay whilst he was filming, going so far as to improvise on the set, which was contradictory to his usual method of meticulous preplanning.

Although Evan Hunter wrote shot directions in the screenplay, and was rather facetiously encouraged by Hitchcock to extensively do so, the director for the most part decided to ignore them. In an interview just before *The Birds* was released, Hitchcock explained his method of working on the story with his screenwriter. 'I do it verbally with the writer, then I make the corrections and adjustments afterwards. I work many weeks with him, and he takes notes and everything. I apply myself two thirds before he writes and one third after. And I will not, and do not, photograph anything that he puts on the script on his own, apart from words. Cinematically, how can he know it? He doesn't know it. I correct the dialogue sometimes.' It was now up to Hitchcock and the technical crew he would assemble to turn the screenplay into a cinematic reality.

NOTES

1 Interview with Joseph Stefano, 28 September 2000, Los Angeles
2 Interview with Norman Lloyd, 30 November 2012, Los Angeles
3 Interviews with Evan Hunter, 31 August 1998 & 18 August 2000
4 Kyle Counts, 'The Making of Alfred Hitchcock's The Birds', *Cinefantastique*, Volume 10, 1980, p. 18
5 Alfred Hitchcock to François Truffaut, unpublished interview, August 1962
6 Bill Krohn, 'Roundtable on *The Birds*', *Cahiers du Cinéma*, 1982
7 Evan Hunter, *Me and Hitch*, Faber & Faber, London, p. 13
8 Interview with Evan Hunter, 28 August 1998, Connecticut
9 Jay Presson Allen & Evan Hunter, *On Writing*, Publication of the Writers Guild of America East, 24 March 1993

10 Alfred Hitchcock to Peter Bogdanovich, unpublished interview, 12 February 1963
11 Charles L P Silet, 'Writing for Hitchcock: An Interview With Ed McBain', Mystery Net
12 Howard Gottlieb Research Centre, Evan Hunter files
13 Evan Hunter, *Me and Hitch*, Faber and Faber, London, p. 9
14 Interview with Anita Hunter, 28 September 2012, New York
15 Interview with Richard Hunter, 14 September 2012, Connecticut
16 Evan Hunter, *Me and Hitch*, Faber & Faber, London, p. 49
17 Donald Spoto, *The Dark Side of Genius*, Little Brown, p. 457
18 Interview with Evan Hunter, 28 August 2000, Connecticut
19 Memo from Hitchcock to Hunter, 30 November 1961
20 'The Making of Alfred Hitchcock's The Birds', *Cinefantastique*, p. 28
21 François Truffaut, *Hitchcock*, Simon & Schuster, 1985, p. 290

THE CAST AND CREW

'There was a particular reaction I had when the little boy whistled at me, and that's what got Hitchcock's attention. There may be more to this woman in the commercial.' – Tippi Hedren

INTRODUCING 'TIPPI' HEDREN

It was Friday 13 October 1961 and, while the screenplay of *The Birds* was still being developed and written, Hitchcock was breakfasting with his wife Alma at their Bel Air home. They were watching NBC's *Today* show, which was beamed from New York on network television. A one-minute television commercial for a Pet Milk diet drink named 'Sego' caught Hitchcock's attention. It wasn't the product that interested him, but the woman in the commercial, an attractive and slim blonde, who turns her head amiably to a little boy's wolf whistle. In his own words, Hitchcock saw in the woman 'a certain quality and charm in the way she moved'.[1]

Like many of Hitchcock's previous leading ladies, including Madeleine Carroll, Grace Kelly and Kim Novak, Tippi Hedren was an elegant blonde with a cool, sophisticated manner. 'Hitch always liked women who behaved like well-bred ladies,' explained Robert Boyle. 'Tippi generated that quality. He was quite taken by the way she walked.'[2]

Hitchcock immediately called his agents and asked them to 'find the girl and bring her out from New York'. As it happened, 'the girl' was living in LA and her name was Tippi Hedren, born Nathalie Hedren in Lafayette, Minnesota, to parents Dorothea and Bernard Hedren. She also had one older sister named Patricia. Her paternal grandparents had been born in Sweden, her maternal grandfather in Germany and her maternal grandmother in Norway. 'Tippi' was an affectionate Swedish nickname for Tupsa, given early on by her father and meaning 'little girl'. She weighed 6 lbs 7 oz at birth.

Tippi was raised in Minneapolis until her second year of high school. She won her first modelling job at age 12, and was engaged as a teenage model and fashion coordinator by a Minneapolis department store. The family then moved to Huntington Park, California and Tippi completed high school and enrolled at Pasadena City College as an art major. After graduating, she returned to modelling and soon became a favourite subject of photographers in New York. With blonde hair, green eyes, a height of 5' 4", weight of 109 lbs, a 22-inch waist and 35-inch hip, Tippi was so linear that she wore clothes beautifully so that they just hung.

'We were both junior models and worked for magazines such as *Seventeen*, *Mademoiselle*, *Coronet* and *Junior Vogue*,' remembers Dolores Parker, another model at the Eileen Ford Agency where she and Tippi worked. 'Modelling at the time, in the late 1940s and early 1950s, was a brand-new business. Tippi and I had the same look. We were both blonde, cute looking and smiled a lot. Very often they would pair us together for double or triple shots and it was mostly junior fashion modelling we did.'[3]

Tippi married the actor Peter Griffith, three years her junior, in 1952, and they had one child, Melanie, born in 1957. Dolores Parker was married to Jerry Adler at the time, who would later become a noted theatre director and actor, and they lived in the same neighbourhood as Tippi and Peter in New York. 'Tippi had no interest in acting whatsoever,' remembers Jerry. 'She was a lot of fun, young, but I remember she was having trouble with her husband Peter.'[4] Tippi and Peter finally divorced in 1961 and Tippi was faced with the responsibility of bringing up a little girl as a single parent through her modelling work.

Eileen Ford was businesslike and ran a very good agency, and both Dolores and Tippi had significant careers throughout the 1950s. With the advent of television came the commercials and these paid well, and were easy work. 'Some of the photographers did come on to you,' remembers Dolores Parker. 'I never had any problems except once. I could handle it and most photographers knew their place.' Tippi worked for Eileen Ford for 11 years and also appeared in television commercials for products like Gleem toothpaste and Chesterfield cigarettes, which paid well.

In 1959, Tippi began acting lessons with Claudia Franck, the dialogue coach in New York. Franck offered a 'sensational opportunity to get all-important experience before live television cameras' and clients were advised to take advantage of this professional training. 'We have developed a hard-hitting professional service to give you every possible phase of training "on camera". You are the future of television,' an advertising slogan read. Tippi hoped that this would also help with her commercials and further her work as a model-actress, as she was now a single mother and keen to support herself and her daughter.

The ethos behind Claudia Franck's coaching services was to make the voice and the visual personality match each other in those who came to her for training, or were sent to her by the film studios. And it wasn't just aspiring board walkers who came to her. Opera singers, who had just secured their first film assignments, came to her to brush up on their acting techniques, actors who had been given difficult character roles, requiring perhaps an Italian or Indian accent, built the character on her advice. Some of the actors groomed by Claudia Franck included Joan Caulfield, Vera Ellen, Dinah Shore, June Vincent, Robert Merrill, Joan Roberts, Maria Gambarelli and Armand Tokatyan. Tippi took advantage of Franck's coaching and decided to try and break into Hollywood.

After her divorce from Peter Griffith, Tippi moved west with her four-year-old daughter Melanie. 'My little girl Melanie was growing and I wanted her to have her independence and freedom. So we picked up the puppy and moved to LA.' Tippi was 31 years old and had no fears. 'I thought I could continue my career as it had been in New York, so I rented a very expensive home. I thought everything would be just fine, and it wasn't. So I thought, "Well, I don't type, what shall I do?"'

Tippi and Melanie first moved to Olive Street in Huntington Park. On 14 March 1961, Claudia Franck wrote a letter to Tippi there: 'In thinking over your situation I felt it might be best to send you to a very active and excellent agent who handles very few people. He is a good friend and will be very honest as to what he can do for you. It might be good to have him see any of your commercials, even though silent, if they are available to you out there. His name is Jerry Lauren and I am enclosing a copy of my letter to him. There is no sense in giving you a lot of names, because you don't want to cheapen yourself by running around.'

As well as meeting Lauren, one of the first people that Tippi met after moving to LA was Noel Marshall who owned an agency that handled television commercials. Noel was a tall, lean man from Chicago, with sandy hair and blue-green eyes. He started up a talent agency with his first wife Jaye Joseph and they had three sons. After they divorced they carried on working together at the agency. When Noel met Tippi he was immediately smitten by her, but it wasn't until a year after they met that they started dating.

Soon Tippi acquired Noel as her agent and, by September 1961, she was renting a house on South Bentley Avenue in Westwood. This was just on the south side of Sunset Boulevard, coincidentally very near to 10957 Bellagio Road where the Hitchcocks lived. It would seem that fate was destined to bring Tippi and Hitchcock together. Indeed, something fateful did happen, appropriately on Friday 13 October 1961. Tippi received a phone call from an agent asking if she was the girl in the Pet Milk commercial, which she confirmed she was. He asked if she would go over to Revue Studios that afternoon with her portfolio and reel, which she did. She was told that a producer had seen her in the commercial and wanted to meet her and was asked to leave her portfolio and reel of 13 commercials over the weekend. Tippi was reluctant to do this, saying she needed them back as they were an essential tool for her work. But she did, and spent the rest of the weekend wondering who the producer was that was interested in her. She had a small party that Saturday but still her agent wouldn't say anything.

On Monday, Tippi went through several meetings with high-level executives, not knowing which producer was interested in meeting her or why. They just said, 'Would you go over to MCA tomorrow morning and meet with Herman Citron?' who was an agent there. Tippi went over and met with Citron. As she sat down, he said, 'I suppose you're a little bit curious as to who this director is.' She said, 'Yes.' He said, 'Alfred Hitchcock wants to sign you to a contract if you will agree with the terms.'

Tippi was stunned and didn't know whether to laugh or cry. Citron said, 'If you are in agreement with this, we will go over to Paramount Studios and meet with him.' By pre-arrangement, Citron called Hitchcock.

'How does she look?' Hitchcock inquired. 'Fine,' answered Citron. 'Then sign her,' said Hitchcock. 'I'll meet her in my office tomorrow.' In retrospect Tippi said that this was a very kind thing for Hitchcock to do because, if she'd known he was the director in question, she would have worried about what to wear or what to do with her hair. Her nervousness would have prevented her from being who she really was, so the meetings had been handled very considerately.[5]

Four days after the commercial had aired, on Tuesday 17 October 1961, Tippi Hedren and Alfred Hitchcock met for the first time. He opened the door to his office and stood there with his hands over his belly and welcomed her. They talked about food, wine and travel and, as Tippi had travelled the world after college and as part of her modelling work, she felt able to contribute to the conversation. Hitchcock asked what dramatic work she had done and Tippi replied she had been coached for two years by Claudia Franck, especially diction lessons. Hitchcock later said he had signed Tippi without seeing her in person, because she displayed 'jaunty assuredness, pertness, an attractive throw of the head'. When he first met her, Hitchcock also observed, 'She walked in with her hair in a beehive, making her face look tiny, and wearing a dress of some awful colour, probably turquoise blue.'

By the end of the week Tippi had signed a seven-year contract with Alfred J Hitchcock Productions. 'And a lovely one,' as she described it. Her starting salary was $500 a week, which she accepted because she felt it was wiser than the unpredictable money earned from modelling. Why did Hitchcock hire an unknown who had never acted before for the lead part? At the time, Hollywood was desperately short of new stars, and its future depended on creating new talent pools. 'We're out to amass the greatest array of new talent we can find,' announced the Music Corporation of America, which owned Universal Pictures. 'Screen tests for all comers – that's our new motto,' declared 20th Century Fox. Many of the old stars had passed away and little was being done to recruit suitable replacements. 'We've been recovering from TV,' explained one studio executive.

'Studios are always looking for new people,' producer Norman Lloyd commented of that time. The result of Hollywood's post-television torpor meant that the few big-name stars remaining could make fantastic salary demands, and often did. It was hoped that the search for new stars would leave Hollywood with a surplus of talent, changing the status of the star from dictator to employee. MCA said that, under the new programme, its roster of new young players under contract had jumped in a few months from 67 to 131 'and we've only just started'. Typical of the new stars were Paramount's 16-year-old Bridgett Barnett, Vince Edwards, Richard Chamberlain and Troy Donahue.[6] 'We had such a shortage of women,' Hitchcock would remark years later on why he hired Tippi Hedren.[7]

Three weeks after meeting with Hitchcock, on Thursday 8 November, and just a couple of days after the devastating Bel Air fire, Tippi was given an extensive colour screen test that lasted two days at Revue Studios and cost $25,000. Martin Balsam was flown in from New York to play her leading man. 'I thought that was a little strange, as if there were no leading men in Hollywood,' Tippi would later joke.[8]

Sets were erected on a sound stage and fully decorated for the screen test, and a complete crew was employed with Bob Burks as the DP. Hitchcock explained why he went to such elaborate lengths. 'It's no use doing the typical Hollywood screen test. It consists of putting a young girl in front of a camera, hiring a stock actor to feed lines to her, and hoping she will prove herself. To determine the real potential of a newcomer, a test must create all the conditions of a feature motion picture set.'

Edith Head designed Tippi's clothes for the screen test, which included cocktail dresses and ball gowns, and Columbia hairstylist Helen Hunt was employed to do her hair. Hitchcock rehearsed with Tippi one afternoon before the test, going over the script with her, and she wasn't nervous. She was given the text of *Rebecca* to read as she would be re-enacting one of the scenes. 'I worked a whole week on my text, reading over again Daphne du Maurier's book to get well into the mood of the part.'[9]

Tippi tested for scenes from *Rebecca*, *Notorious* and *To Catch A Thief*, three entirely different women. After those scenes were filmed, Hitchcock directed Tippi in clothes and different hair styles in ad lib improvisation scenes. Martin Balsam was very nice and helpful throughout the test, which had been planned to the smallest detail, and Tippi even had a bungalow dressing room on the set, with her name on the door and her own named chair. With all this, she felt like a movie star, although she didn't realise she was receiving special treatment. 'I just thought that was what happened to anyone who goes under contract.'

Hitchcock tested Tippi in every way he could think of and she loved every second of it, as she would later say to Claudia Franck. He also did everything he could to throw her off guard, including telling her ribald stories about doughnuts and their manufacturer. And, to Hitchcock's delight, Tippi memorised dialogue quickly: 'That was an unexpected bonus.' Hitchcock was adamant that none of Tippi's old publicity photographs were to be used in the future. Tippi's test was apparently so successful that Hitchcock turned 'ice-cream pink' with delight. When Tippi herself saw her screen test she was happily surprised, as she had much more authority than she thought possible on screen.

Soon the press heard about Hitchcock's new star. By Wednesday 29 November, Mike Connolly of the *Hollywood Reporter* wrote, 'Tippi Hedren zipped out of her cigarette commercial chores to go the Grace Kelly route, starting with a $20,000 colour test for Alfred Hitchcock.'

That same day, three weeks after the screen test, Tippi was invited to Hitchcock's favourite restaurant, Chasen's, for dinner with the Hitchcocks. Lew Wasserman came over to the table and glasses of champagne were placed in front of everyone except Tippi. A toast was then made to her. Wasserman was sitting to her left and Alma and Hitch to her right. Hitchcock then placed in front of her a very beautifully wrapped package from Gumps, one of his favourite stores in San Francisco. Tippi opened the box to find a beautiful pin of three birds in flight, with the seed pearls and gold. Tippi thanked them, thinking this was Hitchcock's way of telling her that her test was good. But then Hitchcock said, 'Look at it, what are they?' Tippi looked again at the pin. 'Birds,' he said.

Tippi glanced up at Hitch, and he said, 'We want you to play Melanie in *The Birds.*' Tippi, of course, had heard about *The Birds* and knew that the screenplay was being written by Evan Hunter. She had heard them discussing it for over a month now at the studio, but never dreaming they were even considering her for a role. Hitchcock said he had become convinced she was right for the part after they had rehearsed the scenes that one afternoon. She was overwhelmed and couldn't believe it, and even started to cry. So did Alma and Lew Wasserman. All the while, Hitchcock sat there looking very pleased with himself. 'Well, I cried, and Alma, Hitch's wife, cried – even Lew Wasserman had tears rolling down his face. It was a lovely moment.'

'I had no idea that I would be associated with *The Birds,*' Tippi would later say. 'I knew it was being made, but it never occurred to me that I would be in it. I thought perhaps there would be a couple of years of acting on Hitchcock's TV shows or some kind of dramatic training.' 'She wasn't what you'd call a regular commercial actress at all,' Hitchcock said. 'She was a girl out of a TV commercial!' Hitchcock would later joke, calling himself the 'victim of an insidious commercial'.[10]

'I felt that one should have anonymous people,' Hitchcock replied when asked why he chose to cast an unknown as the lead in *The Birds*, 'because the subject matter was not as facetious as some of my other films. Anyway, the stars of the film were the birds; anyone else was secondary.' 'He wanted a star all of his own,' Jay Presson Allen, the screenwriter of *Marnie*, would say years later. 'The nurturing and grooming of stars is hard, and he felt that he was too old and that he didn't want to go through that anymore.'

With his actress cast, Hitchcock's next job was to turn Tippi into Melanie Daniels. Melanie's character is described in the script as 'a young woman in her mid 20s, sleekly groomed, exquisitely dressed'. On 24 February 1962, a few days before they were due to go to Bodega Bay, Hitchcock met with Tippi to go over the script. These taped transcripts are fascinating and are held at the Margaret Herrick Library in Beverly Hills. Hitchcock did most of the talking with Tippi speaking to query or raise a point.

'We know that she is very well appointed, very well dressed. She is smart, sophisticated... obviously a woman with a sense of humour, otherwise we wouldn't talk about her going in for practical jokes,' said Hitchcock. Tippi agreed that her character was perhaps disillusioned, but added, 'There's a great need in people like Melanie. She was a very hurt girl and therefore did things to cover up that hurt, like practical jokes.'

Hitchcock also mentioned that Melanie Daniels would have frequented The Hungry I in San Francisco, a famous nightclub in North Beach that was popular in the 1950s and 1960s. In the script, Melanie is also mentioned as having been thrown into a fountain in Rome, which reinforces Hitchcock's view of her as 'a shallow, wealthy playgirl'. All the while, Hitchcock was coaching Tippi, giving her scripting and voice lessons. 'I probably learned in three years what it would have taken me 15 years to learn otherwise,' recalled Tippi, who sat in on meetings concerning all phases of the production. 'I learned so much from Hitchcock. He's an absolutely fascinating person. He has a mind like an IBM computer. He can pull from his past any number of things he has learned and apply them to a particular scene or character.' Tippi acknowledged Hitchcock's control over her characterisation and her contribution as a creative actress. 'Melanie Daniels is his character,' she explained. 'He gives his actors very little leeway. He'll listen, but he has a very definite plan in mind as to how he wants his characters to act. With me, it was understandable, because I was not an actress of stature. I welcomed his guidance.'

ROD TAYLOR

With the part of Melanie cast, Hitchcock was seeking a leading man to play the part of Mitch Brenner, who is described in the script as 'a tall, good-looking man in his early 30s. When we first meet him he seems to be a knowledgeable city dweller, not without a sense of humour, merry nonchalance about him except when embarrassed discussing love birds'.

'Money was always at the forefront of Hitch's mind, otherwise we would have had Cary Grant in *The Birds*,' said Evan Hunter. The screenwriter suggested Chuck Connor in the role of Mitch, who was starring in *Rifleman*, and also Ron Harper, who played Detective Bert Kling in the *87th Precinct* television series as possibilities for Mitch. Evan's own preference ran to Connor, who seemed to have a quiet strength as well as a sense of humour.

On 13 December 1961, Hitchcock watched the Australian actor Rod Taylor in ABC's short-lived series *Bus Stop* and *Portrait of a Hero* in his private screening room. He also watched clips of James Garner, Jack Kelly and Stephen Boyd in consideration for Mitch. John Gabriel was also recommended by Hal Landers as a casting suggestion. Hitchcock, however, invited Rod Taylor to come and meet him in his bungalow in January 1962.

Rod had come to Hollywood in 1955 from Sydney, Australia and, prior to *The Birds*, had worked his way up through bit parts and TV films. He had been the winner of the Newspaper Critics Best Actor of the Year award and won a plane ticket to London, stopping off in LA. He liked Hollywood so much that he stayed. His first American film was *The Virgin Queen* (1955), followed by playing Elizabeth Taylor's fiancé in *Giant* (1956). His most famous role to date had been George the inventor in MGM's time-travelling adventure *The Time Machine* (1960). At 5 ft 11 in, 175 lbs, with light brown hair and blue eyes, Rod was a natural athlete, expert at tennis, surfing and swimming.

Rod went along with his agent, Wilt Melnick of the Louis Shurr Agency, to Hitchcock's bungalow in January 1962. 'The initial meeting with Hitchcock was a disaster,' recalls Rod. 'I called him by his first name,

Alfred this and Alfred that. He went totally white for 20 minutes, and had total misgivings about our meeting.' Rod thought he didn't say all the right things and remembers commenting, 'I hope the birds and things don't kind of totally outshadow the people.' Of course, that's the story... they're supposed to. So that was number one. Wrong. But then we really talked about "making movies" and how I loved it, and how I was interested in his work. I brought that up and said the right thing. We didn't get into any deep discussions about the movie itself at all. No "What do you think of the character?" – none of that. It was taken for granted that I loved it and wanted to work with him.'

When they left Hitchcock's office, Rod said to agent Wilt, 'Well, you can forget that movie.' Two days later, Rod got a call from Hitchcock offering him the part.[11] Rod believes that Hitchcock was influenced by Lew Wasserman, who knew him from films such as *The Time Machine*. Wasserman backed Hitchcock to the hilt and often suggested actors to appear in his movies, and Rod himself was absolutely flattered and astonished that Hitch would want to work with him.

By 2 February 1962, columnist Hedda Hopper in the *LA Times* was reporting that Hitchcock had signed a four-picture deal with Rod over the next six years, which was negotiated by Wilt Melnick. At the time Rod was engaged to the Swedish actress Anita Ekberg, who famously jumped into the Trevi fountain in Federico Fellini's *La Dolce Vita* (1960). Interestingly, the character of Melanie Daniels is also mentioned 'jumping into a fountain in Rome', possibly as a sly reference to Ekberg and the *La Dolce Vita* years of the early 1960s.

Rod was to be paid $50,000 for 12 weeks' work and three weeks additional. He would end up working a total of 16 weeks because of overruns on the film's special effects. The four-picture deal was to commence 31 December 1962 and Rod started work on *The Birds* on 5 March 1962. By 28 May, a multiple-feature contract had been issued between Rod Taylor and Alfred J Hitchcock Productions.

JESSICA TANDY

For the part of Lydia Brenner, Hitchcock turned to Hume Cronyn's wife Jessica Tandy. As already noted, at the beginning of 1962 Hitchcock had sent his friend Hume Cronyn a copy of the script for comments. Tandy and Cronyn were living in Rome at the time and, when Cronyn was making comments and revisions on Evan's script, he paid close attention to the part of Lydia, aware that his wife was under consideration.

Born in London in 1909, Jessica Tandy spent most of her career in the United States. In 1948, she won the Tony Award for her performance as Blanche Dubois in the original Broadway production of *A Streetcar Named Desire*, and she had starred in an episode of *Alfred Hitchcock Presents* called 'The Glass Eye' in 1957.

On 23 January, Hitchcock sent a cable to Mr and Mrs Hume Cronyn: 'Pondering completed and character adjustments made accordingly. In reference last twenty words in postscript your letter 12 January I will fight this in the town, the villages, the streets, and ditches and then in the cashier's office. See you soon, Jessie. Hitch.' The last 20 words in Cronyn's jokey postscript that Hitchcock was referring to said that if Jessica's agents, General Artists Corporation, were making 'unreasonable difficulties, please let Jess know – not, of course, that I won't be delighted to see her take every penny from you that she possibly can.'

Hume Cronyn had also made substantial notes and suggestions with a view to improving the character of Lydia Brenner, Mitch's mother, who starts off strong but it's just a façade. As Hitchcock said, 'She's the weak character in the story.' Lydia has been substituting her son for her husband and is fearful about being abandoned. Through her agent, Hazel McMillan, Jessica was hired for eight weeks, beginning 7 February, for $5,000 per week, with two additional weeks. On 19 February, Hitch sent a further cable to Jessica in Rome: 'I am afraid it looks as though we may need you earlier than the dates indicated in your telegram the reason for this is because we have cover sets and bad weather would necessitate us going into these cover sets. A further problem is the need to put in hand the making of a wig for you this will be used in the scene where the birds come down the chimney. We have had excellent mechanical small birds made whose wings flutter violently and these will be inserted or entangled in this wig.'

Jessica flew first class from Rome to LA on 6 March where she met Edith Head for wardrobe and wig fittings, before reporting for location filming at the Gaffney Ranch on 16 March.

SUZANNE PLESHETTE

'I wasn't at all intimidated by Alfred Hitchcock, I found him so divine' – Suzanne Pleshette

The role of Annie Hayworth, the schoolteacher who nurses an unrequited love for Mitch, was originally written for someone much older than 26 years. On 19 January, casting agent Jere Henshaw sent Hitchcock a memo with suggestions for the role, which included the actresses Barbara Rush, Janice Rule, Angie Dickinson, Virginia McKenna and Suzanne Pleshette. A note by Suzanne's name remarked that she 'may be too young'. Another agent, Helen Ferguson, sent, on 23 January 1962, a packet of photos of Dina Merrill. Evan Hunter, too, weighed in with his opinion. 'It is too bad there isn't an Anne Bancroft looking for work these days. She would make a marvellous Annie. Do you think someone like Julie Harris or Kim Stanley would be interested in taking a featured role?' he wrote in a letter to Hitchcock. Hitchcock, however, took up Henshaw's suggestion and invited Suzanne Pleshette to come in for a chat with her agent.

Suzanne was born and raised in New York City and her father worked at the Paramount Studios. As an only child, she'd often go out to dinner in New York with her family. She was brash, funny and very likeable. By 1962, Suzanne was one of the hottest properties in showbusiness and had recently been chosen by the Theatre Owners of America as the year's 'Most Exciting New Star'. Suzanne had starred in a few feature films such as *Rome Adventure* (1962) with future husband Troy Donahue and done some work on television, including *Hong Kong*, which also starred Rod Taylor.

'Hitchcock saw me on television,' Suzanne recalled in an interview. 'My agent (Herb Brenner) called and said it's very strange, we got a call from Hitchcock's office, and he'd like to see you for *The Birds*. I said, I don't know why, because there's no part. I mean, there was the kid, there was the mother, and there was Tippi, and there was a 49-year-old schoolteacher who lived in the community. So I said, what do I care it's Hitch! So I went to meet him and I had a grand old time. He said what do you look like without all that hair on your face? And I said, well I guess I look like a bald fellow! So he said, well this is a part of a 26-year-old schoolteacher – my agent swallowed his cigarette – he just liked me, so he rewrote everything.'[12]

Suzanne was sent along to hair and make up together with Tippi. According to Suzanne, her dark looks were in danger of stealing the limelight away from her co-star. 'And you know, brunettes, there's a lot of power onscreen, if you put a brunette and blonde side by side on screen then boom if you're going to be photographed kindly. So Hitchcock got nervous and he was going to let me go. And he told someone else to do it because he was such a coward.' When she went to the wardrobe department, Suzanne recalled later, 'They are giving me Virginia Mayo's wool pants with wool garments underneath, a sweater and a jacket, and I arrived on location and no one had fired me, so Hitch said, well she's here. And the cameraman said to me, I have to apologise now for what I'm about to do to you. So I said, I don't care, I'm an actor. And I wasn't at all intimidated by Alfred Hitchcock, I found him so divine.' Suzanne was to be paid $1,250 per week for 10 weeks of work beginning on 10 March.

VERONICA CARTWRIGHT

Still to be cast was the role of Cathy, Lydia Brenner's daughter and Mitch's younger sister. Hitchcock turned to child actress Veronica Cartwright for the role. She had just appeared in a movie called *The Children's Hour* (1961) with Audrey Hepburn, Shirley MacLaine and James Garner and Hitchcock had seen her.

Veronica Cartwright was born in Bristol, England in 1949. After the war, her father was trying to build a house, and supplies were hard to come by, but the family had an aunt in Canada who sponsored their move overseas. The Cartwright family then moved to California when Veronica was six years old, and a friendly landlady suggested putting Veronica and her sister Angela forward for modelling jobs because they were both cute. They were introduced to an agent named Mrs Robinson, and Veronica and Angela entered showbusiness.

'I had thousands of freckles, long blonde hair, blue eyes and looked like the all-American girl,' remembers Veronica. 'I ended up doing peanut butter and cereal commercials – and my dad worked as a technical artist doing commercials. After seeing me in *The Children's Hour* Hitchcock requested to meet me.'[13] Veronica was 12 years old at the time she went to meet Hitchcock in his bungalow at Universal Studios. On meeting the great man, she says, 'I wasn't really nervous – I had already done a couple of Hitchcock shows including "The Witch" and "Short Medical". He was that guy who introduced those shows and he was always so pleasant and nice to me.' Hitchcock knew that Veronica had been born in Bristol and started to tell her of great wines to get, because that's where his favourite wine cellar was. 'We talked and talked. I was there for quite some time, while my mother waited in the outer office. He had a nice office and asked me what I liked.'

The Birds shoot would be long and arduous for any child and Hitchcock wanted to make sure that his child actress was grounded. 'He taught me how to cook a steak,' remembers Veronica. 'He said you have to cook it at a high temperature and then cover it with tinfoil so it seals and continue to cook it in all the juices. He said to me, you need to know these things for when you get married. I think he wanted to see how grounded I was and that I wasn't flighty.'

Veronica went to a regular school so, during the location and studio filming, provisions were to be made for a teacher to be on the set. 'I wasn't that much different from other kids, but I was opinionated. I had to deal with adults and I was always able to handle myself. Not like some of the kids today.' Because Veronica had very long hair at the time, Hitchcock asked her to cut it shorter, because in the storyboards and sketches her hair was short. 'My mother wasn't convinced that I shouldn't have long hair – so we had it put in a pony tail,' Veronica recalls. She was to be paid $625 per week for location work and $550 per week for studio work over an eight-week period to start on 9 March.

ROBERT BOYLE – THE ART DESIGNER

'It was a meeting of equals: the director who knew exactly what he wanted, and the art director who knew how to get it done'
– Robert Boyle

The first crew member to be hired was Bob Boyle (Figure 7). In order to capture the spirit of Daphne du Maurier's novel, Hitchcock needed an excellent art director, so he put in a call to Bob in late summer of 1961, to get his assistance in determining just how the film could be visually realised. Bob was the production designer on *Saboteur* (1942) and *North* by Northwest (1959). 'The production designer is responsible for the space in which the film takes place, you have to start thinking like a director,' said Boyle. According to Norman Lloyd, 'Hitch loved him. Whenever Bob Boyle came in Hitch called him "Bobby". He was a very loveable guy and totally devoted to Hitch.' Bob's contract began on 31 July 1961 and he was paid $600 a week for the first year, with an increment of $50 in the second.

'I had worked on North by Northwest and shortly after that I got a call from Mr Hitchcock, asking me to come to the office. He wanted me to read a novella by Daphne du Maurier called The Birds, and it was a small mood piece, really. He said, "Would you read it and see if, physically, it creates too many problems." There was as yet no screenplay from which to work, so Boyle read the du Maurier story to get an idea of what might be required.

When Bob read the story, he saw it as a mood piece, not as a melodrama. 'And I was bowled over by its strength. I just made some little sketches and I must admit that what I saw was Munch's "The Scream", which I thought was to be a symbol of the terror that birds can strike in the hearts of many people.' 'The Scream' was the name given to four versions of a composition created by the Norwegian artist Edvard Munch. It shows a woman standing on a bridge holding her head and letting out a terrified scream. Bob Boyle wanted to keep the same desperate mood in The Birds, by muting the colours and keeping the skies grey and cloudy. So expressionistic art was at the very heart of the film's conception.

Bob spent the rest of the night working on the preliminary sketches (Figure 4) using 'The Scream' as his inspiration. The mood sketches he painted in both watercolour and charcoal show a man and child on a footbridge being attacked by hovering seagulls and crows that have been hiding in the reeds. 'I saw ['The Scream'] as a kind of icon for the whole thing. It was a scream about what was happening in the world.' This was the time just before the Cuban Missile Crisis, but at the start of the Vietnam War.

Bob talked to Hitchcock about how birds were such an important part of human history and human mythology, constantly in man's conscious or subconscious, as Freud had mentioned. Hitchcock often dealt with the subconscious in his films and so it seemed an appropriate subject matter. He asked Bob if he thought the film could be made and asked him how. To determine what processes were available to realistically combine the birds with the actors, Bob started to investigate. 'I decided to do a little survey, and I went all around town, talked to people in many studios. Everything pointed to the fact that in those days we knew we were going to have mattes of some kind. Some of it would be superimposed, but many places we would have to have travelling mattes.' The result would mean many different studios and departments coming together and sharing resources to achieve the level of technological perfection a complex film like *The Birds* would require.

ROBERT BURKS – THE DP

The Birds needed a top director of photography who could work with all the special effects, so Hitchcock turned to his long-time collaborator, cinematographer Bob Burks. Born in 1909 in Los Angeles, Bob had found a job in the Warner Brothers lab when he was 19 and was able to observe some of the best cinematographers at work in the industry's largest special-effects facility on Stage 5. Bob's natural talent soon led to him being promoted to assistant cameraman and he was able to work with, and learn from, some of the top cameramen in the business. It was out of Stage 5 at Warner Brothers, the special photographic effects stage, that some of Hollywood's pioneering work was done, and Bob had the advantage of being a photographer there. He became a director of photography himself in 1939.

Hitchcock discovered Bob and asked him to be his cinematographer on *Strangers on a Train* (1951). A collaboration on ten other Hitchcock films followed, including *Rear Window*, *Vertigo* and *North by Northwest*. Hitchcock didn't like new faces. When he felt comfortable with someone he wanted them back all the time, and he felt this way about Bob. *The Birds* was to be Bob's eleventh feature with Hitchcock; it was to be in colour and was going to be an expensive movie. 'Hitch insists on perfection,' said Bob of his collaboration with Hitchcock. 'You never have any trouble with him as long as you know your job and do it.'

JAMES H BROWN – THE AD

The first assistant director on *The Birds* was Jim Brown, who was originally from Texas. As a UCLA student, he majored in film and gained a job in the mailroom at MCA in 1953. 'I started in the business at the age of 23, 25 when I became a second AD and first AD at the age of 27.'[14] The mailroom job led to his promotion to second assistant director in late 1955 and Jim's duties included 'paperwork, doing all the chasing and setting the background. Getting actors out of their dressing rooms, getting extras onto the set.' Being a junior administrator without an office, Jim would grab a table on the set and make out the next day's call sheets by hand.

Jim's talents – a likeable personality and willingness to go the extra mile to help the directors to whom he was assigned – quickly led to him being promoted to first assistant director, and he began working with extras to stage the background action, which led to some assignments on the various television series being made at Revue Studios. His first decade in television was spent at Revue, the independent company, a part of the MCA Empire, which had bought Universal Studios and grew into the biggest in television production.

But Jim hankered for location work at the time and was able to direct a couple of Wells Fargo Westerns. 'I didn't like working on the stage that much, my background was early television doing Westerns, I loved working outdoors,' recalls Jim. 'Any time I was on the stage I got claustrophobic.' Jim started working with Hitchcock when he took over from Hilton Green as Hitchcock's first assistant on the television series *Alfred Hitchcock Presents*. Jim's love of location work made him a natural choice for being the first AD on *The Birds*. Jim was 32 at the time, the same age as Rod and Tippi. More than any of the other directors he worked with, Jim was impressed by John Ford and Alfred Hitchcock's effortless command of their sets. 'They were the best teachers I ever had,' he would later recall. Foster Phinney and Lee Katzin would be the second ADs on the picture.

HAROLD MICHELSON – THE PRODUCTION ILLUSTRATOR

The complicated set-ups, and combination of process shots and optical effects, needed careful storyboarding by an expert illustrator. Bob Boyle had worked with Harold Michelson on one other movie before *The Birds* and recommended him to Hitchcock. Harold himself had previously worked for Hitch when he was at Paramount on *Rear Window* and *The Man Who Knew Too Much*, but he had never met him. 'We would do our sketches and they were handed to him.' (Figure 8)

After serving as a bombardier during the war, with many sorties over Germany, Harold left the United States army in 1949. He then went to New York to become an illustrator. 'But I soon realised that wasn't the place for me,' Harold later observed, so he moved his family to LA. He took his illustrations around the various studios and then received an unexpected call from someone he hadn't approached asking, 'Are you the guy who did those drawings? I said yes, so whoever did those drawings may now be selling insurance!'

Harold started to sketch a tremendous amount of illustrations for *The Birds*, including the schoolchildren running down the street being chased by crows. 'I was given the script and with Bob Boyle, who was the production designer, we would discuss the scene.' He would also give the storyboards as much detail as possible: 'I like to give shadows but not diagrams like football stick figures.' Harold drew some sketches which he was very proud of and took them to show Hitchcock. 'He said these are very good but I can't use them here [for this scene]. That's when I knew that we were doing a symphony with the low notes and the high notes. The director has to put it all together and know where.'[15]

'We all felt Hitchcock was a complete filmmaker. When you lay out a storyboard and you get a criticism from him, it's a very good criticism, he's telling you why,' Harold later remembered. As Hitchcock wore a shirt and tie to work, so did those working in the art department, as they knew Hitch liked that. 'This is the first time that I worked with a fairly close-knit group and it was very satisfying,' affirms Harold. In the early stages of research, Bob Boyle and Harold were also very dependent upon the archives of Harold's wife, Lillian, who ran the Universal Studios research library, to find out more about bird behaviour. 'We needed to find out which birds we could use best,' recalled Bob.

When the production crew went up to Bodega Bay to shoot, Harold stayed behind at Universal, as they usually didn't take a sketch artist with them on location. 'So, in many cases, I was on my own interpreting the script. And I did stuff for a few weeks, and then I got a call to come up there. So, evidently, what I was doing was right. And Hitchcock's method of shooting – moving in on a subject slowly, or an objective or subjective way of shooting, which I hadn't come across before – I, of course, went along with it, and learned an awful lot about how to make a movie.'

ALBERT WHITLOCK – THE MATTE ARTIST

The Birds needed an excellent matte artist to create the moody skies for the backdrops, because the weather in Bodega Bay was so unpredictable. Sometimes sunny, sometimes cloudy, mattes were essential if the production were to have consistently gloomy skies, in keeping with Bob Boyle's inspiration from 'The Scream'. *The Birds* was also to be a very complicated film in which some real locations would be combined with composite shots. Albert Whitlock's job was to put the magic skies in.

Born in the East End of London in 1915, Albert's family was originally from Ireland. He had no formal training in art, and didn't go to art college, instead being taught by British matte painting pioneer Walter Percy Day. Albert's long career began in London in 1929 when, at the age of 14, he worked at Gaumont Studios, where he built sets and worked as a grip.

Trained as a sign painter, Albert began a life-long association with Hitchcock by painting all of the signs for *The 39 Steps* (1935) and *The Lady Vanishes* (1937), as well as assisting in the miniature effects for *The Man Who Knew Too Much* (1934). Being both from England, the same part of London, and of the same generation, Albert and Hitch shared the same sense of humour and the two maintained a close professional relationship. Albert liked to wear the typical English gentleman look, with open shirt and trousers.

Albert and his family left England in 1954 to move to America, 14 years after Hitchcock's own move. As his widow, June Whitlock, remembers, 'We were all set to move to Australia because they wanted people over there, but then Albert got an offer from Disney, and California was the logical place for him to go.'[16] So Albert, June and their young children moved to California where Albert worked as a billboard painter, before taking a job at Disney painting mattes for live-action features. The head of the matte department at Disney was a fellow Londoner and near-exact contemporary named Peter Ellenshaw. Both Peter and Albert were two of the greatest matte artists of their time, and it was at Disney that Albert successfully mastered the impressionistic approach to matte painting that he would become known for. Albert worked at Disney for the next seven years, but there could only be one 'prince in the palazzo', and that was Peter Ellenshaw. So when, in 1961, Universal made an offer to Albert, he jumped at the chance.[17]

It was as head of Universal's matte department that Albert resumed his collaboration with Hitchcock, and he ended up working on all of Hitchcock's films from *The Birds* to the uncompleted *The Short Night*. 'He was a delightful man, short in stature, always well dressed when he painted. He wore a cashmere jacket, never got paint on his hands and clothes,' remembers colleague Bill Taylor who worked with Albert in the 1970s.[18] (Figure 9)

'Albert was a very good explainer and teacher, who taught me so much about lighting and understood the effects of light,' remembers Syd Dutton, who also worked with him at Universal. 'He noticed things in the most essential way, with simple draughtsmanship.' It was Albert who would often talk a director out of things if he didn't think the shot was working, and he would develop that strong relationship with Hitchcock on *The Birds*, often acting as his confidante.

RAY BERWICK – THE BIRD TRAINER

Ray Berwick was born in Dalhart, Texas in 1914 and, from an early age, wanted to be a cowboy. By the age of seven he could jump on a bull and ride it. But he started to develop brain swellings from falling off, so he had to abandon that. All his life Ray was interested in animals, as they were the only ones who wouldn't judge him, and by the time he was ten he had been hired by the Mills Brothers Circus.

'My parents were both in the travelling circus,' remembers his daughter Tamara. 'There were only four major animal trainers at the time, my dad being one of them, and he worked with animals in the 1950s. He became interested in bird training in 1943 when he produced a touring stage show called "Animal Stars of Hollywood". In that show was a raven that became his pet and launched his career as a bird trainer.'[19]

Ray started doing guest spots on the *Johnny Carson Show* with Nosey the raven. Nosey, a large, intelligent raven, was one of the first birds Ray acquired in the 1950s. Ray's first feature film working as a bird trainer was *The Bird Man of Alcatraz* (1962), starring Burt Lancaster as a convict on Alcatraz who became a world authority on birds. For the film, Ray trained small, cheepy birds like finches and sparrows. 'He trained those in our bathroom and would lock himself in, much to my mother's disconcertion,' remembers Tamara.

Ray had heard that Hitchcock was going to make *The Birds* using mechanical birds. So he wrote a letter to Hitchcock at Paramount, detailing how it could be done with live birds. Having read Daphne du Maurier's short story, Ray was already thinking how it could be translated to the big screen. Hitchcock was interested and called him in for a chat, where Ray described how he could do it and convinced Hitch to use live birds. He would end up working on *The Birds* for a year and a half, which was a sizeable commission. But his first job was to catch the 25,000 birds that would be used in the film, and just how would he go about achieving that?

VIRGINIA DARCY – THE HAIRSTYLIST

When Hitchcock was filming *To Catch A Thief* with Grace Kelly in the south of France in 1954, he hired a local hairdresser to do Grace's hair. But that didn't turn out well, because it would take hours to attain the right shade of blonde that Hitchcock wanted, and that took precious time out of the production schedule. He vowed never to film in Europe again without an American hairstylist, as they tended to use Clairol hair products that suited his blonde leading ladies.

The need for a location hairdresser arose again when Hitchcock was due to go to Morocco to film *The Man Who Knew Too Much* in 1955 with Doris Day and James Stewart, and someone at Paramount recommended Virginia Darcy. Born in California in 1921, Virginia's parents were from England and she started working in the film industry as a hairstylist in the mid 1940s, first at MGM and then later at Paramount Studios.

'I think he needed a professional hairdresser who could deal with Doris Day on location,' remembers Virginia Darcy.[20] 'Hitchcock only said one word to me at Casablanca airport when I met him. He felt my first name was wrong and said, "Why would anyone name a girl Virginia when it only lasts until she is 17?" I said, "I'm a virgin for sure but not for long!"' And, of course, Hitchcock loved that sort of answer.

Hitchcock and Virginia shared the same sense of humour and, while Doris Day would fret on location about Hitchcock's lack of attention to her, it was up to Virginia to smooth things over. 'Doris used to say, "Hitch doesn't talk to me, he never says anything." And I would say, "That's good, it means you're doing well, you don't want him to say anything."'

But the very professional Doris was anxious to please and the lack of communication between Hitchcock and herself would cause endless worry that she later mentioned in her biography.[21]

'She was scared to death of him, and she got stressed on that picture because he never talked to her,' remembers Virginia. 'He was so busy making it bigger and different (from the original *The Man Who Knew Too Much*, made in 1934).' Virginia worked with Hitchcock for a couple of weeks on location in Morocco before the production moved to London.

After filming *The Man Who Knew Too Much*, Virginia went to New York for four years and became in charge of hairstyles for NBC Television. When the need for a hairdresser came up on *The Birds*, Hitchcock asked his camera operator Leonard South, 'Where is that hairdresser we had with Doris Day?' Lenny said that he thought Virginia was working in New York. 'I don't care where she is, get her out here! If she can handle Doris, she can handle the birds,' Hitch said.

'Hitchcock just got in touch with me,' recalls Virginia. 'I was working at Paramount and he asked me to come and see him. I said I'm very busy, but I'll make arrangements to take a long lunch hour. I went to Sue, his secretary, and asked "What's this all about?" and I went through *The Birds* script. Then Hitch said, "Hello, nice to see you." He said, "Would you come and watch some film and tell me what you think?"'

Virginia watched Tippi's screen test with Hitchcock and, indeed, she did look beautiful. He also showed pictures of Tippi from recent hairstylists they had worked with, and many, like Columbia's Helen Hunt, were the best in the business. 'I don't like to criticise my colleagues in the industry,' remembers Virginia, 'but I knew what Hitchcock wanted. He said he wanted her to look like Grace Kelly. And I had worked with Grace for her wedding in Monaco.' Previously, Virginia had been Grace's hairstylist at MGM on films such as *High Society* (1956), so had been specially requested as the hairdresser for Grace's wedding and travelled with her to Monaco.

The hairstyle for Melanie Daniels in *The Birds* had to be very elegant and composed to begin with. 'I did a couple of hair dos, and knew you had to have a shocker. You can't have anything loose and pretty, because there's no shock when the bird comes, nothing comes apart. I knew what he was thinking. We were very sympatico on that, which is why we were so good together.'

So Virginia set to work designing the upswept trademark hairstyle for Melanie. According to Virginia, 'Hitchcock wanted Tippi to look very sophisticated like a high-class lady. As he wanted her to look like Grace Kelly, we had to colour her hair a lighter shade of blonde. We gave it special colouring, not peroxide, but Clairol, which is used in the salons today. Then, when the bird hits, we had to make her look dishevelled.' That's why Virginia had Tippi's hair in a French twist at the back with a wave in the front, which she describes as 'an updo with a French twist' (Figure 10). As Tippi's facial features were different to Grace's, Virginia had to create a new look that framed her face.

'I also said to Hitch, "How are we going to get the bird shit out of her hair? You know it's going to take me a while." But he said, "My dear, we have mechanical birds." I said only you would have birds that don't shit!' laughs Virginia. 'I got to know him very well on *The Birds*. We became very good friends and worked together well, because we were both perfectionists. I was very lucky because he was wonderful, and I really had great feelings for him, and we were close on *The Birds* and *Marnie*. Not many people get to know him, but when he gets a liking to you it's a real privilege. He was very generous and was always telling his dirty jokes – I had a raucous laugh, and he enjoyed that.'

EDITH HEAD – THE COSTUME DESIGNER

The famed costume designer Edith Head was born in California in 1897. She was hired as a costume sketch artist at Paramount Pictures in 1924, but later admitted to borrowing another student's sketches for her job interview. Edith worked at Paramount for 43 years, where she collaborated with Hitchcock, beginning with *Notorious* (1945). She also designed Grace Kelly's luminous wardrobes in *Rear Window* (1954) and *To Catch A Thief* (1955) as well as Kim Novak's in *Vertigo* (1958).

'Ms Head was an affable woman,' remembers Helen Colvig, the head of Revue Studios' women's wardrobe department. 'She was very fond of publicity, and she was well recognised by the actors and actresses, they trusted her, especially Hitchcock, who was 100 per cent behind her, because she had designed so many things for him.'[22]

For *The Birds*, Hitchcock felt there was something about Tippi that suggested a 'certain withdrawal, a chaste, cool quality',[23] so Head created the soft green suit Melanie wears throughout the film. Edith not only designed the costumes for Tippi to wear on the screen, but also the clothes for her to wear offscreen, too, including those for promotional appearances. 'Hitchcock has a very psychological approach to costumes,' Edith added.

Working under Edith Head during the pre-production of *The Birds* was 32-year-old Rita Riggs. Born in Arkansas in 1930, Rita joined the Hitchcock crew as a costume supervisor on *Alfred Hitchcock Presents*, working on Hitch's intros. 'That was so wonderful, it was like being given dessert while you were good. You got to work with him, see great actors at work, and the scripts were always fascinating. That's how I became associated with them.'

Rita's job on the series was matching, which involved making sure that the jackets were buttoned and the ties straightened. When all of Hitchcock's television crew got to work on *Psycho*, so did Rita. *Psycho* was her first experience working in film, and she would go on to become the wardrobe supervisor on *The Birds* and *Marnie*, working with Edith Head.

She describes Head as 'a well-educated woman, very sensible and a great diplomat. She spoke three or four languages and her French was so much better than Hitchcock's. It was a wonderful learning experience. I was much younger than my colleagues, and it was a great learning curve for me. My first three films were with Hitchcock; I could have been spoiled forever. Everyone knew each other and liked each other, and trusted each other. It was a very dignified set.'

Rita ended up working on *The Birds* for seven months, beginning in 1962. 'It was very carefully orchestrated, as were most of [Hitchcock's] looks, and it was very tidy,' remembers Rita. 'I learnt the ability to visualise an overall look and work with the production designer and the art designer. It was a team effort.'

With such an intricate and complex film ahead, Hitchcock's crew needed to trust each other. The various departments had to be able to work efficiently together to begin the complicated pre-production, where many planned shots included birds, and it required everyone to know what was happening. This involved careful scouting, storyboarding and training of the birds to realise the many planned special effects in the film.

NOTES

1 Jack Hamilton, 'Tippi Hedren, Hitchcock's New Grace Kelly', *Look Magazine*, 4 December 1962

2 Robert Boyle, BBC *Omnibus*, Hitchcock Documentary, 1986

3 Interview with Dolores Parker Miller on 8 December 2012 in Manhattan, New York

4 Interview with Jerry Adler, 2 December 2012 in Roxbury, Connecticut

5 Ronald L Davis 'Tippi Hedren interview', 24 July 1984, Margaret Herrick Library, Los Angeles

6 Jim Gibbins, 'Jim Gibbins in New York', *Sydney Morning Herald*, 19 May 1963

7 Hitchcock to Janet Maslin, *Alfred Hitchcock: Interviews*, 1972

8 Tippi Hedren, 'Tippi Hedren in Conversation' at The Genius of Hitchcock, BFI, 16 August 2012

9 Odette Perry, 'The Suspense Triumph of Tippi Hedren', 10 August 1963

10 'Hitchcock's New Grace Kelly', *Look Magazine*, 4 December 1962

11 Interview with Rod Taylor, 1 June 2012, Los Angeles

12 Stephen J Abramson, Interview with Suzanne Pleshette, 2 September 2006

13 Interview with Veronica Cartwright, 29 November 2012, Los Angeles

14 Interview with Jim Brown, 1 September 2000, Angels Camp, California

15 Interview with Harold Michelson, 5 September 2000, Los Angeles

16 Interview with June Whitlock, 26 June 2012, Santa Barbara, California

17 Interview with Bill Taylor, 8 September 2012, Los Angeles

18 Interview with Syd Dutton, 8 September 2012, Los Angeles

19 Interview with Tamara Mellett, 14 July 2012, Escondido, California

20 Interview with Virginia Darcy, 5 September 2012 in Santa Barbara

21 A E Hotchner, *Doris Day: Her Own Story*, William Morrow & Company, 1975

22 Interview with Helen Colvig, 3 December 2012, Los Angeles

23 Kyle Counts, 'The Making of Alfred Hitchcock's *The Birds*', *Cinefantastique*, p.23

PRE-PRODUCTION

'Q: How did you get the birds to act so well?'
A: 'They were very well paid'
– Alfred Hitchcock

BODEGA BAY

'Up the coast about 60 miles north of San Francisco'
– Mitch's neighbour to Melanie

When Hitchcock was adapting *The Birds* with Evan Hunter he decided early on to drop the Cornish village setting of Daphne du Maurier's story. '*The Birds* needed a present-day atmosphere,' Hitchcock stated. 'And in order to get the photography of the birds in the air, we needed an area with low land, not high mountains or a lot of trees. In a pictorial sense, it was vital to have nothing on the ground but sand so that we had the entire sky to play with. Bodega Bay had all of that.'[1]

Located 60 miles northwest of San Francisco and 20 miles southwest from Santa Rosa, Bodega Bay, Bodega Head and the neighbouring town of Bodega made up a picturesque hamlet in Sonoma County, Northern California. Bodega Bay was discovered on 3 October 1757 by Spanish lieutenant Juan Francisco de la Bodega y Cuadra. At that time the whole area was deep in old-growth redwoods that stretched from the coast into the valleys and all the way down to San Francisco. In 1841 the first saw mill was built in Bodega by Captain Stephen Smith, and commercial logging of the redwoods made the area prosperous. Money brokers came from San Francisco and invested in property but, after the timber was cut down, the area had to rely on other resources. Today Bodega and Bodega Bay are supported by the crab, fishing and tourist industries, though in 1961 it was still very rural with beautiful scenery, few people and thousands of birds.

Hitchcock had known about the area since 1942 when he was filming *Shadow of a Doubt* with Teresa Wright and Joseph Cotten. During the first few days writing *The Birds*, on Wednesday 20 September, Hitchcock and Evan Hunter scouted San Francisco. Production designer Bob Boyle was assigned to explore Bodega Bay and find the film's key locations, including the Brenner house, the schoolteacher's house and the school. Bob spent three days in the area from 25–27 September 1961 and, when he arrived, agreed with Hitchcock that the location offered many scenic values to meet the needs of the story, with the ocean to the west, the broad expanse of bay to the east and south, the dramatic green hills rising from the water's edge and the picturesque bay community nestled against the shore.

But the bay alone had its drawbacks. The fishing community was small and there was little to recommend it except a fishing pier, a motel and a few other buildings. The larger area, which included Bodega and Bodega Head, offered more potential as there was a school house and an old church. Also, the surrounding habitat was just too sunny and picturesque to suit the film's eerie and moody background, in keeping with Bob Boyle's inspiration from the Edvard Munch painting 'The Scream'. Later some critics would remark that the film didn't exploit the beauty of Bodega Bay enough but, as Bob stated, 'We weren't making "A Bright Day at Malibu" type picture.' He and Hitchcock wanted the movie to look gloomy, to the extent that 'it was necessary to subdue the colour of many of the scenes in the film lab to get the proper effect'.

When Bob returned from his scout, he met with Hitchcock on the morning of Tuesday 17 October to go over some of the shots and locations that were key to the film, and Hitchcock instructed the following:

1) Organisation of the farm and buildings – make various layouts with combination of sketches

2) Make a list of long shots
   - Girl's POV of boat
   - POV of the approach in the car when Mother comes back from back part of house looking down
   - We will need to shoot towards the south west. We will not need to shoot with our back to the south west
   - New road
   - Girl's POV of house with jetty
1) Work out the joining up of school and town
2) Lay out the back lot set in relation to the Tides
3) Lay out the town and school combined for matte shots
4) Girl drives up to teacher's house with matte of bay with town in background
5) Lay out dummy map of town and how it works

Accompanying Bob on one of his next trips to Bodega Bay was matte artist Albert Whitlock. The film would need a number of complicated matte paintings to unite the geography of the Bodega locations and create mood, in keeping with its subdued and gloomy look. In the past, Albert had created his impressionistic paintings with the aid of photographs, but for *The Birds* he researched locations with Bob and made a series of sketches from which to work.

At first, Albert and Bob were very wary of each other, but soon they became great friends after having dinner one night. Albert painted many mattes for *The Birds* and was very pleased with his layouts. In total, he created about 50 oil paintings to show mood, because that was what interested Hitchcock, who once remarked while looking at them, 'Don't forget. Let me not lose the mood that you have in these paintings.' But as soon as it started to rain, Hitchcock would duck for cover, and only fine weather would coax him out to shoot, so Albert had to paint in the gloomy skies retrospectively.

While on location in Bodega Bay, the crew built a small plywood barge to hold the second unit camera to film scenes from the water and across the bay. It was used for approximately three weeks and then was destroyed (Figure 14).

THE SCHOOL HOUSE

While scouting Bodega and Bodega Bay for locations, Bob found two existing buildings that would lend themselves well to the film. The first was an old school house located in Bodega, seven miles inland from the coast. Built in 1873 of old-growth virgin redwood, it was known as the Potter school house after County Sheriff Potter, who donated the land. There were two classrooms downstairs for grades 1–8, and upstairs was a multi-purpose room. By the fall of 1961, however, the school house had been boarded up for storage and listed as unsafe in the event of earthquakes, with no water supply to the property.

Bob met with Lena Piazza, the clerk of the school board in Bodega Bay, about using the school house. She had already talked to almost all the members of the board and she felt that there would be no objection to the use of the school. After negotiating a fee, Bob instructed his crew to repair the school house and added a fence and a nearby jungle gym, which would later figure prominently in the crow attack. Since being abandoned, the interior of the school house had mainly been left intact, with desks, chairs, maps and a chalkboard. The front room was the only part of the interior repaired for the classroom scenes, a portrait of George Washington was added, and a small cloakroom was fitted near the front door.[2]

Next to the school house, Bob built Annie Hayworth's home. Only the front of the house was erected for exterior scenes, such as when Melanie meets Annie for the first time, and later for Annie's death scene. It is during the latter scene, when Mitch and Melanie discover Annie's body, that Saint Teresa of Avila, a Roman Catholic Church, can be seen in the background. The church was made famous by the American photographer Ansel Adams. After filming was complete, the Potter school was sold at auction in April 1963 for the sum of $3,150, and today it's a private residence owned by Leah Taylor.

THE TIDES RESTAURANT

The other important building for Bob to find was a restaurant, which was to be the focus for many key scenes in *The Birds*. He found the ideal one in the Tides Wharf Restaurant in Bodega Bay (Figure 12). Bob immediately saw that the restaurant and parking lot could be used for the café, gas station and boat dock scenes. The owner at the time was a man named Mitch Zankich, a resident of Bodega when Bob came knocking. Another Bodega local was Hazel Mitchell who was working as a waitress at the Tides. She later recalled that Mitch told Bob that he would allow them to film in the restaurant for free if they would call the community in the movie Bodega Bay, and if they gave him a small speaking part. (He was the man who passes Mitch and Melanie on the docks after she is first hit by the gull.) Bob agreed.

Later, when the crew came to film, Hazel served lunch and waited on Hitchcock, who only wanted 'green beans and filet of sole and nothing else, miss'. In keeping with the theme of documentary realism, the waitress in the finished film bears an uncanny resemblance to a youthful Hazel.

The entire inside scenes were recreated very specifically from the original buildings back at Universal Studios. The Tides Wharf was completely rebuilt in the 1990s and today is located across Highway One from the Visitors Centre.

FINDING THE BRENNER HOUSE

Bob continued to look all over Bodega Bay for a suitable property that could be used as the Brenner house, and it turned out to be the most difficult location to find. Hitchcock was very specific in his requirements, because he wanted the house to be isolated with no suggestion of neighbourly support. This was very important towards the end of the film when the house is under attack by the birds. The isolated house is prominent in other Hitchcock movies such as Manderley in *Rebecca* (1940) and Minyago Yugilla in *Under Capricorn* (1949), where the house becomes a character in its own right and a trap for the suffering heroine.

The house also needed to have an entrance or dock that could be reached by boat for the scene when Melanie arrives by water. Bob eventually found the ideal building on Westshore Road, which was part of Bodega Head, in an almost completely enclosed bay. Here he found a 100-year-old ranch house, built around 1849 by colonising Russians, that had gone to wrack and ruin. Many Russians lived on the coast at the time and, when the Russians owned Alaska, they used to come down to hunt for seals. Eleven miles north of Bodega Bay is the Russian River and a town called Sebastopol lies 16 miles east towards Santa Rosa.

In 1962, the house was owned by 65-year-old Rose Gaffney, a local rancher (Figure 11). Rose had just achieved local notoriety in a successful crusade against Pacific Gas and Electric's proposed nuclear power plant. In the early 1960s, PG&E had selected Bodega Head as the future site of one of the first commercial atomic power plants. Rose, who was an ardent environmentalist, made headlines by battling their plans to build a power plant on her land.

Naturally, the feisty Rose was suspicious when Bob Boyle approached asking to use her ranch house. She reportedly asked, 'Who is Alfred Hitchcock?' But, as Bob later remembered it, 'We charmed her into it.' A contract was issued on 12 October 1961, offering $1,200 to allow the film crew and independent contractors the right to alter the premises for filming purposes. Rose signed two days later. More specifically, it was up to crew member Bob Luthardt, who was part of the production design team, to placate Rose, and it was his job to be very friendly to her at all times.

Renting the ranch house from Rose Gaffney was only half the battle. Although the location was ideal, the condition in which it was discovered made Bob grimace. 'The house was nothing but a shack when I first saw it. Rose used it as extra property and hadn't kept it up very well over the years. We had to literally make a new house out of it by building over it.'

Set construction began on location on 19 February, and included the interior of the Brenner house, the exterior with yard and dune, the boat dock, and the road leading up to the house. As there was hardly any house existing, the crew built a front. The outbuildings and barn behind the main house were deemed too far away for filming, so an exterior barn was erected to group the structures closer together. Bob and his set decorators refurbished the main house and a small pier was added to the front of the property, where Melanie could land her boat. A gazebo was also built for the birthday party sequence and the overgrown grounds and trees were trimmed, the lawn manicured and spring daffodils planted.

Sadly, all of these structures burned down in the late 1960s. The Gaffney property had been sold to the Regents of the University of California and it became the site of the Bodega Marine Laboratory, which began construction after the filming of *The Birds*. Today, if you stop at the entrance to the marine lab, just before the dormitories, and look out into the marsh, about 100 yards away, you can see the old entrance road which was built. The sand dunes where Mitch and Melanie climbed are now behind some cedar trees and, although the house has been demolished, the ancient trees look much the same as they did in the film.

VALLEY FORD FARM

The other farmhouse that was to feature in *The Birds* was that belonging to Dan Fawcett, the neighbour who is killed by birds in his home. Bob Boyle found a 640-acre dairy ranch in picturesque Valley Ford on 15000 Highway One. Valley Ford Farm was originally owned by a wealthy landowner in Sonoma County with the ironic name of Hollis Hitchcock. The farm was then bought in 1918 by the Bianchi family, who had emigrated from Northern Italy in the early 1900s. They first settled in Port of Marin and then moved to Valley Ford.

In 1962, the farm was owned by John Bianchi and his wife. Bob Boyle thought that the farm would be suitable for the Fawcett place, and offered $3,000 for a couple of weeks. The Bianchis turned out to be easier to persuade than Rose Gaffney and they accepted the offer, excited that a Hollywood film crew would be filming on their ranch. Paul Bianchi, John's son, was 20 years old when filming took place. 'They were here for two weeks, and Mr Hitchcock was smart and intelligent,' Paul remembers. 'Rod Taylor wanted to know how to milk a cow because he had never milked one before, so I took him to a barn and showed him.'[3]

Very importantly for the art department, the farm had a long road leading up to the house that could be used in a crucial long shot which occurs when Jessica Tandy drives her truck along it as she goes to check on her neighbour, Dan Fawcett, to find out why his chickens aren't eating either. Hitchcock was careful to show the actual arrival of the truck by watering the road down so that no dust would arise. 'I wanted it to rise on the way down. That truck seen at a distance to me, tremendous speed, expressed the frantic nature of her mood,' Hitchcock remarked in an interview. 'This is when you are taking an emotion – it means a lot to me when you are expressing it through a truck, this is an emotional truck. The sound should have a cry – it should go oohhhhh! If this electronic sound is going to mean anything, it will give an extra use as a dramatic device.'[4]

PHOTOGRAPHIC REALISM

Although *The Birds* was based on a fantastic premise, that of birds attacking humans, it retains, like other Hitchcock films dealing in fantasy, such as *North by Northwest*, a sense of being very vivid and real, almost like a nightmare, because it's photographed realistically. Hitchcock intentionally wanted to keep it real and once said, 'My suspense work comes out of creating nightmares for the audience. When you have a nightmare, it's awfully vivid if you're dreaming that you're being led to the electric chair. Then you're as happy as can be when you wake up because you're relieved. It was so vivid. And that's really the basis of this attempt at realistic photography, to make it look as real as possible, because the effects themselves are actually quite bizarre.'[5]

For Hitchcock, the juxtaposition of the ordinary with the fantastical is what made his plots interesting. The wilder the storyline, the more realistically it should be told. Just as he strove for realism in his previous film *Psycho*, when he sent a photographer to Arizona to take pictures of secretaries, their offices and apartments, so he did the same for *The Birds*. This was to be even more important in Bodega Bay where the townspeople would also appear as prominent extras in the film, with the town itself becoming a character.

Bob Boyle sent out a roll call asking for the townspeople to appear as movie extras, and inviting them to come to the Tides restaurant for auditions. Glenice Carpenter was a 30-year-old Bodega Bay resident at the time of the auditions. 'It was exciting because Bodega Bay wasn't very big,' she remembers. 'All the townspeople had their pictures taken in the dining room of the Tides Wharf if they wanted to be extras and I, too, went along.'[6] Hitchcock later said, 'I had every school child photographed in the area and every living person photographed, so that there would be no mistake in the wardrobe. And had the characters photographed.'[7]

SET DECORATION

The attention to realism extended to the set decor, especially for the Brenner house. In a memo dated 24 January 1962, Bob Boyle laid out the set requirements for furnishing the interior. 'The first consideration should be that the Brenners are reasonably educated and literate people' and that 'the general atmosphere of taste and character would be, it would seem, to combine that of the mother and her son'.

In a pre-production conference Hitchcock described the Brenners as 'pleasant people, and, as I say, literate, educated. I imagine if they hadn't had the money, they would have been kind of bohemians almost, you know.'[8] A character study written for Lydia Brenner surmised that, after her husband died four years earlier, she had sold their apartment in San Francisco to live permanently on the farm in Bodega Bay, taking some key furniture items with her and giving the rest to Mitch for his apartment in the city.

Bob's memo went on to suggest that the crew should rely upon photographs taken of a number of interiors around Bodega Bay, and that these should be taken from the house of such a character as Rose Gaffney. The idea was to look inside the homes of the most well off of all the residents of the Bodega Bay area, including a home owned by a wealthy family in the area, the Chancellor family.

The second set which was to be carefully dressed was that of the home of Annie Hayworth, the schoolteacher. The memo noted that 'Annie Hayworth is about 27. She taught when she was somewhat younger at a private school in San Francisco. For emotional reasons, she has moved into Bodega Bay and has secured the job of teaching at the local school'. The memo surmised that Annie's one-storey home would contain a large number of books she had brought from home and school, along with recently acquired paperbacks. She would also have one or two prints on the walls of her living room. They would be Braque, maybe something Mexican from the Museum of Modern Art, and perhaps she might even be catholic enough in her taste to have a Grant Wood print. Annie's artistic sensibilities are most evident during the scene when she and Melanie sip brandies against a background of Cubist and Modigliani prints on the wall.

The memo recommended that the research for Annie's interior should be conducted in three different places: the house of the actual school teacher in Bodega Bay; a slightly upgraded teacher's home in San Francisco; and finally, perhaps, a female professor's rooms at Berkeley or Stanford. For the third interior, the home of farmer Dan Fawcett, it was recommended that the crew take pictures of the master bedrooms of some of the biggest families around Bodega Bay, or some of the even bigger ones near Valley Ford.

COSTUMES

The most famous costume in the whole of *The Birds* – and, indeed, in Hitchcock's entire oeuvre – is Tippi Hedren's green suit. Aside from the opening scene in the pet shop, Tippi wears the cool green suit for the entire length of the movie (Figure 20). 'That was what Mr Hitchcock wanted,' remembers Rita Riggs, the costume supervisor. 'If he was going to be in the editing room every day and watching his lead actress on screen, there was no question that he wanted to see his favourite colour.'[9] Hitchcock loved green and specifically chose the shade celadon. Celadon is a term for ceramics, invented in ancient China, and is a light shade of green. Grace Kelly had worn a celadon-green, mid-length jacket with collar and matching skirt in *Rear Window* (1954), and the influences for its shape and style, such as the soft round shoulders and stand collar, can be attributed to Cristobal Balenciaga and Charles Creed respectively, both popular designers of the time.

'Green is very pleasing on the eye, especially if you have to look at one colour throughout the whole of the movie,' Tippi observed. 'That's why doctors in surgeries are said to wear green, because it's a very calming colour and that's what Hitchcock wanted.'[10] So Rita Riggs went searching for the right shade of green and fabric for the suit in LA. She swatched and swatched and eventually found a heavy bolt of green Irish tweed fabric that would be perfect, from a shop called Beverly Hills Silks, which is now long gone. This silk shop had fabric stacked high to a 20-foot ceiling, with trims and buttons and haberdashery that came from the glory days of MGM.

'As a young design assistant I would find gorgeous silks and I would hide them, so that when I needed something like that again I would go back and know where they were. I still have things I bought there which were left over from *Gone with the Wind*,' reminisced Rita. 'It was such fun to be put in a car, driven all over the city, and to come back with wonderful things for Ms Head.'

Edith Head took the fabric and adapted it into a Chanel-style suit for Tippi to wear. 'We made six of those suits and lived with them for a long time,' says Rita. 'Ms Head made a sleeveless dress and a jacket to wear, and it was so much more interesting than wearing a silk blouse. The sleeveless dress was very much a trademark of Ms Head, and it was handy to wear with the coat.'

'Hitchcock had a fondness for simple and elegant things like scarves and mink coats,' Edith Head once recalled, 'so these things also became a part of her wardrobe.' On working with Edith, Tippi has said, 'I just adored her. We became such good friends. And the thing that I really loved about her, during meetings with her, and Hitch, was how she manipulated the director or producer around what her ideas were. Making him think it was his. She was brilliant, absolutely brilliant.'[11]

Aside from the green suit, the next most famous piece of costume is the mink coat that Melanie Daniels wears (Figure 19). 'The mink was to give her economic status,' stated Rita. 'It was before fur was taboo.' When filming was completed, Hitchcock, as a grand gesture, gave Tippi the mink coat for her own personal use. 'You can afford it,' said Evan Hunter. But, in the 1970s, Tippi 'hocked' it to pay for maintenance and food for her lions at the Shambhala animal preserve she started.[12]

For the opening pet shop scene, Edith Head designed a two-piece black suit, made of flecked nubby wool, with a white silk blouse for Tippi to wear. Just as he had carefully selected the wardrobe and jewellery for Eva Marie Saint in *North by Northwest*, Hitchcock did the same here. He chose one bracelet, a ring and a single strand of baby pearls, which he liked because, for him, they expressed gentility. These were bought from the upscale store Gumps in San Francisco on 9 January 1962 for Tippi to wear during the production. To complete her costume, a yellow-gold, Florentine-finish, mesh bracelet watch was bought from William Ruser, jeweller to the stars in Beverly Hills, at a cost of $313. After the production, Hitchcock made Tippi a present of the watch.

And it wasn't just Tippi's costumes that kept the wardrobe department busy. The birds did too. 'We made hoods for the birds made of black silk stockings,' remembers Helen Colvig. 'They acted as blinds for the birds and they would be lined up on the wires. And they'd sit there because they couldn't see so wouldn't fly away.'

MATTE PAINTINGS

The multiple locations that Bob Boyle had discovered, some in Bodega, others in Bodega Bay or Bodega Head, needed to be tied together to keep the look of the picture ominous and moody. Many aerial and faraway shots were needed to amplify the size of the town, so Hitchcock relied on matte painter Albert Whitlock. Before the arrival of digital effects and computer graphics, these matte paintings were crucial to alter the landscape and provide the background for the live action and special effects.

Albert's 12 matte paintings, produced without the help of an assistant, took more than a year to complete. 'The first matte used was in the scene near the beginning where Tippi Hedren looks out from the post office to see the Brenner house across the bay,' recalled Albert in an interview.[13] 'That was done above the hills, above the Tides restaurant. I painted the foreground in on a reverse angle. It was really just a hole in the middle of the shot with the Tides and the motorcars all around; the sides, bottom and top were painted into this along with the sky.'

Hitchcock's bungalow and the art department were close to Albert's studio, and a painting could take a week and a half for him to complete. He liked to paint his mattes on brown butcher paper, sprayed with shellack first so the oils wouldn't be absorbed into the paper. His matte paintings were typically 3 ft by 3 ft, very flat, and his favourite brushes were a one-inch Grumbacher and a two-inch short bulletin stroke. As Albert's background was as a scenic painter, he produced the matte effects using the minimum of paint. His palette of Winsor & Newton oils was made up of titanium white, alizarin crimson, ultramarine blue, cadmium yellow, raw umber, burnt sienna, yellow ochre, Winsor green, and mars black. With this limited palette Albert felt he could mix any colour he needed, though he rarely used black in his paintings except to darken the sky. Very much a visceral painter, Albert would draw everything out carefully and his technique was to get a shape going, and he was always looking for happy accidents in his paintings.

Whereas Edvard Munch inspired Bob Boyle, Albert was influenced by the English romantic painters John Constable and William Turner when painting the Bodega Bay skies. One particular Constable he admired was 'The Hay Wain', plus several of Salisbury Cathedral, and these artworks were reflected in the clouds he painted for *The Birds*. He would often copy a Constable on brown paper, 'for my own amazement' he would say.[14]

For the sequence of Tippi crossing Bodega Bay in the outboard motor, Hitchcock asked Albert to make a matte painting of the skyline (Figure 27). Albert blocked out the top of the frame, just above Tippi's head in the boat under the line, and painted an idealised version of Bodega Bay. It was to be his first painting for *The Birds*, and it bore his signature. As he never usually signed his paintings, he must have regarded it highly.

'When the girl is going across the bay in a motorboat,' remembered Albert, 'the sky was repainted in a couple of different angles to give it mood; the weather that day of shooting was clear, and the sky was bald. When you see her coming in the boat towards the house, the background – the hills and sky – is a matte shot, grouping it all together in one piece and making a township around the Tides where previously there was none.'[15]

Hitchcock rarely offered any criticism of Albert's matte paintings but, on one occasion, Albert remembered, he did: 'The very first time the birds were seen was when Rod Taylor was saying good night to Tippi after that first evening that they had become friends, and it was the only time that Hitch actually criticised a matte shot. I mean not just on *The Birds* but forever after. It was a night shot with the car driving away, and I had to do a moonlit sky, you know, and rows of birds on the telephone wires. That was the shot. They were standing there and this was merely the background. Hitchcock called me in and he said, 'The sky is too dramatic, Al. I don't want the audience alerted at this time. I want them to see the birds, but they're just on the telephone wires, and he was right, actually.'

STORYBOARDS

Along with Albert Whitlock's first-class matte paintings, the production was reliant on continuity sketches because of the enormous technical problems and challenges in the film. Hitchcock loved to work that way anyway, as the main thrust in all of his work was preparation and storyboarding. As Bob Boyle said, 'Matter of fact, he sometimes facetiously said he was bored with shooting the picture. The excitement came with the ideas that were generated in the preparatory portion of the filmmaking process. He liked to have it all clear in his mind so that, before he started to shoot, he saw the whole movie in his mind. There are very few people, directors or otherwise, that can hold this kind of a concept.'

As Harold Michelson was the main production illustrator on *The Birds*, it was his task to sketch almost all of the storyboards. As Bob Boyle affirmed, 'Harold has an extraordinary sense of film. He only draws what the camera sees. He reproduces storyboards of what the lens sees exactly. From his storyboard you could tell what lens you should use, what the angle of the camera was. Harold was a master of his technique and his storyboards always represented a shot that you could get with the camera.'

Harold learnt the art of draughtsmanship while working at Paramount. Some storyboards have a tendency to produce ultra-wide shots that can't be photographed, but Harold always drew what the camera could encompass and Hitchcock would follow these storyboards in the finished film. 'If there were any variations on the storyboards,' said Bob Boyle, 'they were mostly variations on the interiors, but usually they didn't make continuity drawings for a two scene in a living room. That was up to the actors and Hitch. We began to think like Hitchcock because he allowed us to do that. Many directors these days seem to be afraid to let others in on the secret.'

An example of the art department visualising Hitchcock's concept can be seen in the jungle gym sequence (Figures 21 & 22). Although Harold drew these storyboards, both he and Bob Boyle affirmed that the execution was Hitchcock's idea. Bob remembered, 'He said that Melanie will come out of the school, we hear the children singing in the background, and she's very relaxed no problem, she goes down and sits by a fence, we see a bird come in. We're in a loose shot (a full shot) of Melanie, she gets a cigarette and starts to smoke a cigarette, very relaxed we see another bird come in. Then we're in a little closer, another bird, and we do this several times, when we finally get to a choker shot, we'll hold it until the audience can't stand it anymore. Once you've heard that, you know how to draw!' Bob's story shows how skilled Hitchcock was when it came to articulating his visuals to his production crew, and how he was mostly interested in generating feelings in the audience.

Bob then relayed the scene to Harold who would draw out the storyboard. 'When [Melanie's] sitting in front of the jungle gym, the shot back and forth, and moving closer and closer, I did that but it wasn't my idea, we got ideas from Hitch and tried to interpret them. He's a very visual guy but he was able to communicate what he wanted.'

Although it was initially Hitchcock's idea, he wasn't above giving his production crew credit for their work. 'He shot my storyboards as was and that, for me, was credit,' remembered Harold. Bob agreed that 'he wasn't against giving people credit, not at all, in fact he was so secure in his own professionalism, it didn't bother him that other people got credit.' Harold's storyboards were then passed on to the various departments, including the cinematographer, the special-effects people and the wardrobe people, so that everyone was working towards the same vision (Figures 21 & 22).

FILMING THE BIRDS

Harold Michelson's storyboards were very important for the crew and bird trainers in determining the answer to the inevitable, million-dollar question: how to film the bird attacks. This was the dilemma facing the crew from the very start and Hitchcock never dared admit to himself that what they were attempting to do had never been done before. If he had succumbed to any doubts, the film would never have been made, so the production crew decided to play it by ear.

When Bob Boyle started work, his most immediate thoughts were about how to film large flocks of birds, so he called Arnold Small, who was recommended as the most authoritative birder on the West Coast, regarding the best times and places. Small suggested the Sacramento National Wildlife refuge at Willows, California, and Bob put in a call to the director, Edward O'Neill. He was informed that there were three main wildlife refuges and that the largest flocks of birds would be ducks, white geese and Canada geese.

Bob also spoke to Doyle Nave about any cameraman familiar with wildlife photography similar to those used in the Walt Disney nature series and asked whether any of the Disney photographers could photograph in 35mm. The answer was no. Bob was advised to speak to cameraman Alfred Milotte about when and where to photograph birds, and Milotte recommended the San Francisco city dump as a good place to film flocks of seagulls. A camera crew was then dispatched to photograph the gulls at the dump. On 26 January 1962, production manager Norman Deming wrote to Milotte: 'What we are getting from you and the other camera crew in San Francisco is certainly good and usable film, but it all seems to be the same thing and, until we can agree how to more successfully plan our work, we have decided to ask you to stop and ship back all the gear. Many mechanical problems have been solved by seeing the film you sent us, but how to put it together convincingly and how to make it appear the birds are attacking people are problems we have not yet solved.' Filming birds in the wild was not convincing enough, so the production had to look at other means to create the bird attacks.

THE MECHANICAL BIRDS

To begin with, Hitchcock and his crew started to look at miniatures, and entertained the idea of using artificial birds, mechanical replicas with motorised wings. Over $200,000 was spent building and testing these models and Hitchcock had them in mind very early on in the production when the script was being developed. On page 15 of Hitchcock's script notes from 28 October 1961, he wrote, 'This sounds a little facetious, but would it be possible if, when we go to a close shot of Melanie's car going around curves at speed, we show an insert of the lovebirds on the floor of the car, both huddled together on the perch and swaying from side to side, as the car negotiates the curves to the sound of screaming tires?' The leaning lovebirds could only be achieved through the use of miniatures.

An expert model designer was needed so the production turned to Larry Hampton, who had been a special-effects department head with RKO and Fox and who had a long and varied experience in his field. He came highly recommended by Buddy (Arnold) Gillespie at MGM for his recent work on *The Four Horsemen of the Apocalypse* (1962) and *Mutiny on the Bounty* (1962). Other credits included creating miniatures for *It's A Wonderful Life* (1946) and the mechanical animals and birds for Disneyland.

On 3 January 1962 a memo was sent from Norman Deming to Hitchcock advising that 'Larry Hampton has been engaged on a week-to-week basis as special-effects supervisor for our picture *The Birds* for a salary of $400 weekly. His credits are mostly for wire-work and miniatures which concern flying birds and airplanes.' Larry started to build the prop birds, generally made from papier-mâché, and he also built the electronically controlled mechanical birds. Despite numerous successful experiments with these birds, Hitchcock always believed that the drama, horror, and the spirit of Daphne du Maurier's original short story had to be achieved by the use of live birds, and this was to achieve long lasting notoriety later on in the attic scene.

Some of the mechanical replicas of the birds had motorised wings. 'I must say we tried to use mechanical birds, and we did use a few, but mechanical birds that moved didn't work out too well,' said Bob Boyle. 'Some tests had been done at Universal using mechanical birds, but they were very phony looking,' agreed Bud Hoffman, who was hired as an associate editor on the film. Previously he had worked in the special-effects department at 20th Century Fox. When Bob Burks, the DP, saw the crude designs, he agreed with Bud that the mechanical birds would have to be abandoned. Hitchcock concurred, though a few mechanical birds were used in scenes where bird training was not possible, such as the swaying lovebirds mentioned in the script notes, and the gull that pecks the little girl at Cathy's birthday party.[16]

Bobby Bone was the prop master on the production, and he spent a further $24,225 on dummy birds, which included 300 plastic gulls, 400 plastic crows, 2,000 doves strung on wires, 400 plastic robins, 700 stuffed and painted robins, 1,000 winged jays and 1,000 winged swifts (Figure 25). But the combination of mechanical birds and dummy birds still wasn't enough to instill the terror that was needed, so it soon became clear that real birds would have to be used. After all, Hitchcock wanted to outdo *Psycho* for shocks, especially the shower murder.

Hitchcock and Bob Boyle thought about how they were going to physically film real birds attacking, and Bob said, 'Well, the only thing is getting the birds into the frame.' It was decided to rely on the more tried-and-tested methods like travelling mattes, superimpositions and blue screen, and that trained live birds were needed for these optical overlays. In those days, blue screen was used for travelling matte backgrounds, and often produced a halo or fringe around the subject. Bob knew that if they were to shoot small birds with fast-moving wings, the result could be unconvincing.

Bob Burks and Bud Hoffman thought that using real birds was the way forward and produced some test footage to demonstrate what the attacks would look like. They worked with Universal's optical department, creating shots of birds and people intermingled that looked 'passable' in the words of Bud Hoffman. Hitchcock was sufficiently convinced that this test footage was an improvement on the mechanical birds, but it was clear that many refinements would have to be made to the matte process.

Ray Berwick, the bird trainer, had thought all along that only real birds would give the right effect. 'I don't think Hitchcock knew what he was letting himself in for. He quickly had to give up any idea of using mechanical birds if he wanted realism.' The fundamental problem with getting any bird behaviour on film was getting close to them. The only thing that induces them towards man is food, and even their hunger is sometimes overruled by fear. Furthermore, no book or ornithologist could give the crew guidance on controlling flocks of wild birds.

It was by training the birds that Ray Berwick would be able to orchestrate scenes in which gulls swoop down on humans, strike and fly away; or 300 ravens chase a group of schoolchildren drown the street; or 1,500 finches fly down a chimney through a fireplace, and into a living room to attack people. But first they had to catch the birds – and that was far from easy.

CATCHING THE SEAGULLS

In January 1962, a film crew had spent three days at the San Francisco garbage dump filming hours of footage for use by the special-effects department. 'The crew went to the dump area and raked together all the garbage they could,' Bud Hoffman recalled.[17] A large number of seagulls regularly scavenged there and, when they saw what had been laid out for them, they dove right in for the food. The camera crew photographed reel after reel of birds using a 70mm lens, including individual birds, birds flying in the air, birds sitting on the dump, either singly or in pairs. In total, to get the few shots needed, some 20,000 feet of film was shot of the gulls flying above the dump, and in doing so the camera crew pioneered an early form of natural history filmmaking (Figures 15 & 16).

Ray Berwick decided to go along with the crew to the garbage dump to try and catch some gulls, so that he could experiment with teaching them simple tricks. A permit was issued by the Department of the Interior Fish and Wildlife Service on 9 January 1962 lasting six months: 'Permission is hereby given to Norman Deming of Alfred Hitchcock Productions Inc, Revue Studios, Universal City, California, to take, possess and transport not to exceed thirty live California or herring gulls and not to exceed twenty dead specimens of the above species for photographic purposes in connection with the motion picture production of Revue Studios located at Universal City, California.'

The seagulls were canny but, when Ray managed to catch one, he was bombarded by trash from other gulls, before finally ending up with the ones he needed. 'I found the gulls on the whole to be vicious and ornery, not very intelligent at all,' recalled Ray. 'I never came across one in all the time we were shooting that was affectionate, either towards another seagull or a human being. But they could be quite easy to trap and, in some ways, easy to train. They responded quite quickly to the food reward system, and the rest was patience on my part. I could trap a bunch down at the San Francisco garbage dump and, by the end of the day, have them doing stunts.'

From the second week of January until 21 March, Ray managed to catch 26 seagulls and transport them to Universal. The death rate was approximately one in ten birds and a couple managed to escape during training practice. In approximately two-week intervals, additional seagulls were caught to replace the escapees and, by 21 March, the full quota of 50 seagulls had been reached on location.

For Ray, the essence of training a bird was patience and soft, slow movement. Since there was no way to discipline a bird, Ray used positive reinforcement, like a food-reward system, using a signal like a buzzer, to make them do tricks. With this technique he could get a chicken to turn the pages of a book in half an hour. Similarly he could teach a bird to lie down or do a somersault.

A decade later, Ray wrote a book called *How to Train Your Pet Like a Television Star* where he expanded on this positive-reinforcement technique. 'In the terms we use it, it means that when you train your pet and he does something you want him to do, then you do something in return for him. It could mean just a friendly pat on the head. Usually it means something to eat. A treat. The treats should be in small bits so you only give a little bite at a time. Otherwise, very quickly your pet will be full and the training session will be over. If at the end of the training session he has not had enough to eat, feed him whatever amount he needs from your hand. A good rule of thumb with a bird is to feel his breast bone (keel) and if it begins to feel sharp then he is not getting enough to eat.'[18]

As well as catching the seagulls, some of the birds were raised from eggs. Because the gulls were a protected species, permits and permissions had to be obtained from the Society for the Prevention of Cruelty to Animals. The gulls were easy to handle because they'd go for food which was put on the end of some sticks. 'But they lost a lot of gulls in the process,' remembered Bob Boyle. Later, the US Fish and Game

Commission claimed that the production abused the film's permit to catch seagulls. They counted 54 live seagulls as opposed to 30, and 40 dead seagulls as opposed to the 20 allowed. In addition, they found 60 songbirds in cages, none of which was covered by the permit. On 28 March, Norman Deming was asked to appear before Judge Adele McCabe at a hearing. The production was subsequently fined $400 and the federal permit to collect gulls was revoked. With only days before the studio filming, this could have been a major setback. But by contracting other bird collectors such as Leo Yates from Colusa, California, the production was able to circumvent the ban and obtain an additional permit for collecting the gulls needed for the studio filming.

Bob Boyle recalled, 'Like all animal trainers, Ray was very persuasive when we talked to him. We didn't have too much fear except getting state clearance on the gulls, and the little birds we could buy, the linnets and that sort of thing. But the crows – well, we figured those would be the easiest to work with, and Ray said "No problem." This would be a case of famous last words.

CAPTURING THE CROWS

Getting the large numbers of crows and ravens for filming was far from easy, as they are among the most intelligent of all birds. At first the production was told they could have all the crows they needed but, because of their wiliness, they proved almost impossible to get. First, Ray had to hunt down 25,000 birds – and he started in his own backyard. He remembered an old rookery out in the valley, 'A big old tree out in Encino.' So he set a trap and caught a crow. The production thought capturing the rest would be straightforward and that Ray would simply put traps all over but, after that, not one crow was caught in the whole of San Fernando Valley. The clever birds avoided Ray's traps so he had to go further afield to catch more. A bounty of $10 was also offered to professional trappers for every bird brought in, but this failed to bring in any birds.

As Bob Boyle remembered, 'The reason we started with crows is obviously because they have an intelligence that most birds don't have. You could train a crow. But because they were so intelligent, they were also hard to capture. So we finally had to go with eggs – growing crows. That didn't take as long as it sounds, because they were very young. I think there are still some of the original crows flying around here. They live a long time!'

Even brainier than the crows, and harder to catch, were the ravens. Ray discovered that ravens in the wild are highly intelligent, communicative and social. 'We had a chance to study one flock of more than 3,000 ravens when we were trying to trap them. We discovered there were twelve scout birds always on the lookout around the fringes of the flock. And after we had trapped four or five birds we could never get another one to fall for the same kind of trap.'

In December 1961, Ray had to go further afield for almost a month to catch the ravens, and one of his best achievements was the capture of a great flock in their breeding grounds in Wilcox, Arizona. There were some 20,000 ravens in the rookery and the task was made particularly difficult because of the flock's efficient organisation and communication. The raven leaders spotted Ray and his assistant coming by car, and switched their roosting places without warning. He and his assistant finally caught the flock at night by wearing black masks and using black nets while the ravens roosted. Using this camouflage technique they were able to capture 25 ravens each night. Only once did Ray feel fear, one night at dusk, when a silent black cloud of ravens swirled over his head. 'I thought, could Mr Hitchcock's story be right after all,' remembered Ray. After he captured the birds he worked with the leaders of the flock to train them en masse after a close study of their flock habits.

CAPTURING THE SPARROWS

As Ray Berwick was busy catching the crows, ravens and gulls needed for the film, another bird trainer was employed to gather together the 1,500 small birds that were needed to invade the Brenner chimney. Jim Dannaldson was an expert animal handler who, together with his wife Beth, provided animals for such sci-fi B movies as *The Land Unknown* (1957) and *Earth vs the Spider* (1958). Jim kept snakes, including pythons and rattlesnakes, lizards, bugs and parrots. He employed a young animal trainer named John 'Bud' Cardos who had a pet mountain lion and worked with him at Universal Studios. Bud would go on to become an actor and director and, in 2013, remembered, '*The Birds* was the biggest film I worked on.

My job was to catch English sparrows, they are all over California and aren't native.' The English sparrow was introduced to the United States in 1851 and in the next few years colonised California. 'I started collecting the small birds before filming began,' says Bud. 'I used to go out at midnight and put out nets in cracks between hedges and trees. I was watching the nets and catching these English sparrows. One night a police car was following me, and the policeman kept his lights off. When he approached me, he asked what I was doing, so I explained the whole thing and he cracked up laughing. That story made the local newspaper!'[19]

Bud's perseverance made him successful in catching about 50 sparrows a night, and altogether he caught under 1,000 sparrows. This still wasn't enough small birds for the numbers required for the chimney scene, so they were supplemented by other birds bought from pet stores. 'We had to buy some finches because we couldn't catch enough sparrows,' recalls Bud.

POSITIVE REINFORCEMENT

Once Ray Berwick had caught the ravens, crows and seagulls, he kept the birds in 40 pens, or dog runs, at Universal studios, where he trained them. 'We built these runs on the back lot of Universal and looked after them seven days a week,' remembers Tamara Berwick, Ray's daughter, who was 12 years old at the time. 'They were usually fed by me and some keepers. We would weigh the birds and feed the ravens, crows and gulls horsemeat. It would not have been useful to feed fish to the gulls while he was trying to train them.'

With the seagulls, Ray trained them on a line the same way he would the crows, by enticing them with meat so they would fly straight at the camera. The seagulls, being greedy, would fly at the lens if food was placed just behind the camera or right on top. 'We were especially amazed at the seagulls,' remembered Ray. 'No one had ever before trained a seagull but we found they learnt even faster than ravens. In three days we could teach them to fly at a person's head. However, they can't learn as many things as a raven and they don't retain as well.'

'I remember my dad, coming home and his hands would be bleeding,' remembers Tamara. 'The seagulls have a vicious hook on the end of their beak.' Ray trained them using positive reinforcement and his philosophy was to watch the animals, to see what they would do naturally. He would check for the clever birds and pay them off with food. He didn't believe in formal training sessions, but used short bursts of six minutes to get the best results, after which he would put them back in their cages.'

Ravens were the easiest birds to train, according to Ray: 'The raven is the chimpanzee of the bird world. Ravens learn faster than dogs, and they can learn a variety of tricks. After 20 years of training birds, I'm still amazed at their reasoning powers.' As ravens and crows are meat eaters, the best kinds of treats were horsemeat, but, as the birds are also notorious thieves, they often tried to grab the treats from Ray before the training session was over.

Ray developed a great affection for the birds he trained as 'they had a capacity to get into your heart', remembers Tamara. Pun-Kin was a one-year-old raven that was Ray's favourite. He liked to eat raw hamburgers and answered his master's voice. 'He was called Pun-Kin for endearment and he loved that bird,' Tamara recalls.[20] Nosey, a five-year-old raven, liked to eat raw hamburger and could play 'Bye Bye Blackbird' on the piano. He'd put a cigarette in Ray's mouth and light it and was able to bring the morning paper in from the front porch at their house in Van Nuys. But Nosey could also be mean and had to be given his own place, away from the other birds.

In total, 25,000 birds were used in the film, 3,000 birds trained, with 30 specials, 2,000 finches, 700 English sparrows, 50 ducks and 125 ravens. The gulls and assorted larger birds consumed 100 pounds of shrimp, anchovies and ground meat per week. Before the film was finished the tab for this provender came to about $1,000, which, as production manager Norman Deming declared, 'ain't hay.'

SODIUM VAPOUR PROCESS

If the bird attacks using the trained and rehearsed live birds were to be believable and terrifying, Hitchcock knew he would need excellent special effects and composite photography to have the birds interact with the actors. Some of the shots could be superimposed but, in most cases, they would need travelling mattes to act as backgrounds. The matte process was not unknown, but to get the birds with fast-moving wings into the film was a problem.

It was the task of Bob Boyle, being the film's art and production designer, to find out what processes were available. He had a meeting with Hitchcock who asked, 'What do you think, can we physically attack this project?' And Bob replied, 'Well, the only thing is getting the birds into it.' The only system of travelling matte background that was really known at the time was blue screen, a colour separation process using a special cobalt-blue paint on muslin or blue dye on a transparent screen. The painted muslin was lit from the front using any convenient light, and the advantage of this method was the availability of equipment. The disadvantage was that colour, particularly in the blue range, was practically impossible unless the blue was very light, and it often resulted in lines around the figures, like a rather disturbing fringing or a halo in hair. Bob knew that if they were to film small birds with fast-moving wings then it would be just a messy blur and, while blue screen had been essentially perfected in 1958, it was still not quite to the level that Hitchcock wanted.

Bob started to research other matte systems available and came across the sodium vapour process, an older system developed by the Motion Picture Council. The sodium system had been designed by an English inventor named Holt at the Rank Studios and was a filter system that subtracted the wavelength from visible light. It was a method of combining foregrounds and backgrounds that were photographed at different times in an optical printer in postproduction.

Like blue screen, sodium vapour was a colour separation process. The screen was muslin painted yellow and lit by sodium vapour lamps. The advantages were that, since the sodium band was not affected by yellow pigment colour, a complete range of colour was available in foreground subjects. Extremely fine details, without the usual line or halo, were also possible, including moving objects like birds, which tended to be fuzzy. Unlike blue screen, the sodium screen process generated a virtually flawless matte with no discernible traces of separation between the photographed elements.

The main disadvantage of the sodium vapour process was the lack of special equipment. However, Walt Disney Productions had the only sodium vapour lamps available, and they had brought the sodium process to a high level of perfection. So Bob decided to approach Ub Iwerks, the head of Disney's special processes department (Figure 30). Iwerks had met Walt Disney in Kansas City in the early 1920s and together they co-created Mickey Mouse, bringing Disney into the spotlight. Iwerks had animated the first Mickey Mouse cartoon in 1928, after being requested to start drawing new character ideas.

At the time it wasn't uncommon for studios to share techniques and various processes were available on a rental or lease process, such as 20th Century Fox's Cinemascope. Fox would lease anamorphic lenses to any studio that wanted to make a film using that process. The same was true for Paramount with VistaVision, as Paramount had special 8 perforated 35mm cameras, sound blimps and other support equipment.

According to Iwerks' son, Don, 'My dad did not know Hitchcock prior to the filming of *The Birds*. They became acquainted once the studio approved the working relationship... [Hitchcock] wanted the best process of composite cinematography. Somehow he heard about the Sodium Travelling Matte Process that was being used by Disney.'[21]

Ub Iwerks was in charge of Walt Disney's research and development and had his own optical printer for experimental work. He used that printer to accomplish the sodium combination work. The original sodium vapour system had not worked particularly well and was on the verge of being abandoned when Iwerks took possession of it, modified the basics and turned it into a sophisticated, reliable process. He had been awarded a special Oscar in 1959 for 'Improvements in Optical Printing'.

By 21 March 1962, an agreement had been made between Revue Studios and Walt Disney Productions: 'We hereby agree to furnish you with the following: the necessary number of sodium vapour lamps; one closed-circuit television for viewing foreground and background images together; the services of one technician; and the services of one assistant cameraman.'

This would involve the studio leasing the sodium travelling matte system to Hitchcock, which included Iwerks' time to supervise the scenes on location and to handle the postproduction work of combining the footage of the actors and the birds. Iwerks conferred with Disney, got the go-ahead and immediately went to work. As outlined in the agreement with Revue, all special effects and combination printing were to be executed under Iwerks' supervision, with special design work and all the first-generation optical printing his prime responsibilities. Revue agreed to furnish, at their own expense, yellow screen, a Technicolor sodium process d-7 camera, camera parallels, foreground lamps, and rigging and striking. The sodium vapour shooting days were scheduled between 25 April and 5 September, with the majority taking place in June.

Finally, Bob Boyle had a process whereby the birds could be filmed against a screen to create footage that would later be superimposed on the actors. Everything now depended on how well both the sodium vapour and the birds would perform on camera inside the studio. But first there were six weeks of demanding location shooting to contend with, and everyone knew that the Northern California weather could be notoriously unpredictable.

NOTES

1   Kyle Counts, 'The Making of Alfred Hitchcock's *The Birds*', *Cinefantastique*, p.16
2   Interview with Leah Taylor, 9 November 2012, Bodega
3   Interview with Paul Bianchi, 7 November 2012, Bodega
4   Truffaut interview with Hitchcock, 1962
5   'Hitchcock talks about Lights, Camera, Action', *Hitchcock on Hitchcock*, University of California Press, 1995, p. 303
6   Interview with Glenice Carpenter, 1 August 2012, Bodega
7   'Hitchcock on style', *Hitchcock on Hitchcock*, University of California Press, 1995, p. 300
8   24 February 1962, taped transcript between Hitchcock and Hedren, Herrick Library
9   Interview with Rita Riggs, 5 September 2012, Los Angeles
10 Interview with Tippi Hedren, 18 June 1999, Acton, California
11 Rob Christopher, 'Bird Talk with Tippi Hedren', *Chicagoist*, 3 April 2012
12 Tippi Hedren with Theodore Taylor, *The Cats of Shambhala*, Century, 1986
13 Albert Whitlock, 'Roundtable on *The Birds*', *Cahiers du Cinema*, 1982
14 Interview with Syd Dutton, 8 November 2012, Los Angeles
15 'The Making of Alfred Hitchcock's *The Birds*', *Cinefantastique*, p. 17
16 'The Making of Alfred Hitchcock's *The Birds*', p. 16
17 'The Making of Alfred Hitchcock's *The Birds*', p. 16
18 Ray Berwick, *How to Train Your Pet Like a Television Star*, Armstrong Publishing Company, 1977
19 Interview with John 'Bud' Cardos, 10th January 2013, Los Angeles
20 Vince Johnson, 'Pet Ravens Are Living It Up,' *Pittsburgh Post Gazette*, 4 April 1963
21 Interview with Don Iwerks, 29 October 2012, Los Angeles

ON LOCATION IN BODEGA BAY

'I can remember being up until two or three in the morning discussing how we would do it the next day' – Robert Boyle

Getting 120 people to Bodega Bay, with all their equipment, for six weeks of location work, was a challenging logistical feat. During the week of 19 February 1962, the advance party of key crew was getting ready to travel there in order to prepare all the locations and be ready to receive the filming equipment. The film gear was borrowed from Revue Studios where Hitchcock was making his television series, and *The Birds* was the first film he had made not to have a releasing agreement in place with a major studio. 'We didn't get a cent from Paramount on *Psycho* until we delivered the negative and, for that, they got 20 per cent of the picture,' said Hitchcock. 'You might say we're doing this one on television money.'[1]

When asked by columnist Herb Caine if *The Birds* was one of the scariest films he had ever made, Hitchcock replied, 'Undoubtedly – I paid for it myself and I am terrified of losing all my money.'[2] A report in the *New York Times* suggested that Hitchcock was indeed using his own money to finance the film. The article went on to speculate that, 'Sources for the money might be the Music Corporation of America, the talent agency and one of the major producers of the television show. Mr Hitchcock is a client of the MCA. His television show is filmed at the Revue Studio, which is owned by MCA. It was said that Mr Hitchcock had decided to finance his own movie because of the huge profits he earned from his last film, *Psycho*. This movie, which was distributed by Paramount, cost about $750,000 and is said to have grossed about $14m so far. Mr Hitchcock is reported to have earned about $7m from the movie.'[3]

Just as during the making of *Psycho*, the financial risks he had undertaken weighed upon Hitchcock throughout the making of the film. As Albert Whitlock remembers, 'All the way through *The Birds*, he kept saying, "I wonder if we haven't taken on too much here." That was a thought of his all the way through the picture, and rightly so.'[4]

Trucks carrying the equipment left LA on the morning of Thursday 21 February and arrived in Bodega Bay the next day. The main crew, comprising Bob Boyle, Albert Whitlock, Bob Burks and Hitchcock, flew up to Santa Rosa on a charter plane on the morning of Tuesday 26 February and immediately went to work that day in Bodega Bay. The location work was to run close to 30 working days, without allowances made for impossible weather conditions. The majority of the cast and crew stayed at the El Rancho Motel at 2200 Santa Rosa Avenue in Santa Rosa.

On arriving in San Francisco, Hitchcock and Alma stayed at the Fairmont Hotel, a favourite in the city. The Hitchcocks loved San Francisco, and preferred places to go shopping in the city included Dunhill's for cigar shopping and Gumps for buying gifts. Hitchcock thought San Francisco was a very cosmopolitan city, like an American Paris, and he enjoyed the atmosphere, food and mild climate. In the evenings they would dine at Jack's or Ernie's, the latter restaurant having featured in *Vertigo*.

Every day Hitchcock would be driven by his elderly chauffeur the 67-mile, 90-minute journey to Bodega Bay, and the first big problem they encountered on location was the weather, which caused delays. The company finally began shooting at the beginning of March, after being held up for several days by hard, cold continuous and gloomy rain. 'We seemed to be filming in Bodega Bay for a very long time,' remembers costume supervisor Rita Riggs. 'It was windy and difficult and we had every kind of weather imaginable. I remember standing out on the pier every day waiting for the sun to come out.'

To achieve the desired moody, overcast look, it was decided that *The Birds* should be filmed even during inclement weather. On 25 January

1962, Norman Deming, the production manager, wrote: 'It is our intent to photograph in all types of weather, except in pouring rain or zero visibility fog, which will help prevent running much over our schedule.' Later, Norman's colleagues would praise him: 'He was a production manager in the true sense and a great gentleman,' remembers Rita Riggs. 'And things just ran smoothly, and there was please and thank you.' Harold Michelson also remembered, 'When I was up in Bodega Bay and it was freezing, a truck would come up at the right time with coffee and doughnuts. Norman had set it up. But, more importantly than the amenities, it was the creative juices that flowed.'

While on location, Hitchcock didn't like being exposed to the weather and would often stay in his trailer until just before it was time to shoot a scene. Harold Michelson, who had been asked by Hitchcock to join the production on location, recalled, 'I remember we were outside the house in Bodega Bay, Hitch's car drives up, it's freezing. He rolled the window down, and Bob Boyle came over to Bob Burks and I. Hitchcock said, "Where is the camera cutting her? Is it cutting her here?" Yes. Good. And the camera was about a quarter of a mile away. He just rolled up the window and took off. I don't know who else directs like this!'

The gloomy weather didn't keep the crew's spirits down, however, and there was enormous camaraderie among them. 'After work we'd go up to Bob Burks' hotel room, which had a well-stocked bar, and talk about the picture and mix Manhattans,' said Harold. 'We were all so enthused about the picture that we'd carry on talking late until the night, and then suddenly remember we hadn't eaten so go out for dinner around 11pm and try and find a restaurant that was still open.'

'It was the most cooperative effort that I've ever worked on,' affirmed Bob Boyle. 'Where we were on location for one thing, which makes it a little easier because you're with each other from early until late at night. Very often, when we'd have a problem, I can remember being up until two or three in the morning, discussing how we would do it the next day.'

FILMING AT THE TIDES

One of the first sequences to be filmed was outside the Tides restaurant and wharf from Monday 5 March through to Wednesday 7 March, when

Mitch helps Melanie after the first gull attack. Various restaurant scenes, portions of the gas station fire, and the boat dock scenes with Melanie were also filmed in the first week. The crew later returned to film at the Tides on Tuesday 20 and Wednesday 21 March. As depicted in the photographs (Figures 17 & 18) a few cars were burned in the parking lot. 'That was very exciting,' remembers Bodega resident Glenice Carpenter, as the filming of the fire attracted large crowds from Bodega Bay[5] (Figure 13). John Bressie was a 24-year-old freelance photographer living in Bodega Bay at the time, who had heard that the film crew were looking for extras for the attack on the townspeople. In 2013, John remembered, 'I was instructed to run around in the parking lot of the Tides restaurant and pretend that we were being attacked by birds. It was pretty chaotic and we waited a long time between the different takes.' John also recalled Jim Brown, the assistant director, walking around with a megaphone and in tennis shoes, directing the 30 odd extras who were instructed to run around. Of Hitchcock, John observed, 'He was pretty funny. His expressions and mannerisms were unique and a little bizarre. He seemed extremely engaged in the whole process of the movie.'

Most of the actual fire was later filmed in a parking lot at Universal Studios with a mock up of a gas station, Highway One and the Tides Wharf. The fire was also filmed from a helicopter, the footage later being superimposed on a matte of the town and wharf that Albert Whitlock had painted. As Harold Michelson remembered, 'The Tides and the parking lot came up to a road where a gas station was supposed to be, but there was no gas station there. That's how close we were cutting; because the gas station was down in the Universal back lot. And when the gasoline poured down from the gas station, you were here, and in a reverse you were where the gasoline was going down. I mean, they pushed both things together and, of course, they were five hundred miles apart.' Boyle said later, 'We actually showed the gasoline running down and followed Harold's storyboards very carefully on that.' (Figures 17 & 18)

When the crew returned to Universal Studios, Ray Berwick used a live gull trained to skim the head of the man who is pumping gas. He was a stunt man and exaggerated his reaction to make it look like the impact of a punch in a boxing match. Evan Hunter was on set that day and remembered, 'They were shooting the exterior for the bird attack on the man at the gas station. They had a guy wired so that the fake bird would be on to hit him on the head and move on. And they had all the pyrotechnics set for the gas to get on fire.' By a combination of mattes, location and later studio work, Hitchcock and his team were able to craft the sequence together.

FILMING THE SCHOOL HOUSE

On Thursday 8 March, the crew located seven miles inland to Bodega to film the sequence of the schoolchildren singing inside the school house and then running down the street. 'One of the first sequences we filmed was the school house where we sang the song,' remembers Veronica Cartwright. 'We worked regular hours, an eight-hour day, they weren't excessive and I had my three hours of schooling every day.'

For the part of 11-year-old Michelle, Cathy's school friend, Hitchcock cast child actress Shari Lee Bernath. 'I started working at the age of four, and I was always the little girl being killed,' remembers Shari. 'I was killed by horses or machineguns, maybe because I was thin and waif-like.' Shari also recalls the first time she met Hitchcock. 'I can remember Mr Hitchcock standing in a hotel. He treated me very well, and asked me a couple of questions, like did I mind wearing the glasses. I said no, I didn't mind. Then he asked me if I was afraid of birds. And I said no. Then they gave me two sets of clothing to bulk me up a little bit.' Shari and her mother moved to Bodega Bay for a two-month period and stayed with the rest of the crew at the El Rancho Motel in Santa Rosa.[6]

Shari Lee and Veronica worked the longest hours out of all the kids on location. 'Hitchcock was very blunt to me, but I came from a very blunt family, so it didn't bother me and I had a quip of my own to answer back, which he liked,' remembers Shari Lee.

For the attack of the crows on the children, many of the press were invited on location and it generated a great deal of interest. The children started running in Bodega, by the school house, and, in the film, ended up in Bodega Bay. So Hitchcock made one town out of two – Bodega and Bodega Bay. The shots of the children running downhill were filmed on Taylor Street in Bodega Bay above the Diekmann's Bay Store. The close-ups of the running children and Melanie would later be filmed in the studio on a treadmill.

Hitchcock let his assistant director Jim Brown, who enjoyed location work, direct the crow attack on the children. There were about 20 children

a Penguin Book   3/6

The Birds
and Other Stories

Daphne du Maurier

Figure 1. Portait of Daphne du Maurier (© The Chichester Partnership)

Figure 2. Book cover by Virgil Burnett
for the 1963 paperback reprint of *The Birds
and Other Stories* (© Penguin Books Ltd)

Figure 3. Polridmouth coast, Cornwall, setting for *The Birds* (© The Chichester Partnership)

Figure 4. Mood sketches for *The Birds* by art designer Robert Boyle (© Alfred Hitchcock Collection)

Figure 5. Alfred Hitchcock and his wife Alma (© Alfred Hitchcock Collection)

(Clockwise from top left) **Figure 6.** Evan Hunter and his wife Anita (© Richard Hunter), **Figure 7.** Robert Boyle, the art designer (© The Estate of Robert F Boyle), **Figure 8.** Harold Michelson, the production illustrator (© Lilian Michelson), **Figure 9.** Albert Whitlock, the matte painter (© June Whitlock/Bill Taylor),

Figure 10. Tippi Hedren, with wardrobe supervisor Rita Riggs and hairstylist Virginia Darcy
(© Alfred Hitchcock Collection)

Figure 11. Rose Gaffney's Ranch
(© The Estate of Robert F Boyle)

Figure 12. Jib outside the Tides restaurant
(© Marc Wanamaker/Bison Archives)

Figure 13. The Tides restaurant filming
(© Marc Wanamaker/Bison Archives)

Figure 14. The Bodega Bay camera boat
(© Marc Wanamaker/Bison Archives)

Figures 15 & 16. Natural history filming of the seagulls at San Francisco dump (© Marc Wanamaker/Bison Archives)

Figure 17. Filming the gasoline explosion outside the Tides restaurant (© Marc Wanamaker/Bison Archives)

Figure 18. A truck on fire outside the Tides restaurant (© Marc Wanamaker/Bison Archives)

Figures 19 & 20. Tippi Hedren costume sketch of the fur coat and the green dress
(© Edith Head Motion Picture & Television Fund)

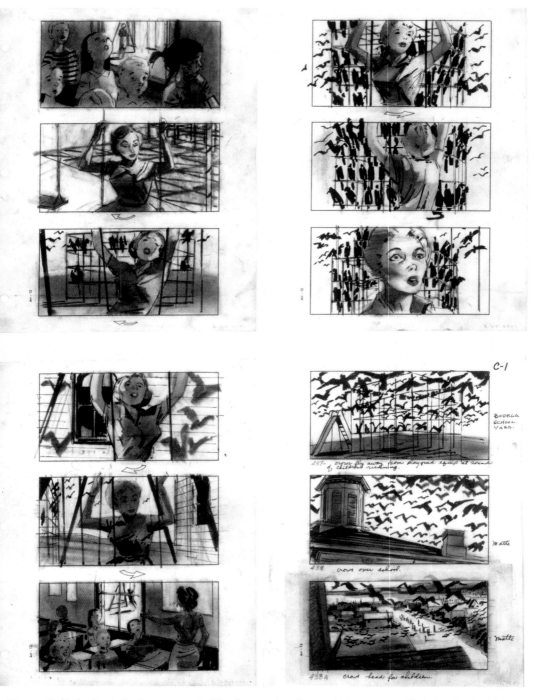

Figure 21. Early sketch for the crow attack. The shots getting closer to Melanie were added after Hitchcock's specification and the swing was replaced by a bench. (© Alfred Hitchcock Collection)

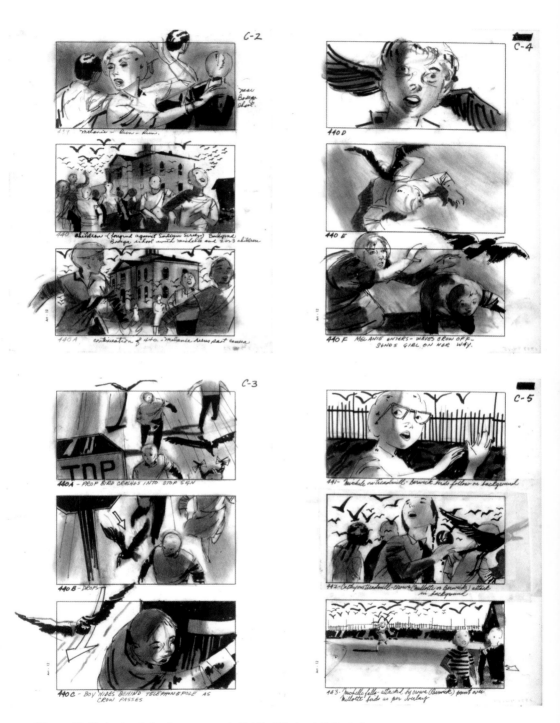

Figure 22. Early sketch for the crow attack (© Alfred Hitchcock Collection)

441N

441P - ANNIE DRAGGING SLOW CHILD

Figure 24. The storyboard ending for The Birds shows the destruction that has been wreaked on Bodega Bay
(© Alfred Hitchcock Collection and The Estate of Robert F Boyle)

Figure 26. Rod Taylor, Alfred Hitchcock and Robert Boyle on location in Bodega Bay
(© Universal Pictures/TCD)

Figure 27. Albert Whitlock's matte painting forms the backdrop when Melanie crosses the sea by boat
(© Deutsches Filminstitut, Frankfurt)

in the scene, but much more frightening than running from birds that weren't there was a huge camera truck rolling rapidly down the hill on their heels. After several takes on the mile-long hill, the children, Tippi Hedren and Suzanne Pleshette were getting tired of running.

'In the scene when we are running down the hill, when the children are being attacked, I didn't have the birds,' remembered Suzanne, as the crows would be double printed on afterwards. 'I had to swoop up one of the children and run. For me it was more of a case of exercising than worrying about being killed.'[7]

Evelyn Casini, a Bodega resident, ran the Casino bar and restaurant, a landmark roadhouse located at 17000 Bodega Highway, just near the school and the church. She was in her thirties when the movie was filmed. 'I remember the kids running down the hill. Some of them had mechanical birds tied to them, so it looked like they were pecking them. It was something exciting and different, and an insight into how a movie was made. Hitchcock was a genius and very meticulous. We used to feed the cast and crew whatever they wanted, like roast beef or steak and potatoes.' According to Evelyn, Hitchcock and the cast kept themselves to themselves.

Hitchcock later admitted to Bob Boyle that he had let himself become distracted by the presence of the press during filming of the crow sequence. Maybe he was keen to show off his new actress or else he was proud of what his crews were going to accomplish. Commentating on his technique with actors, Hitchcock elaborated: 'I tell them why they are doing what they are doing. I show them how a particular shot fits into the movie. I just explained to Miss Hedren why she had to look back as she stopped to pick up a child. Because, in the movie, the next shot will be a close-up of a raven flying at her head.'[8]

FILMING THE CROWS ON THE WALL

Next to be filmed were the crows gathering on the jungle gym outside the school. The close-ups of Tippi smoking a cigarette would be filmed later in the studio, but the long shots of her and the crows on the bars were filmed on location. As Tippi was a model who had featured in cigarette commercials such as Chesterfields, she was well practised in the art of smoking for the camera. At the time, Tippi smoked in real life, but she would give up smoking two years later, at the end of *Marnie*, just before filming the final scene on the San Jose railway platform.[9]

When it came to filming the scene of the crows on the roof of the school house after the attack, Bob Boyle came up with the idea of attaching little magnets to their feet. 'Brilliant idea was that if I had little magnets which I could attach to the feet of the birds, and put the birds on the gutter, which was metal, they couldn't fly off. We'd have them kept there,' Bob reasoned. So he did this, then waited on the roof ridge for Hitchcock to call 'action' – after which he immediately heard him call 'cut'. When Bob went to look, all the crows were hanging upside down, as they had tried to fly away and fallen in this position.

Bob crawled around on the roof, trying to pick the birds up, but, as fast as he'd pick them up, they'd fall back down again. Some of them were tied on with string and were hanging from the roof, as they didn't have magnets. Down below, Hitchcock was getting very upset at the whole operation and, as Bob said, 'Suddenly, I find that he was blaming me for the whole thing, and it was Ray's [Berwick's] idea. And just before I was trying to drag these birds into an upright position, he thought that I was the real villain. Of course he was terribly afraid of the Society for the Prevention of Cruelty to Animals.' The SPCA was on the set a lot of the time. One of the script girls on the production also started to become a great protector of the birds and, in fact, an aviary was built on the set where she would take care of any that had been hurt or injured.

In other shots detailing the aftermath of the crow attack, the production used some cardboard-cut-out birds and some stuffed birds made by Larry Hampton. Veronica Cartwright was on location and, ever the curious child, asked Hitchcock, 'Well, isn't it going to look fake on camera?' But Hitchcock replied, 'No,' because he had interspersed a few real birds with the stuffed ones. He said, 'Your eye – it's the illusion. You see movement from one bird, you assume they're all moving.' So, in this way, Hitchcock created the illusion that the whole flock was alive, rippling feathers and cawing after the attack. 'I just kept asking questions, and he never seemed to mind answering them, either,' says Veronica. 'I never felt intimidated by him. I liked him; maybe I reminded him of his daughter.'

FILMING THE CHILDREN'S PARTY

On Friday 17 March, Hitchcock and the crew moved to Rose Gaffney's house to begin filming the exteriors of the Brenner house. This included the filming of Cathy's birthday party, when the children are attacked by seagulls. The cast were joined by veteran actress Jessica Tandy, filming her first scenes, who had arrived from Italy a couple of weeks earlier.

When Hitchcock had distributed copies of Evan Hunter's script to the production personnel back in November 1961, Bob Boyle had had the idea that it would be more interesting if the bird attack took place while the children were playing blind man's buff, so that Cathy would be blindfolded when attacked. 'Of course, we could have the entrance of the cake about the same time,' he noted.

Glenice Carpenter, a Bodega Bay resident, was playing one of the mothers in the party sequence, who runs into the house with two kids after the gulls attack. 'We wore our own clothes,' remembers Glenice, who wore a pale green dress. 'And my sons were both in the film as the kids who ran under the table when the birds attacked. The old Gaffney farmhouse had a false front built on it. They set up the tables in the yard and Tippi Hedren, Rod Taylor, Jessica Tandy and Suzanne Pleshette were all there, while the children are having their little birthday party.'

'Those gulls at the children's party were all trained every one,' said Hitchcock in an interview. 'To dive at the little boy, dive into the food, go into the food, it's incredible what that bird trainer has done.' They put a pin on the front of the beaks so that they fly in and puncture the balloons.[10]

Ray Berwick had a trained seagull named Charlie, attached by a long string to the handler, his beak and claws bound with loose wire. From the top of a tall ladder, Ray coaxed Charlie to swoop down and attack Veronica Cartwright, who was blindfolded, as the children are playing blind man's buff. Seed was placed on Veronica's hair so that, on cue, the gull would dive down to her. But Charlie's string broke, and he started flying out towards the bay.

As Ray had very loosely wired the beak of the seagull so that it wouldn't hurt the children, he was worried for the bird's survival after it had flown away. He went to Hitchcock and said, 'We have to stop filming for the rest of the afternoon because I have to find that bird.' Otherwise it would starve to death. Charlie the gull landed on a mud flat far out in the bay, so Ray had to go out after him while the whole crew watched and waited anxiously. The bird also watched and waited until Ray was within a few feet of him. Then the gull took off and flew directly to one of the other trainers on shore and was caught.

Because of such setbacks, the whole sequence took a week to film, remembers Glenice Carpenter. 'Mr Hitchcock was very friendly to the people on the set. The most friendly and outgoing of all the actors was Suzanne Pleshette. Everyone seemed to like her because she was so open and friendly and a good actress.'

Hitchcock was keen to film the bird attacks from the point of view of Melanie's character. 'Melanie really represents to the audience the growth of the attack of the birds,' he said during pre-production. 'You see it reflected in her. In other words, we rely upon a storytelling point of view, this is where we're relying upon Melanie to convey to the audience there's something very strange happening here with these birds.'[11]

Later, Hitchcock would recreate the entire scene in the studio, taking the same clothes that the children had worn so that child doubles in LA could also wear them. The other children in the party sequence were given mechanical birds whose wings moved when the children squeezed them, a rubber bulb type of thing, so they could make it look as if the birds were attacking them.

FILMING AT VALLEY FORD FARM

On 28 March, Jessica Tandy's scenes of her character Lydia's discovery of Dan Fawcett's body were filmed at Valley Ford Farm. Hitchcock spoke about her truck being an emotional truck after the shocking discovery of his mutilated corpse.[12] On the journey up, Hitchcock had the road watered down but, on the way back, dust rears up as the truck tears down the road to convey Lydia's distressed emotional state.

Bob Boyle said Hitchcock was a very subjective director: 'The scene also dictated how it was going to be subjective. If the scene is working, even a long shot can be subjective because it's expressing what the character is feeling. It might be a standard viewpoint shot of what the character sees. Sometimes a great long shot, a long vista could be revealing what a character felt. He was mostly interested in feelings.'

The soundtrack in the sequence after the discovery of Dan Fawcett's body is also vital. As Hitchcock noted, 'I had [Jessica] run up from a distance and then bring her up to a big head when she's inarticulate. The sound of her running feet should match the size of the image and, when she gets into the truck, the sound of anguish, which I hope to stylise, will be the whine of the engine on the truck. In other words we are really experimenting here by taking real sounds and then stylising them, so we can abstract a little more drama out of ordinary sounds than we would normally do.'

To emphasise the starkness of the soundtrack when Lydia runs out of the Fawcett house, a faint echo was added to Jessica Tandy's footsteps. Hitchcock had her run from a long shot to a close-up and open her mouth to scream. But, where we expect her to scream, because she is so shocked, almost catatonic, she can only produce a guttural silence which is another example of effective counterpointing.

It was when filming at such isolated farmhouses that Hitchcock found out more about the mysterious behaviour of the birds in the real-life attacks. 'In all the accounts that I have read about bird attacks, they were pretty localised, no matter how violent,' said Hitchcock. 'Oddly enough, when I first arrived in Bodega Bay, one of the farmers said to me, "It's funny you should come up here to do a film about this. I've been losing a lot of my lambs with the birds attacking and pecking their eyes out."'[13] This isolation appealed to Hitchcock and is perhaps part of the reason he was reluctant to film an ending where it might be interpreted that the bird attacks in Bodega Bay were part of a larger phenomenon.

WORKING WITH THE ACTORS ON LOCATION

In the weeks leading up to the location filming, Hitchcock had been working closely with Tippi Hedren, talking her through the script line by line, feeling by feeling and reaction by reaction, as they developed the character of Melanie Daniels. As she later remembered, he would direct her even to the turn of a head and the bat of an eyelid.[14] Tippi arrived on location ready to work and, indeed, worked very hard during the 75 days of filming, taking only one afternoon off to go to the dentist. Professional and private, she kept to herself most of the time during the filming, eager to do a good job in her first movie role.

'He's a very psychological director. He works on you like putty,' said Tippi about working with Hitchcock. Years later she would also remark how controlling he was. Although, most of the time, she travelled in a cast car with Peggy Robertson and Suzanne Pleshette, sometimes she would ride in Hitchcock's limo to and from the shooting location. Apparently, Hitchcock wouldn't let anyone else ride in the car with them, including co-star Rod Taylor, who would travel in another cast car with some of the male crew members. 'It was a very weird situation,' remembers Rod. 'He was very possessive of Tippi. She was his next Grace Kelly and he wouldn't allow me to ride in the same car as her, which I found very strange.'[15] Rod soon found himself disillusioned with the filming experience as Hitchcock became increasingly more protective towards his leading lady.

But hairstylist Virginia Darcy, in a 2012 interview, defended Hitchcock. 'You had to take Hitch with a pinch of salt. Tippi was an innocent from New York. I don't think she could handle herself then, she had never done a movie in her life, never been around a studio, never knew a director, she only knew guys who were photographers.'[16] (Figure 10)

Hitchcock was undoubtedly very protective of Tippi on location and was beginning to isolate her from the rest of the cast and crew. 'But that was just his way to protect his leading ladies,' argues Virginia. 'I worked with John Ford and he was like that with Elizabeth Allen when we were filming *Donovan's Reef*, but Allen knew how to handle the old guy. Tippi didn't know how to handle Hitch. She was an innocent who had come to Hollywood and she didn't go through the ropes to get where she was.'

For the time being at least, in those early weeks of location filming, Tippi was compliant and grateful, thrilled to be working on her first motion picture and eager to repay Hitchcock for his confidence in her. She was bucking a lot of negativity from some of the executives at Universal who had remarked that it was foolhardy to cast an unknown and inexperienced actress in a major film.

When Rod Taylor arrived on location in Bodega Bay, he, like all the other actors, was looking forward to working with the great director. But he soon found that any direction from Hitchcock was lacking. 'I felt that I was handcuffed. And that he didn't give direction, except for the technical aspects of making the movie.' Of his character Mitch Brenner, Rod says, 'I found him to be cold and distant and lacking in any human warmth or quality, and my attempt to bring any to the character was against Hitch's wishes.'

On the written page, Rod identified with the description of Mitch Brenner being likened to John F Kennedy, who spends summers at his country home and is a proactive leader. 'I was a supporter of Kennedy,' Rod says. Just like JFK, who was credited with protecting America during the Cuban Missile Crisis, Rod's character Mitch is a criminal defence lawyer who can handle San Francisco's toughest 'hoods' and fights for justice. Towards the end of the film, a news story on the radio from San Francisco mentions the attack on the schoolchildren at Bodega Bay and ends with the actual recording of JFK delivering the conclusion of his 1962 State of the Union Address. During it, he refers to America's place in a precarious world, motivating people 'on the move' to work together.

The Brenner family in Bodega Bay is depicted as gentry among the fishermen and townspeople, very similar to the Kennedy family who had a six-acre compound in Hyannis Port, Massachusetts. Both had waterfront property in isolated moorings, partly only accessible by boat. Also, like JFK, Mitch is charismatic, patrician and well dressed.

Ted Parvin was Rod Taylor's wardrobe man on *The Birds*. Whereas Rita Riggs supervised the clothes for all the women who appeared in the film, Ted was her male counterpart looking after the men. He remembers one item of clothing that Hitchcock specifically requested for Rod to wear: 'Hitch wanted a Pig's Whisker sweater, which is a kind of sweater from England, with a crew neck, and white knitted wool. He was very specific about that.'[17] The Pig's Whisker is an English yachting sweater, and Hitchcock's request for Rod to wear it was in keeping with his view of Mitch as gentry, with sartorial elegance like JFK.

Of working for Hitchcock, Ted had many fond memories: 'I found him marvellous to get along with. He would listen to me, answer my questions and explain things between takes. As long as I caught him at an appropriate moment, for example not when he was about to direct a scene, he would always graciously answer them.' Ted's words echo those of many cast and crew members who remember Hitchcock as a marvellous teacher.

Rod Taylor, however, was having difficulty working with Hitchcock. 'Any warmth or masculinity to the character came from me and not Hitch,' he says. There was one scene, for example, where Rod was required to leap off the dock and come to the aid of Tippi who had just been hit by a seagull. Hitchcock wouldn't let Rod show overt physical tenderness towards Tippi during that scene. 'That's because he didn't have any experience of behaving like a masculine and rugged man, whether by jumping off the dock or rushing to a woman in need of aid,' says Rod. 'He had no streak of tenderness for relationships between men and women and he just didn't show tenderness in his movies.'

According to Rod, Hitchcock tried every day to cut off any warmth Rod brought to the character. 'He did give me a few line readings which I ignored.' A famous publicity still of Hitchcock on location shows him leaning over Rod, one hand paternally on his shoulder, as he looks over the body of Suzanne Pleshette. 'That's a very rare glimpse of him standing over me in that still,' says Rod, 'fooling everyone into believing that he was fond of me and how gentle he was. Wrong!' For Rod, the photograph was pure showmanship for publicity's sake on Hitchcock's part.

As filming progressed, Rod continued to try to bring warmth and normality to Mitch's character. 'When Tippi is trapped in the phone booth, and goes into the café, I enter and go to embrace [her] and Hitchcock shouted "Do Not Touch!" I just felt the whole thing so weird.'

During the working week, Rod stayed with the cast and crew at the El Rancho motel in Santa Rosa, which he disliked, but at weekends they were free and Universal Studios generously put them up at the Fairmont Hotel in San Francisco. 'If we had time, we would socialise after hours, but Hitchcock tried to keep me apart from Tippi. It was her first role with a very famous director, and she came across as a real trooper,' Rod remembers. His overall feeling about working with Hitchcock was that he was a magnificent manipulator who surrounded himself with a lot of other talented artists, such as Albert Whitlock. 'Hitch depended on him a lot,' says Rod. Nevertheless, Rod took the opportunity to learn from the master at work and showed a keen interest in the entire movie-making process. He spent hours talking to Hitchcock about directing techniques (Figure 26), and, with cameraman Bob Burks, he talked about photographic composition and even the mechanism of the camera. With art director Bob Boyle, Rod chatted about set design, especially from an actor's viewpoint, which interested him.

The third young star of *The Birds*, Suzanne Pleshette, arrived on location feeling like she was second best because she wasn't blonde. She also felt that, being a brunette, she would draw attention away from the film's blonde and believed Hitchcock tried to be make her look ugly. According to Suzanne, when she turned up on location Bob Burks, the DP, said to her, 'I have to apologise now for what I'm about to do to you.' She was then dressed unprepossessingly in grey slacks, a vibrant chunky red sweater (Hitchcock very seldom used red), and her face soiled as if she had just been gardening.

Evan Hunter was on location some of the time as he was in discussions with Hitchcock over *Marnie* and had been invited to watch some of the filming. He was introduced to Suzanne and later wrote in his memoirs, 'It didn't help that Hitch dressed this beautiful woman like a grocer's wife, lighted her badly, and shot her from the most unflattering angles. Three minutes after we'd been introduced on the set, the first words Suzanne said to me were, "The blonde, he gives a mink coat. Me, he gives wedgies and a house dress." I fell in love with her at once.'[18]

The first meeting between Annie and Melanie was filmed on location outside the schoolteacher's house that Bob Boyle had built. Hitchcock said to Tippi during pre-production, 'It's a nice scene, I think it should be played, I'll photograph it to get the benefit of these looks, but we should observe every nuance, because every look and every pause, you can see in every beat and give us a meaning, you see. And I'm sure when you get together with Miss Pleshette, you'll be able to work out the timing which is so important. ...So there's plenty in it, Tippi. Plenty in this scene to play, a lot to play. A lot of coming in and going here with the changes in attitude between each other. First she's mysterious, then the other one's mysterious.'[19]

Suzanne wasn't intimidated at all by Hitchcock during the filming. He appreciated her sense of humour and she in turn liked his Cockney charm. 'I'm pretty bawdy, he loves those things that are a little dirty, and I made him laugh.'[20] In looks, humour, background and style, she presented a complete contrast to Tippi, both onscreen and off.

On one occasion Hitchcock said to Suzanne, 'You're too well behaved, I don't like it.' So Suzanne said to him, 'Hitch, can I change a line? And he said, "You mean add a line." I sat on his lap and read him back the line. People were shocked, thinking, "What is she doing to Alfred Hitchcock?" But we had a divine relationship and he wanted to sign me to a multiple-picture deal. I said to him, "This is not going to work, because I know you and the blondes."'

To lighten the mood and break up the monotony between camera set-ups, one day Suzanne put on a blonde wig and turned up on location. She said to Hitchcock, 'MCA is a little insecure, they think you prefer blondes.

Can't I do the role?' When Hitchcock saw her he said, 'Take off that awful wig – you look like a female impersonator!'

Suzanne died in 2008, but all her fellow cast and crew members recall her very fondly. Veronica Cartwright remembers, 'Suzanne was very funny. She was a good spirit and had a good sense of gung-ho.' Rod Taylor, who had worked with Suzanne previously on the ABC television series *Hong Kong*, says, 'She had a great sense of humour and was like one of the guys.'

Hitchcock's vast experience in film led him to use a different approach with each of his quintet of leading actors, Rod, Tippi, Jessica, Suzanne and Veronica. As Suzanne remembered, 'With each actor he was a different director. With Tippi she had nowhere near the emotional experience, so he would talk her through the emotional life to bring her to the moment of that scene. Whereas he would say to me, walk through the door, you know what to do. So he could be a genie with her, and with me like a traffic cop.'[21]

Suzanne's recollections of working with Hitchcock, when interviewed only a couple of years before she died in 2008, are very perceptive. 'And as you talk to all the women who worked with Hitchcock, you will find, if they had experience, and if they could be trusted to use that experience to benefit the film, he in fact welcomed it. Those who were less experienced had to rely on his experience to take them through the various stages of the film.'

She remained intrigued that Hitch had the whole movie planned in his head. 'I was ingenuous and said, what if I did this and this and this, but he was not looking for an associate. But I was so stupid, it didn't occur to me, having worked in the theatre. [However,] he never once made me think that I shouldn't want to do that, and that was very generous of him. For me, he was wonderful, generous and loving, and I had a wonderful experience with him. We've heard many stories about how controlling he was, and what I think Hitchcock was trying to do was protect his vision of the film, which most directors do, some more subtly than others. But I, coming from the theatre, am used to collaborating and didn't know that Mr Hitchcock didn't want to collaborate with me. So, instead of not listening to me, he was very attentive, and sometimes even listened to some of my ideas, and he always made me feel that I had something to say and that what I had to do was valuable. He was very generous. The only people who don't welcome that kind of collaboration are insecure people who aren't very good.'

The death scene for Suzanne's character, Annie Hayworth, required the expert make-up of Howard Smit to work on her face, clothes and hair, to create tears and scratches from the crow attack. Albert Whitlock was on location that day and was dubious. 'I said to Hitch, "Something's bothering me. What does Suzanne die of, because she only has a few scratches?"' Hitchcock's amusing reply was, 'Who knows?'

All around, the crows were placed on the rooftops at the front of Annie Hayworth's house and the nearby school. Suzanne had to lie on the front porch, perfectly still, with the crows above and around her. As she remembered, 'I was never afraid of birds, so it wasn't a problem for me, but when I had finished I had a very healthy respect for them. My sequences were all with the crows, which were very bright birds. And I learned to be careful. When I am lying dead on the porch, and all the birds are on top of the roof, with my eyes closed I felt terribly vulnerable, because we had one of the crows try and peck out the eye of the trainer. I, fortunately, had no bad experience with them.'[22]

One of the crows flew over and did poop on Suzanne during her death scene, and everyone on location was hysterical with laughter. Virginia Darcy remembers Suzanne wailing and crying out for tissue. On a more serious note, Hitchcock later said that her character, Annie, dies because of her sense of duty to the school and compares her death to Mr Memory's in *The 39 Steps* (1935). 'The whole idea is that the man is doomed by his sense of duty. Mr Memory knows what the 39 Steps are and, when he is asked the question, he is compelled to give the answer. The schoolteacher in *The Birds* dies for the same reason.'[23]

Location filming in Bodega Bay was completed on Saturday 31 March. By all accounts it had been a very successful shoot, 'due in great measure to your unending cooperation' said production manager Norman Deming to the cast and crew. A wrap party took place in the lounge of the El Rancho motel that evening and local crew members were also invited. The Bodega Bay Area Chamber of Commerce was also pleased and Ray Ruebel, who ran it, wrote to Hitchcock saying, 'We wish to express our deep appreciation that you chose Bodega Bay as the site for filming your picture *The Birds*. You have helped us economically. The winter and early spring months often bring little money in to this community. This year was expected to be an especially poor one money-wise, due to a shortage in market-size crab, usually the source of income for our fishermen during this time of year. The money you have spent here has helped many families. You are to be complimented on the excellent conduct of those whom you employ. They have been friendly, gracious and considerate, and their behaviour has been correct at all times.' Hitchcock replied that he was glad he had remembered Bodega Bay from when he was at Santa Rosa in 1942.

SAN FRANCISCO

Before Hitchcock returned to Universal, the final location shooting took place in San Francisco for what would be the opening of the film. Melanie Daniels crosses Union Square on her way to Davidson's pet shop, and looks up to see a flock of gulls massing ominously overhead. The Dewey monument is distinctly seen in the background.

As Hitchcock was instantly recognisable to the public, and drew crowds that hampered work when he filmed *Vertigo* in the Bay Area, he had to shoot the opening of *The Birds* on busy Union Square in absolute secrecy. While the actors could wander freely, the barest glimpse of Hitchcock, whose seven years on television had made him instantly recognisable to millions of viewers, would draw fans on the run.

An elaborate plan was devised to enable Hitchcock to direct the opening of the movie. A studio truck was dressed in Hollywood to resemble a furniture van and dispatched to San Francisco, where it was parked at the corner of Geary and Powell at 6am on the day of shooting. The tailgate of the truck had a specially built camera enclosure with a slit for the lens that would allow for a 200-degree panning shot of Tippi Hedren as she crosses the street. Then the camera turret was carefully covered with tarpaulins. Only the slit of the camera enclosure was exposed, making it appear to be an odd piece of furnishing lashed to the van. On the day of filming Hitchcock jumped into a nondescript car and was driven to the waiting van where the car was double-parked long enough to allow him to transfer himself into the furniture truck, hidden by dummy packing cases on the sidewalk. A one-way mirror installed in the rear of the van allowed him to watch prearranged action from within while he was blocked from outside view.

The local police cooperated by allowing the traffic signals at the intersection to be controlled by Hitchcock's crew during the filming. Tippi Hedren and 20 movie extras intermingling with pedestrians took their cues for action from the position of a passing cable car. Hitchcock wanted the cable car in the shot to establish the San Francisco locale right at the beginning. As the chime of the cable car passes, Melanie crosses the street with Union Square in the background. As Melanie passes a billboard, Hitchcock cleverly cuts to the interior of the studio. In less than an hour, the crew had captured the opening of the film, allowing Hitchcock to slip back into a double-parked car, and were prepared to fly back to LA.

The rest of the opening scene would be filmed in the studio where a little boy wolf whistles at Tippi outside the front of the pet shop, in a direct reference to the Sego commercial that had caught Hitchcock's attention. Peggy Robertson wrote to Ralph Pasek of the Gardner Advertising Company which owned the rights to the commercial, 'As this proposed sequence would closely resemble the commercial your company made for Sego's Pet Milk – I would appreciate if you would send me a letter stating that your company and the Pet Milk Company agree to our company filming the above mentioned sequence.' Pasek gave his consent two months later.

Hitchcock wanted a light opening to the film, to establish the theme of a complacent society. 'Generally speaking, I believe that people are too complacent,' he said. 'People like Melanie Daniels tend to behave without any kind of responsibility, and to ignore the more serious aspects of life. Such people are unaware that catastrophe surrounds us all. But I believe that, when catastrophe does come, when people rise to the occasion, they are all right. Melanie shows that people can be strong when they face up to the situation, like the people in London during the wartime air raids. The birds basically symbolised the more serious aspects of life.'[24]

Tippi Hedren's entrance into the pet shop also affords Hitchcock his famous and characteristic cameo early on in the film, as he walks out with his two prize Sealyham terriers, Stanley and Geoffrey. Albert Whitlock remembered that they were fed choice cuts. 'Oh, I mean, those dogs ate better than most people in the world. He would go to the store and get the finest cut of meat and have them ground it up for these dogs. They were wonderful! He would bring them to work. They would be in his office, and he loved them dearly.'

The location work had been successfully completed but filming was far from over, as the complicated studio work - including the many bird attacks, using actors, live birds and the sodium vapour process - was about to begin.

NOTES

1   Thomas McDonald, 'Watching Birds: Happy Hitchcock films Terror-Ridden Tale', *New York Times*, 1 April 1962

2   Alfred Hitchcock to Herb Caine, *New York Times*, March 1962

3   Murray Schumach, 'Hitchcock Paying for Latest Film', *New York Times*, 22 March 1962

4   Albert Whitlock, 'Roundtable on *The Birds*', *Cahiers du Cinema*, 1982

5   Interview with Glenice Carpenter, 1 August 2012, Bodega

6   Interview with Shari Lee Bernath, 4 November 2012, Malibu

7   Interview with Suzanne Pleshette. *Movie Classics*, 2006

8   Thomas McDonald, 'Watching Birds', *New York Times*, 1 April 1962

9   Interview with Tippi Hedren, 18 June 1999, Acton, California

10   Hitchcock to Bogdanovich, 14 February 1963

11   Hitchcock and Hedren transcript, 24 February 1962, Margaret Herrick Library

12   Hitchcock to Truffaut, August 1962

13   Arthur Knight, 'Conversation with Alfred Hitchcock', *Alfred Hitchcock Interviews*, University Press of Mississippi, 1973, p 143

14   Donald Spoto, *The Dark Side of Genius*, Little Brown, p. 456

15   Interview with Rod Taylor, 1 June 2012, Los Angeles

16   Interview with Virginia Darcy, 5 September 2012, Santa Barbara

17   Interview with Ted Parvin, 16 October 2012, Chicago

18   Evan Hunter, *Me and Hitch*, p. 27

19   Hitchcock and Hedren transcript, 24 February 1962, Margaret Herrick Library

20   Stephen J Abramson, interview with Suzanne Pleshette, 2 September 2006

21   Abramson, interview with Suzanne Pleshette, 2006

22   Suzanne Pleshette interview for *Movie Classics*, 2006

23   François Truffaut, *Hitchcock*, p. 98

24   Hitchcock to Truffaut, August 1962

ON THE SOUND STAGE

'Hitch was always in complete and affable control of any and all problems that came up' – Evan Hunter

As soon as the cast and crew arrived back in LA from location, they set straight to work with the studio filming. Work began at Revue Studios on Monday 2 April and lasted until Tuesday 10 July 1962, a total of 15 weeks. Hitchcock sent flowers to Tippi, Jessica and Veronica's dressing rooms, and, to Rod and Tippi, he gave a box of Vendome liquors. Veronica remembers how kind Hitchcock was to her throughout the filming. 'He was really terrific to me and every afternoon at 4.30pm I would bring him a cup of tea in a china cup, and Peggy Robertson would make it. And he would have me sit there next to him while he drank his tea.'

Hitchcock would also tell dirty jokes on the set, everyone would laugh, and Veronica would go along with it. 'I didn't know what they meant at that age, but I laughed, too.' He would often break the cast and crew for tea and tell stories. 'He liked to hold court,' said Tippi. 'He would hold court on the set, sometimes we would hear the same stories over and over, but we all listened and laughed because of the way he told them and what a special storyteller he was.'[1]

Many cast and crew members often recalled how quiet and disciplined everything was on a Hitchcock set. As Albert Whitlock affirmed, 'That's what he was trying to do, create an atmosphere, so you were circumspect in your dress and circumspect in your behaviour. That's what he wanted, he wanted discipline.'[2]

There were few people that Hitchcock feared at the studio, but Albert noted that Hitch took an intense dislike to Jim Pratt, the studio manager at Universal. From 1946 to 1952, Jim Pratt had been head of feature productions there, but left to work for Disney Pictures. Pratt returned to Universal in 1962 to work as an executive production manager, at the time when *The Birds* was being filmed. He controlled the budget and Hitchcock tended to fear people who had power.

THE SPARROW ATTACK

For much of April 1962, the interiors of the Brenner house were filmed, including all the scenes involving Jessica Tandy, as the actress was only contracted until the beginning of May. The sparrow attack was one of the first of the several large-scale bird attacks to be filmed inside the studio, culminating in the attic attack on Melanie. The scene drew upon real-life events and inspiration in La Jolla, California in 1960 when swifts suddenly came racing down chimneys to the bewilderment of homeowners.

For the scene to be authentic, 1,500 small birds were needed to rush down the chimney. 'The birds in this scene are supposed to be [swifts],' remembered bird trainer Beth Dannaldson in a 1962 interview. 'Actually they are a mix of sparrows, finches, buntings and other varieties. Most of these species are imported birds.'[3]

The sparrows had been caught locally by Bud Cardos, but the finches were bought through suppliers from the Philippines and the buntings came from India. Jim and Beth were on hand during filming to protect the birds and see that they had good working conditions, plenty of air and water, and that they didn't work too hard when they got tired. Also on the set was Paul Ridge, a representative of the American Humane Association. Birds, especially small ones, tend to get very nervous when faced with stressful conditions and too much excitement can give them a heart attack, so it was very important for the bird handlers to keep them calm.

When Melanie sees the first sparrow come out of the fireplace, the bird handlers put a little rubber band around its wings so it couldn't jump and fly away. To prevent the small birds from escaping, the living room of the Brenner house was enclosed by polyethylene walls, enabling light to still penetrate and illuminate the set. The camera lens was poked through a small aperture in the cellophane, so that the birds couldn't fly though the hole. Once the actors had slipped through the cellophane curtain, it was promptly sealed behind them. The birds were then placed in opaque cages, which rested atop the prop chimney. On cue, the bird handlers opened the trapdoors in the cages, and, spotting the light below, the birds would fly down the chimney, and into the cellophane bubbled set. The birds then swooped up but were contained by the plastic ceiling above. Air hoses handled by grips prevented the birds from roosting and kept them on the move.

'After we dumped all the birds out of the fireplace, it took a while, a good hour to recapture all the birds,' remembers handler Bud Cardos. 'There were special trapdoors fitted around the fireplace. We did about three dumps a day, that's all we could do to re-rig the shots. When the birds came down they all came out and flew in a thousand different directions. You couldn't see off the set because they were flying around.'

The purpose of the cellophane envelope was to contain the birds in the room and prevent them flying off into the catwalks. 'That is the obvious one, of course,' remarked AD Jim Brown. 'About 100 escaped but the bird people recaptured 70.' Many of the birds flew up to the rafters and couldn't be caught. As there was no food on top of the stage, birdseed was sprinkled around on the set floor, in the hope of snaring the birds when they came down to feed. Some of the escapees were never caught and, after *The Birds* was finished filming, some birds would still cheep in the rafters and cause sound problems for later movies.

Veronica Cartwright remembers the sparrow attack in the living room as one of the most vivid and challenging scenes to film. '1,500 birds were brought in and came down the chimney. We were filming inside a big plastic bubble, and the birds came down and then they would go up, and then they'd hit the plastic ceiling and they would drop and land on the floor. We learned not to step but sort of shuffle and I remember Jessica accidentally treading on a bird and being beside herself.'

This scene also provided Veronica with an important lesson for projecting her emotions on camera. 'When I was doing *The Birds* I discovered that you can't really sit there and say, "Oh, my dog died at this age and so now I've got to be emotional,"' says Veronica. 'That can only work so many times. I discovered on that movie, if you watched the other people, and listened to what was happening, then you were able to come up with the emotion because you had immersed yourself in it. I just had to look at Jessica Tandy who was totally freaked out. So *The Birds* was the movie that led me to that kind of thinking.'

'Jessica Tandy was a pro, she put up with lots of difficulties, especially when we put the wig with mechanical birds on her,' says Virginia Darcy. Despite the challenges of working with their avian co-stars, the actors quickly learned to adapt. 'I got used to the birds rather quickly,' said Jessica, 'simply by looking upon them as other actors. Although, I must say, I was beginning to wonder in some of those scenes towards the end. I've never had another actor bite me before.' It was a difficult and vexing scene for the actors, and for Hitchcock, yet he remained impressively calm during filming. Director Peter Bogdanovich, who would later interview Hitchcock for the MOMA retrospective, was in LA during the spring of 1962 and an observer on the set: 'The whole area had been netted in with plastic sheets so the little birds couldn't get off the actual room-set. The actors – Rod Taylor, Tippi Hedren, Jessica Tandy, and 12-year-old Veronica Cartwright – were, of course, to react in terror to this invasion. The bird wranglers essentially poured the birds down the chimney chute and into the fireplace but, although the actors ran about in proper fright, the small birds seemed more terrified themselves than threatening. Rather than attacking, they flew around trying to find a way out. Hitchcock, extraordinarily calm and cheerful, called out "Cut!" and told the actors to "slip out" of the set so the wranglers could begin the arduous and time-consuming task of trying to recapture all the birds for another take.'[4]

According to Peter, Hitchcock was in complete and affable control of any and all problems, including the technical ones that came up. Storyboard artist Harold Michelson also remembered filming the sparrow invasion and that, 'Hitchcock's greatest fear was that people would laugh at that scene. He was quite worried that, when the women went screaming and stuff like that, people would laugh.'[5] By 12 April, the scene was completed with the principals, but the sparrow attack was still to be enhanced through optical effects as well as the sodium vapour travelling mattes that Bob Boyle was investigating, which would quadruple print the birds over the actors.

The scene immediately following the sparrow attack gave Hitchcock the chance to show one of his best examples of subjective treatment. Less technical than the bird invasion, it was an opportunity for him to improvise while he was filming, a radical departure from his carefully controlled preplanning and storyboarding. Lydia is picking up the broken pieces of china from the living-room floor and Hitchcock's camera photographs the actress Jessica Tandy going around the room, in various positions, ending with her straightening the picture.

Hitchcock keeps his camera on Melanie to show her watching the older woman. 'The reverse cuts of the girl whose POV it is have to build in a very subtle way, going here, going here and going there,' Hitchcock said. 'This is her increasing concern for the mother.' Melanie, like the audience, can see that Lydia is cracking up under the strain of the bird attacks and Hitchcock keeps the mood by following Melanie in close-up across the living-room floor as she suggests to Mitch that she should stay the night.

'Even when she crosses to the young man and says, "I think I'd better stay the night," I take her in the biggest close-up even though I'm walking her, because I think her concern and her interest must maintain the same size on the screen,' Hitchcock explained in an interview. 'If you go back, I feel her concern has dropped as well. So, to me, emotionally, the size of the image is very important, especially when you are using that image to identify itself with the audience. She represents the audience there – look the mother is getting unbalanced – and she represents the general way I handle these things.'[6] All the while, Hitchcock was carefully coaxing a performance from his novice actress.

'I believe that one should, at all cost, try and use that face in the visual as much as possible. Well, you take, for example, the work that I gave to Tippi Hedren in *The Birds*,' Hitchcock explained. 'Her face was used entirely to register impressions... She didn't say a word until she spoke. But she was taking all that in. Visually.'[7]

Hitchcock found himself in an anxious and emotional state halfway through filming *The Birds*, as he began to improvise on the set, which was unusual for him. 'I ran into some emotional problems,' he confided to François Truffaut. 'I had trouble, you know, this is being, this should be written with discretion. I had trouble with the leading man. I was pouring myself into the girl. I was doing Svengali, you know. Because it needed so much. I taught her every expression – never a wasted one, you see... because I was so emotionally upset in the middle of this picture it seemed to do something, it sharpened my mind.'[8]

THE FAWCETT FARM

On Monday 16 and Tuesday 17 April, the interior scenes of Dan Fawcett's farmhouse were filmed, with Hitchcock directing Jessica Tandy in one of the film's most powerful and horrifying sequences. Lydia goes to call on neighbour Dan Fawcett to find out why his chickens aren't eating, in an effort to determine if there's some kind of bird plague going around. As she enters his house she sees some broken cups hanging on the rails, a reminder of her own china damaged by the birds only the previous night. Hitchcock later remarked that he improvised this link during filming, just as he had done with Melanie's subjective treatment, so that Lydia's character (and the audience) would connect the broken china back to the sparrow attack.[9]

As Lydia walks down a long corridor to Dan's bedroom, she slowly opens the bedroom door and sees that birds have penetrated the room. Hitchcock then uses a masterful triple jump cut to show her reaction to Dan's body, starting with a wide shot of Dan, a mid shot of his face, and ending with a close-up of his pecked-out eyes. 'The three staccato jumps are almost like catching the breath – gasp, gasp, gasp – Is it? Yes it is,' said Hitchcock.[10]

Hitchcock said he used a triple jump cut instead of the more conventional zooming because he wanted to prepare for any censorship problems. 'If I ran into censorship anywhere, you can tape it out you see.'[11] He also said that the visual motif of the pecked-out eyes came from the famous Frederick Browne and William Kennedy case of 1927 in England. They were two car thieves who shot Police Constable George Gutteridge in the face four times, with two of the shots aimed at his eyes. 'A murderer could have the impression that the photographic image of the last scene may be left in the eyes,' said Hitchcock. 'Therefore, to prevent this, the eyes are damaged... Gutteridge was murdered, and both his eyes shot out for the same reason.' Just like car thieves and murderers Browne and Kennedy, birds had pecked out Dan Fawcett's eyes, leaving no witnesses, in deference to the superstition that dead men's eyes preserve the last image they behold in life.

Achieving the maximum effect from the triple jump cut required the expert make-up of Howard Smit. A stunt man playing the role of Dan Fawcett was required to sit patiently for 90 minutes as Howard transformed him into a mutilated corpse. Pyjamas were torn and shredded and fake blood added to the man's legs and torso. To create the effect that his eyes had been plucked out, Howard applied an undertaker's wax known as dumold around the man's eye sockets, which were then heavily blackened with make-up, giving them a deep-set look.

THE ATTACK ON THE HOUSE

Throughout April and the first half of May, studio filming continued on the set of the Brenner house, including the climactic attack of the birds, as the family board themselves in. As they wait, Hitchcock effectively utilises silence to heighten the tension. 'It was one of the most satisfying scenes for me personally,' said Hitchcock. 'You have a boarded-up room with four people in it, sitting there in silence, just waiting for the birds to come. I kept the silence going quite a bit.' There is the first flutter of wings and then the terrifying screech of bird cries.

In order to elicit similar reactions from all the actors when the birds attacked, Hitchcock brought in a drummer to help them respond to what would be an external sound of wings and cries. As he explained, 'I had a drummer on the set with a side drum, and he had a microphone put close to it and then put on a loudspeaker. So every time the actors played the scene there was a side drum roll. To ask them to react to nothing was too much.'[12] The pounding drums were played louder and louder, building up real anxiety in the actors and eliciting similar reactions.

'When we arrived on the set, we saw this drummer sitting there with a huge drum,' recalled Tippi. 'We didn't know Hitch had planned this. In the scene, the tension is supposed to slowly build as the birds start to attack the house. Even Hitchcock, as fine a director as he is, couldn't get a bunch of birds to act that way, so he got the idea of using the drum roll to help us react and to build up the tension. For me, it was the most effective scene in the film.'[13]

During this scene, Hitchcock described two kinds of shots to show the panic of the Brenners and Melanie inside the house. 'I gave the mother and child a dotty movement. Can't find cover. They end up in a corner. The girl retreats from nothing. So her image was emptiness in the foreground, symbolising nothing. And she backs up against the sofa, and starts to climb the wall, rolls around the lamp. I build her up as she goes along. Well, these images are angles chosen to express the fear of the unknown. They're not shot just without any thinking about what the intention is, you see.'[14]

Hitchcock compared the helplessness of the Brenners and Melanie to being 'no different in that sequence than people in an air raid with nowhere to go. Now that's where the idea came from. I've been in raids in London and the bombs are falling, and the guns are going like hell all over the place. You don't know where to go. Where can you go?'[15]

To smash through the heavy balsa wood front door of the Brenner house, hammers with fake birds' heads attached were used. Prop men were standing behind beating the door, so that it looked as if the birds' beaks were ripping through, splintering the wood. As Veronica Cartwright remarked, 'He sort of built up anxiety levels a bit, you know. And he would just show you the blocking of where you would be and then just took the reactions as they came. They had hammer heads with birds' heads on them, and they would have these, like, hand puppets, and all sorts of things that had birds' heads on them so they could control them.'[16]

During the attack, Rod Taylor's character, Mitch, goes to fasten the windows after a gull breaks through the glass. To simulate the birds breaking through the window, candy glass made from spun sugar was inserted into the frame. What appears to be Rod's hand being bitten by a gull is actually Ray Berwick's hand, without any make-up since the gull's razor-sharp beak drew real blood on the take.

'I only had the shutter blow open and the young man try to close the shutter, to tell the audience what it was really like outside,' said Hitchcock. 'Otherwise, I was asking too much of their imagination. So, I gave them a little sample. White shadows go for his hand, bloody it up. I'm saying, "Audience, that's what it's really like outside. Only by the millions, not just two, as I've just shown."'[17]

Just as suddenly as they have arrived, the birds retreat, their cries fading in the distance. Hitchcock uses an impressive low-angle shot to show the weight of the house bearing down on his main characters. First we see Mitch step into the low angle, followed by Melanie, followed by Lydia, each entering from opposite sides of the frame for visual symmetry. Finally, a masterful track back reveals all three standing motionless, listening to the now-distant bird cries, hoping and praying that the danger has passed.

The attack on the Brenner house is a marvellously realised scene because of Hitchcock's use of silence, sound and suggestion. During filming of this sequence, the crew stopped for work to give Veronica a surprise 13th birthday party on Friday 20 April. A huge cake was given to her to share with the cast and crew, everybody sang 'Happy Birthday', Jessica gave her a sweater and Tippi a pair of lovebirds.

Hitchcock signed his autograph and signature profile on a piece of cardboard that Peggy brought over, and wrote the inscription 'To the woman I love, Veronica'. She still has it to this day, framed in archival paper. 'He was very nice to me,' she remembers. 'He was never weird with me and I have nothing but kind words to say about him.' When Veronica returned home that evening, there was a huge bouquet of lilacs and French tulips waiting for her, another birthday gift from Hitchcock.

Rod Taylor's problems with Hitchcock on location continued into the studio filming. On Monday 23 April, during the scene when he is washing up in the Brenner kitchen with Jessica Tandy, the press had been invited onto the set. In Rod's own words, 'I was washing up with Jessica, and people were scattered around the set. I noticed putting away the things that the refrigerator light didn't go on. We had done our rehearsals and Hitchcock said "now go for a take". I remarked to the cameraman Bob Burks that the light in the refrigerator didn't go on when I opened the door. Hitch said very loudly, "We shall now take a two-hour lunch break while Mr Taylor, our technical adviser, shows us how to make a movie."'

Everyone then dispersed, leaving Rod feeling rather foolish. At the end of the day, by way of apology, Hitchcock invited Rod to his office to have a drink with the press. There was a spare seat next to Hitchcock and, when Rod walked in, Hitch said, 'And this is for the one I love, my star.' As Virginia Darcy says, 'You had to take Hitch with a pinch of salt,' as he often said things he didn't mean. In truth, Hitchcock was never close to any of his male leads, with the exception of Cary Grant and James Stewart. He once said that his favourite leading man was Robert Donat who set the style for the wrongfully accused man in *The 39 Steps* (1935). Although he admired the acting techniques of men like Anthony Perkins and Martin Balsam, he was often indifferent to virile and handsome men like Rod and John Gavin who played Sam in *Psycho*.

Veronica also remembers the dynamic between Rod and Jessica's characters as being very interesting. 'Jessica, who played my mother, was 54 at the time. She was in love with her son. My brother, played by Rod Taylor, was older than me – and later journalists often thought he was my father. It set up an interesting dynamic. I knew that my brother was attracted to this lady (played by Tippi) – she was closer to my age than my mother was.'

Hitchcock introduces this Oedipal undertone as soon as he introduces Lydia in the Tides restaurant, by remaining on her in a close-up while other characters are speaking. 'Yes, I was anxious to establish the nature of the woman, because, in truth, the arrival of another girl, right into Bodega Bay, with her son really put her on her guard and she was resisting it, before she even examined who the girl was. To her, she was another good-looking woman. What else could she think when he says she brought some love birds. It shows you that the word love is a word of suspicion.'[18]

In mid May, Hitchcock went on to film one of Evan Hunter's favourites – the debate in the Tides restaurant. As Hitchcock said, 'The scene at the Tides restaurant needed comic relief from the drunk, the woman ornithologist, otherwise the latter half would be too much for the audience. I've always seen the long or short of a scene by the preoccupation of the audience.'[19]

Hitchcock felt that, after the gull attack on the birthday party, the sparrow attack, the man's eyes being pecked out, and the crow attack on the schoolchildren, the audience needed a rest from the horror before going on again, and that they needed light relief, otherwise the latter half would be too much for them as the bird violence escalates. The Tides scene would provide that contrast, as there was a drunk, Mrs Bundy the ornithologist, the desperate mother and Melanie all trying to figure out why the birds are attacking. These were played by excellent character actors who included Elizabeth Wilson, Ethel Griffies, Charles McGraw, Doreen Lang, Karl Swenson, Joe Mantell and Dal McKennon, who all started work on 16 or 18 May.

On the set of the Tides restaurant, Hitchcock was preparing to film a scene with Tippi Hedren and Ethel Griffies who was playing Mrs Bundy. 'We are about to see a scene played by one girl doing her first film, and another doing her 101st,' he remarked to his film crew. The veteran 84-year-old Ethel Griffies had first made her debut at the age of three on the London stage in East Lynne. She was paid $1,000 for a week's work on *The Birds* and Tippi would later remark how fascinating it was to watch Ethel perform.

Hitchcock was keen to show the maturity and growth of Melanie's character during the Tides debate. 'Now we get a very businesslike Melanie,' he said in the pre-production conference. 'She's on the phone to her father, and she's surrounded more or less with a lot of different types from the town: the restaurant owner, the comic old Mrs Bundy, and here, I think, we should see Melanie holding her own quite well. I think she's emerging a little with a practical approach toward what should be done.'

While the actors were rehearsing and filming their roles, so were the birds. Ray Berwick was working with hundreds of seagulls, crows and ravens to orchestrate the chilling bird attacks. 'We had about 12 or 13 crew members in the hospital in one day from bites and scratches,' remembered Ray. 'Some of them were absolutely terrified of the birds and with good reason. They always talk about the danger to your eyes when birds are involved. The seagulls would deliberately go for your eyes.'

A raven named Corvus was trained to bite Rod Taylor's hands. The bird learned this after pecking chunks of meat from Rod's hand a few times and performed on cue without bait the first take. Hitchcock later joked, 'Corvus has now learned one of the basic rules of the actor, always bite the hand that feeds you.' Another raven called Archie took an intense dislike to Rod. As Rod recalls, 'There's a still of me looking terrified with a bandage on or something, and I'm looking at this bird. That's real terror. I hated that bird! That bird – every morning, if I was on the set, we were on the set together, would come over and go "Ungg!" and bite me. And I hated him, and he hated me. Even when we came back to the studio. And I think that shot on the veranda was taken in the studio. I'd walk in and say, "Is Archie working today?" And they'd say, "I don't think so, Rod. I think we're working with seagulls." And out of the rafters would come Archie. And, you know, he hated me. And would lie in wait for me. And I'm sure that bird's still alive!'[20]

Rod remembers that some of the funniest guys on the set were the bird wranglers. They were a bad-tempered bunch and Rod would have drinks with them in the evening. 'You look after a bunch of seagulls and ravens and crows and pigeons and God knows what else and you get very nervous. Ray Berwick was the head bird wrangler. He was a wonderful guy. He indeed had patience. He wasn't as bad tempered as his buddies. He knew his birds backwards. He was like a great old cowboy with horses. He knew these silly looking birds. And he understood them and liked them.'[21]

As well as having drinks with the bird handlers, to relieve the demanding studio filming Rod would also socialise with Ted Parvin, his wardrobe man, and Stanley Smith, the make-up man, and go to the Peppermint West Club in Hollywood and do the twist. It was the 1960s and the twist was the popular dance of choice.

THE ATTIC ATTACK

'I said, "Oh, well, what are we going to use?" He answered, "There's a bunch of ravens and crows."' – Tippi Hedren

The most infamous scene of *The Birds*, both onscreen and off, is the attic attack where Tippi Hedren had birds thrown at her for a week. These scenes were scheduled to be filmed in the last week of May 1962 and would achieve notoriety long after the film's release. After the bird attack on the Brenner house, the exhausted family, except Melanie, are sleeping. Many people have asked the question; why does Melanie go up to the attic in the first place? According to Evan Hunter, Hitchcock originally intended to show Melanie opening several doors in the house, but quickly abandoned this idea. He was very concerned about logic and making everything seem plausible.

'I had her going up to the attic after she heard a bird peeping,' Evan said. 'Hitch asked, "If she hears birds in the house, why doesn't she wake Mitch?" I said, "Because she's not sure there are birds in the house." Hitch persisted. "But if she thinks there are birds in that room, why would she open the door?" I had no answer. He said, "All right, it's a good scene, but let's take the curse off it. Let's have her open a lot of doors and find no birds any place and therefore open the last door believing it's safe to do so."'

In the final film, however, even though the opening of the doors was added to the script, Melanie opens just that one attic door after all. Another aspect of Melanie's character that does not come across in the finished film is that she shuts herself inside the attic to prevent the birds from invading the rest of the house. Hitchcock described this act as 'self-sacrificial' but, in the filmed version, it seems that Melanie is stunned by the birds, accidentally knocking the door shut, rather than deliberately sealing it to prevent the birds spreading. As an early version of the script had indicated, it was Annie that was originally to face the birds, but Hitchcock thought that, as Melanie was the central character, she should experience the ordeal.

'This didn't turn out in the film itself, but when she opens the door to that attic, there is every bird imaginable to mankind in that room,' said Evan. 'I mean there are hawks, eagles, seagulls, anything you can imagine, we see all the birds in the universe in that room, and right at that moment we know it's a unified attack against human beings and not something we're playing with in Bodega Bay. It didn't turn out that way in the film. He just used crows and seagulls.'

Until the day of filming the attic scene, Tippi assumed that most of the birds would be either mechanical like the ones used with the children, or optical as in the case of the sparrow attack down the chimney. But, to achieve the visceral effect Hitchcock was looking for, fake birds wouldn't do. So, unbeknownst to Tippi, birds were trained and a special set constructed for the sequence.

On a Monday morning in late May, Tippi was sitting in her dressing room, accompanied by Buddy, a raven that would hang out with her and jump on the table and play with all her makeup. Buddy was playful, affectionate and hadn't been taught some of the bad things the other ravens had. Tippi grew so fond of him that she put a sign saying 'Buddy and Tippi' on her dressing-room door.

'The morning we were to start the scene,' remembers Tippi, 'the assistant director, Jim Brown, came into my dressing room and seemed to be avoiding looking at me. He looked at the floor. He looked at the ceiling. He looked at the walls. I said, "What's the matter with you?" and he mumbled, "We can't use the mechanical birds." I said, "Uh, well, what are we going to use?" He answered, "The mechanical birds don't work and we have to use real ones."'

When Tippi went to the studio floor she saw that a cage had been built around the attic door where her character was to enter, with a top to keep the birds from flying up into the rafters. Inside that cage were four big cartons of gulls and ravens. Standing by were trainers wearing big, thick, leather gauntlets up to their elbows to protect themselves from being scratched or bitten when they held the birds. Tippi had seen how the trainers needed to protect themselves so that they wouldn't be scratched. Already, 12 crew members had been taken to hospital with bites and scratches and no one wanted any more casualties.

Was Hitchcock deliberately deceiving his actress? He would later be accused by the popular press of misleading Tippi and even being sadistic, putting her personal safety in jeopardy. But Tippi remarked in an interview, 'Well, actually, I think Hitch did a very, very kind thing for me. He told me that they were going to use mechanical birds for that scene. Because it was obvious. I thought, how are they going to do this? And, no problem, mechanical birds. I thought, piece of cake.'[22]

Early on, Hitchcock had given up the idea of using mechanical birds for this scene because he needed realism. It was to be the film's set piece just like the shower murder in *Psycho*, and the rape murder in *Frenzy*, which he was to film nine years later. The sequence depended on montage, the cutting up of little bits of film to achieve the effect he wanted, which required shooting from many different angles. As Hitchcock said, 'The scene will last only 50 seconds on the screen, but it will take me a week to film. What you will see on the screen will be a mosaic of little pieces of film – some of them less than an inch long.'[23]

To achieve the effect of birds flying towards the lens and at Tippi, the birds were often tied to their trainer and meat was put near the camera lens so that they would fly towards it. In total, more than 500 crows and gulls were hurled at Tippi during the filming of what turned out to be two minutes of screen time. The ASPCA was on set every day and an aviary was set up to treat any injured birds.

As Ray Berwick explained, 'For the first few days, we trained the birds to land on Tippi and she would push them away. We finally exhausted that, since the birds began to get the idea and wouldn't go near her any more. Then we'd have to hold the birds at a distance of maybe eight or ten feet and just sail them right at her. In that close-up where she's bitten, we put a little rubber tip on the bird's beak.'[24] Air jets were used to prevent the birds from flying into the camera lens, and the bird handlers enticed them back and forth with food. When Tippi swats a gull away with a torch, a dummy bird was used.

The press had been invited onto the set that week to observe the attic filming. Erskine Johnson from the *Oscala Star Banner* wrote on 27 May 1962: 'The girl slumped to the floor. Director Alfred Hitchcock said "Cut" and then an assistant announced, "One hour for lunch." In his portable office on the sound stage, Hitch sat down to a steak the size of a silver dollar and a cup of black coffee... Alfred Hitchcock, Hollywood's merchant of menace, building suspense and leading up to a climax in *The Birds* which he predicts will be as hair raising as his final scene in *Psycho*.'[25]

Hitchcock, as always, was thinking about his audience and how he was going to top *Psycho*. That was the driving force behind *The Birds* and was at the forefront of Hitchcock's mind when filming the attic scene. As Evan said about their motivation for making the film, 'We were trying to scare the hell out of people, period.' Contrary to popular opinion in the press, he didn't unleash the fury of the birds on Tippi out of sadism or spite. He was getting the job done and, in doing so, secured Tippi cinematic immortality just like he did for Janet Leigh in the shower scene in *Psycho*.

After two days of shooting, the strain on Tippi was beginning to show. The cast and crew were watching anxiously and everyone was worried for her safety, including Rod and Veronica. As Rod remembers, he was standing nearby and wanted to intervene. 'Hitch put her in a corner in the attic and directed those wonderful men to throw seagulls at her. I wanted to step in.'

Hitchcock himself seemed anxious directing the scene and wouldn't come out of his office until Bob Burks was ready to film the scene, perhaps feeling twinges of guilt having to put his inexperienced actress through such an ordeal. As Tippi said in a 1980 interview with *Cinefantastique* magazine, 'It was very hard for Hitch at this time, too. He wouldn't come out of his office until they were absolutely ready to shoot because he couldn't stand to watch it.'[26] She reaffirmed this view in a 1997 interview: '[Hitchcock] felt very badly about it. In fact, he couldn't come out of his office until it was really time to roll the cameras.'[27]

Everyone on the set remarked on Tippi's bravery and about how lucky Hitchcock was to have such a compliant actress. 'It's a miracle she got through it with her face intact,' said Ray Berwick. His daughter Tamara agrees: 'She was one of the few people who wasn't frightened of the birds.'[28] Tippi acknowledged that, too: 'I wasn't really frightened, just tired. That scene took a week to shoot.'[29]

Tippi's hairstylist, Virginia Darcy, was on hand to look after her between takes. Often she would step in and say to Hitchcock, 'If you want an actress tomorrow, you'd better let her go so she can work again. I'm sure you have some other shots you can do. I'd then take her to the dressing room, and I'd massage her, and make a banana milkshake.' The milkshake was to calm her down because she was losing so much weight having birds thrown at her and she wasn't eating.

According to Virginia, sometimes Hitchcock forgot that his actors were real people and treated them like puppets. But she remains adamant that

Hitchcock wasn't doing it out of sadistic delight or to torture his actress. His thoughts were on montage, just as when filming the shower scene in *Psycho*. Still, the popular press later delighted in portraying Hitchcock as a sadistic ogre. 'That's all about not knowing Hollywood and not knowing him,' says Virginia in response to the accusations. 'That's why I stepped in. I was the only one who would tell him. Hitch was a perfectionist, he's not thinking about her, he's thinking about what's on the screen. What he gets on that screen is what counts and everything else dissolves. He used to do a lot of things to get what he wanted out of people, that's why you have to study someone before you work with him. He gets so carried away. He's so involved he doesn't know what's going on. He'd sit in the chair and no one else would talk to him. Bob Boyle would sit next to him. But I would go up to him and say you're doing too much, and Tippi can't take anymore.'

Evan and his wife Anita were on set and remember the birds being thrown at Tippi, and Evan wrote about it in his memoirs *Me and Hitch*, describing her as 'inexperienced, bewildered and ultimately terrified'.[30] Although the process was tiring for Tippi, the results were extremely effective onscreen, rivalling the shower murder in *Psycho*. As Tamara Berwick remembers it, 'Tippi was a real trooper.'

'By Wednesday of the shooting week, I was tired,' Tippi said. 'By Thursday, I was noticeably nervous.' And, on Friday, Tippi was asked to lie down on the floor with the birds tied loosely to her dress with elastic bands. It was the job of Rita Riggs to tie elastic bands around Tippi's costumes. 'We went into all kinds of problems with the birds and the only way we could get them pecking at Tippi was to tie them with rubber bands, which we attached to the clothes,' says Rita. Everything had been carefully storyboarded and the crew was following through on weeks of planning. 'I particularly remember Tippi's bravery. I worked so closely with her every day, and the scenes when she's attacked by crows were actually rather dangerous. We didn't realise we were putting her at risk, but that scene when she was on the ground, and the crows are on top of her, I had rigged with elastics on their beaks, so when they were pulling back, they still looked like they were pecking her. It would take three or four hours to rig one of these shots, and she would lie down patiently while we were doing all this. And the take when there were more birds poured into this small room on top of her, and the direction was that she must keep her eyes open as if in a trance.'

Sometimes the film crew was lucky to get four shots. On that Friday, one of the birds jumped from Tippi's shoulder over her face and nearly clawed her eye. Rita remembers, 'I think the last time she managed to stay still, keep her eyes open, I remember a crow walked right across and near her eye, thank God she didn't move and we got the shot.' But that was enough for Tippi. She threw all the birds off her, picked herself up from the floor, sat down and cried. 'And everybody left me,' Tippi later remembered. She then spent the weekend sleeping, out of sheer exhaustion. When she returned to the studio the following Monday, she lay down on the couch in her dressing room. Makeup man Howard Smit tried to wake her but couldn't. A doctor was called and Tippi was sent home to rest for the entire week.

'But I have nothing to shoot,' Hitchcock complained as his lead actress was in almost every scene. In the end they did find something else to work on and filming continued without closing down the production. As Veronica recalls, 'We shot the scenes with the body double while Tippi was recovering.' These are the shots of Mitch carrying Melanie down the stairs from the attic and giving her brandy on the couch. The insert close-ups of Tippi were filmed later when she had returned to the studio.

The whole experience was an ordeal for Tippi and she coped admirably. But if Hitchcock hadn't been so exacting and persistent, the scene would nowhere near rival other set pieces like the shower sequence in *Psycho* or the crop duster attack in *North by Northwest*. Of the sadistic rumours, Rita Riggs says, 'It's like newspapers, it sells, but I never really thought he was serious. He was a jokester and a prankster and I have only good memories throughout *The Birds*.'

FILMING THE ENDING

Aside from the attic filming, the ending of *The Birds* was to cause much controversy when the film was released. It was still unresolved even while the crew was more than a third of the way into filming. Evan Hunter's intention was to show that the bird attacks were widespread and not just localised to the characters. 'Where we see disaster all through the town, as we see an overturned school bus. We see a farmer with a shotgun, lying across a front porch. We see windows shattered all over town. Dead birds on the road. Police patrol cars, in flames. It's almost as if a war has been waged against the town by the birds.'[31]

While still on location, Hitchcock had gathered cast and crew together one evening at the El Rancho motel, and spun them a story about the ending. Some of the crew thought the story would never end. 'I toyed with the idea at one time of lap-dissolving. They're in the car and they look, and there's the Golden Gate Bridge, covered in birds,' said Hitchcock. 'Now, San Francisco, oh, my God. Yes, that's a belly laugh.'[32]

When Hitchcock returned to LA to begin studio filming, he was still undecided how to conclude the film, so he instructed Robert Boyle, Albert Whitlock and Harold Michelson, who were still in Bodega Bay, to film the widespread-attack ending. Harold had storyboarded the finale, which involved littering the town with dummy and dead birds. Birds lie on the road ahead as the Brenner family drives away with Melanie, and they have also taken over the other houses (Figure 24). As Albert recalled, 'Hitch wanted to do the final scene, which was going to be the car leaving the house and trying to make its way, and he was going to have a sequence in San Francisco. So he wanted the one scene where the car would make its way around the bay, but through this collage, you know, with birds and dead people. So, we're out and it's now getting to be summer. It had been spring, and now it's summer, very hot, blazing blue skies and no mood at all. And we had an old derelict boat in the bay and we draped some dummies over that. We were perspiring and setting all these things up.'[33]

Harold Michelson remembers, 'We actually did it, physically. We started messing up the place. What happened is, I think the prop man went to some butcher place or something, and got a whole bunch of, uh, chickens – dead chickens. And we laid them all over the road, and we had a lot of ketchup, and we would dip rags in the ketchup and throw them against a building, and get a lot of blood.'

The men created a lot of mess on the road for the car to drive through as it headed towards San Francisco. After having brought the dead chickens from the poultry farm, pouring ketchup over them, and laying them down all over the streets, it looked like avian Armageddon. When the Animal Protection people who had been carefully monitoring their activities arrived, all they saw were dead chickens on the road and, misinterpreting the scene, became violent. One woman came up to Bob Boyle and ripped his jacket.

Albert, however, was dubious about the ending. 'I kept saying to Bob, we're wasting our time, and he said, "Hitch wants it. Let's shoot some film at least, and show him what we've done." So the production office was actually in the house – you know, the house on the point, and there was always somebody there to answer the phone, so somebody came out of the door and yelled out Bob Boyle, Hitch wants you. Well Hitch was back in Hollywood by this time. We were doing this all on our own. And Bob came back onto the set, and Harold and I were just standing there dripping with perspiration, and Bob said, "I've got good news for you. Hitch has decided on another ending. We don't need this at all." '[34]

Hitchcock had decided to abandon this ending for the more unresolved one of the family leaving their homestead surrounded by birds. Evan Hunter later said he didn't know why Hitchcock chose not to shoot the ending as he had scripted it. 'In those ten pages, the Brenners and Melanie leave the house and drive through the town, where we see absolute chaos and realise the bird attacks are not a personal vendetta on Melanie and the Brenners but a widespread calamity.'

The other ending that Hitchcock and Evan had devised was of the Brenner family and the wounded Melanie fleeing from Bodega Bay in the convertible. The car is travelling on the same winding road that Melanie drove in on, which was set up early in the film, but now the birds are following the car in a straight line and descend on it. 'And the convertible was also set up at the very beginning of the film; it's a convertible with a canvas top,' said Evan. 'And now the birds land on the top of the car, and they're in the car, and we see the top starting to shred, and it goes back suddenly, and all the birds are hovering over the car.'[35]

This scene was never filmed, and Evan believes that Hitchcock figured that he could achieve the same effect by showing the birds having taken over the house and, by association, the world: 'I think he was very tired by then, and this would have required a lot of work with the scene in the car where four characters are in a tight space and the camera is in with them watching the beaks, and then the scene of the birds hovering, and the birds following, and the helicopter shots, animation, everything. It was just too much to do.'[36]

One Saturday afternoon in the middle of studio filming, Hitchcock went home with Bob Boyle and Peggy Robertson to lay out the whole sequence with the intent of filming it. 'And I started with them bringing the girl out of the attic. I even gave the direction when she saw the birds she says "No, no". I made her speak like a small child. The intonation it would be hard for her; I wanted a kind of distorted reasoning and I made her intonation say

"No, no, I've been among the birds and you're not going to put me among the birds again." And I changed the whole, I threw the whole lot away and I put this new ending in. But this is in the middle of shooting the picture which I'd never done before. It was strange, you know. I wouldn't like to feel that one's best work sometime must be done under strain like that. Because I'm not usually that emotional.'[37]

Hitchcock later explained why he did not find it necessary to film Evan's final pages. 'I excluded those scenes because I felt they were superfluous,' he said. 'Emotionally speaking, the movie was already over for the audience. The additional scenes would have been playing while everyone was leaving their seats and walking up the aisles. We used to call these hat-feeling scenes.'[38] After the film was released he wrote to an exhibitor: 'I did have a further ending with a final attack on the automobile as it raced away, but I cut it out because it was so repetitious that the thing was anti-climactic.'[39]

Evan was still feeling sore that his script had been tinkered with. As he wrote in his memoirs *Me and Hitch*, 'To Mr Pritchett, however, must go the credit (or blame) for urging that the film end on a gloomier note, with the people in the car "looking backwards at the village with fear, rather than forward to the hope of escape". (You will remember that, in my first draft, Mitch Brenner expressed the fear that the birds might be in San Francisco when they got there.) But it was Pritchett's suggestion that translated itself into what became the final scene of the film.'[40] Evan believed that the way Hitchcock ended the film conveyed the idea that the attack on the Brenner house was a random event. But perhaps that was part of Hitchcock's intention and why he rejected the Golden Gate Bridge finale. During the research phase, he had heard from local farmers who said that attacks by birds were often isolated.

The film's final shot, which Hitchcock eventually settled on, showing the Brenners and Melanie slowly making their way across the bird-dominated landscape in the convertible, as the skies of morning break overhead, has been described by Hitchcock as 'my most complicated shot ever', requiring 32 pieces of film.[41] For this shot, birds appear to stretch from the camera to the horizon. Many of the birds seen were tranquillised to temporarily suspend their flying abilities. The crows could be taught to perch, or were bound to their perch; the gulls had to be tied in place atop the house and barn to prevent them from flying away. Stagehands were often required to rescue birds when they lost their footing and fell over the sides, leaving them hanging upside down by elastic bands. 'I remember when Rod Taylor came walking out of the house, and the birds were moving a little bit, we had built the set on the sound stage and had a lot of mounted and live ravens,' says Bud Cardos. Thirty gulls were used over and over again, as this was the maximum quota of gulls allowed. Five hundred ducks were sprayed with watercolour paint in the background to look like distant gulls. It would take editor George Tomasini's expert hand to put all the pieces of film together.

THE SAND DUNE SCENE

One of the most contentious scenes in *The Birds* occurs just before Cathy's birthday party and was filmed on 7 June 1962. Melanie and Mitch wander up to the dunes with a martini pitcher and two glasses whereupon they talk about their mothers and Melanie's frivolous life in San Francisco. Hitchcock, who was dissatisfied with the development in Melanie's character, wanted to add substance and background by providing detail of how she had been abandoned by her mother when she was 11 years old.

The exterior sand dunes that Rod and Tippi climbed on location were filmed next to Rose Gaffney's ranch house. But Hitchcock wanted to shoot the main dialogue inside the studio. As Rod observed, 'Hitch was a studio man. If we were within 100 feet of some beautiful sand dunes, he would go into a studio, build a dune and put sand against a blue background, and we did that to recreate the scene.'

To be fair to Hitchcock, he recreated scenes in the studio so that he could control the lighting and present his leading man and leading lady to their best advantage, despite the set looking obviously artificial. He wanted control and went to great lengths to make his actors look good on stage, and have their makeup freshly touched up before a take. He also wanted the bird attacks to look as realistic as possible and it was easier to control the birds inside a studio than it was on location.

Of the sand dune set, Bob Boyle explained, 'There's no way you can do a set like that and make it look real. You're talking about trying to get sunlight from arc lamps. Sunlight is a single source and impossible to recreate.'[42] There may have been numerous reasons why Hitchcock chose to film the scene indoors, as Bob went on to speculate. 'Was the actual hill too steep to climb? Did Hitchcock want to get back to Hollywood? I have been on many locations with Hitch where he gets very impatient. He'd rather work on a sound stage.'

But it wasn't the lighting and the aesthetics, or the obvious phoney backdrop, that would cause screenwriter Evan Hunter so much consternation – it was the dialogue. Evan was on the set that day in early summer when the sand dune scene was being rehearsed and remembers Rod Taylor coming up to him with script in hand. 'Rod took me aside and asked me if I knew anything about the scene. I read it and told him I'd never seen it before. He said, "We're shooting it tomorrow morning." I said "Well, let me talk to Hitch about it."'[43]

Evan didn't know it at the time, but his script for *The Birds* had been sent out to other writers for a second opinion, specifically to V S Pritchett. At Hitchcock's request, Pritchett wrote the sand dune dialogue mentioning Melanie's mother running off 'with a hotel man from the East' and the effects of Melanie's feeling abandoned, and saying, 'Well, maybe I should go and join the other children.'[44]

As Hitchcock noted in his pre-production conference with Tippi, the Melanie character is starting to feel slightly foolish in the company of the serious Brenners, especially when she talks about teaching a Mynah bird to shock her prim aunt. 'If she'd been telling this in the Hungry I nightclub in San Francisco to a group, it would have all gone down very well. But it seems out of place here,' observed Hitchcock.

Character development or not, Evan wasn't buying it. He went to Hitchcock and stated, 'This is a dumb scene, it's going to slow down the movie enormously, slow down the point where the birds attack the children at the birthday party, and it serves no purpose and I don't think it should be in the movie.' Hitchcock looked Evan right in the eye and said, 'Are you going to trust me or an actor?'[45] But Evan believed that it was Hitch's way of trying to redeem Melanie's frivolous character in three sentences for the audience, and that it just didn't work.

It was during the filming of the sand dune scene that Tippi was also informed by her agent (not by Hitchcock) that she'd be playing the lead role in *Marnie*, on the very day that Grace Kelly publicly announced that she was withdrawing from negotiations in June of 1962.[46] 'I was stunned. I was amazed that he would have this faith in me,' remembered Tippi. But Hitchcock felt, and possibly as a reward for Tippi's hard work and bravery during the arduous bird attacks, that when you started with a new actress, you got a rhythm going with her. He felt that way with Tippi, just as he had done with Grace Kelly and Vera Miles before her.

THE PHONE BOOTH ATTACK

Also to be filmed as part of the sodium vapour process work, on 12 and 13 June, on sound stage 12, was the attack on the telephone booth where Melanie takes refuge during the gull raid on the town. This scene also serves as the pay-off to the line in the bird shop when Mitch says, 'Back in your gilded cage, Melanie Daniels.' As early as the pre-production conference, Hitchcock said, 'I really think that we ought to get the makeup changed toward the end of the telephone booth and, if not there, by the time they arrive at the school to pick up Cathy and we find the dead Annie there. I think she should look washed out, because we're going to have, in the phone booth, real hysteria.'[47]

Real hysteria – that's the effect Hitchcock wanted. All around, birds are flying and attacking the townspeople. Hitchcock wanted to shock the audience, and Melanie, and the scene was devised in the script so that the birds would fly all around and crash into the telephone booth, causing her to retreat back inside. The phone booth was a travelling matte foreground. For some shots, bird trainers would throw live birds at Tippi inside the phone booth. Outside the glass of the phone booth, live action is sometimes seen, and one angle is a full matte painting by Albert Whitlock that has no action built into it, but is simply designed as a background.

As well as the live birds, it was planned for dummy birds to hit the glass for shock effect. It was up to Bobby Bone, the prop master, to send a dummy seagull down on a wire, upon which it would crash into the glass. Tippi was inside and it was assumed that the safety glass of the booth wouldn't break. But, in the event, when the dummy seagull hit the glass, it shattered, and sprayed all over her skin. The makeup people spent the rest of the afternoon picking out tiny bits of glass from Tippi's face. It was an unfortunate accident, but luckily no lasting damage occurred and Tippi went on to film the bird shop sequences with Rod Taylor the next day.

A myth has developed that Hitchcock planned the dummy gull smash to deliberately shock Tippi or even punish her, even though the scene had been written months before in Evan's script. Indeed, why would he offer her the coveted part of *Marnie*, only to intentionally put her in a position a few days later where she might be harmed? Both the hairstylist Virginia Darcy and the costume supervisor Rita Riggs, who were on the set that day, have rejected this notion. As Virginia Darcy says, 'He's not going to do it deliberately. Why would he have her deformed so he can't use her? He had been in the business since the 1920s. That was the prop man's fault because he didn't have unbreakable glass. Mr Hitchcock didn't have anything to do with it. Why would he endanger his lead actress on a $3 million film so that she's deformed for the rest of the movie?' Rita Riggs concurs: 'The scene was dramatic. I was on the set that day. I don't agree [that it was deliberate]. He could be a total Jekyll and Hyde but I never saw that.'

THE PET SHOP INTERIORS

The interiors at the pet shop, which were Rod Taylor's last scenes, were filmed between Thursday 14 and Monday 18 June. Afterwards, Rod went on to star in *A Gathering of Eagles* with Rock Hudson. He still had a multi-picture deal with Hitchcock that would last over the next few years, and his agent duly reported Rod's other commitments to the director, but the deal was not honoured beyond *The Birds*.

Tippi describes the pet shop scene as one of her favourites because they were 'fun and flirty'. She and Rod had good chemistry and they rehearsed the scene together. They were both 32 years old when they filmed *The Birds*, their January birthdays being just a week apart. They soon formed a friendship which lasts until this day, and Rod remains loyal to Tippi, saying she was stoical during the filming.

Of the pet shop scene, Hitchcock said in the pre-production meeting, 'We don't want to make it dull. It'll depend how it's rehearsed... How you and Rod Taylor jump in on each other. But the main thing I want to make clear at this point is that I don't think we should play it with what I call "on the nose", expectant expressions... It's high comedy. It should be played for real high comedy. A high comedy is played like drama.'

Hitchcock continued to devote all his energy to directing Tippi, feeling that her lack of range and emotionless expressions were actually a benefit to the film and his style of filmmaking. He once remarked in an interview, 'I only want on your face what we tell to the audience, what you're thinking. Let me explain to you. If you put a lot of redundant expression on your face, it's like taking a sheet of paper and scribbling all over it. Then you write a sentence, but you can't read it, too much scribble on your face. Much easier to read if the piece of paper is blank. That's what the face is for.'[48]

Later he would boast in interviews, 'There is not one redundant expression on Tippi Hedren's face. Every expression makes a point. Even the slight nuance of a smile when she says, "What can I do for you, sir?" One look says, "I'm going to play a gag on him." That's the economy of it. Dialogue should simply be a sound among other sounds, just something that comes out of the mouths of people whose eyes tell the story in visual terms.'[49]

He would also describe the significance of the line when Mitch puts the canary back in its cage: 'Back in your gilded cage, Melanie Daniels.' Hitchcock wrote that line himself because he said he wanted to express the true nature of Melanie's character. During the seagull attack, when Melanie takes refuge in the telephone booth, it was his intention to show that she was a bird in a cage, but not a gilded one. 'Which is the beginning of her trial by fire, the birds are outside and the human is in the cage.'[50]

By mid June, Rod Taylor's scenes were completed, as Jessica Tandy's and Suzanne Pleshette's had been the month before. Hitchcock could now focus his concentration on the numerous process and travelling matte shots that involved Tippi Hedren and the bird attacks. He always felt that it was very important for close-ups, especially of his leading ladies, to be done under controlled lighting, so he wanted almost all of the close-ups to be done inside the studio.

Bob Boyle had determined that the sodium vapour process was superior to blue screen in filming birds against a background so that they could be superimposed later to give the illusion of attacking birds. On 29 May, the film's production manager Norman Deming wrote to John Grubbs, the production manager at Walt Disney Studios, 'After many unavoidable schedule delays we are now ready to start using the sodium vapour process rather extensively during the next month.' The services of Ub Iwerks and the use of sodium vapour process equipment, plus lab work for optical effects, came to a total of $23,481. Eustace Lycett at Disney Studios supervised the day-to-day production.

As Robert Boyle said of the sodium vapour process, 'It was a wonderful matting situation. It would even matte smoke. It's not used now, because it was very cumbersome. Now, remember, we're talking several years ago. Today, many of these problems would be solved with a computer.' As it turned out, the production tended to use more blue screen than sodium vapour. But there was the added problem that the seagulls would often ruin the blue screen because they would leave excrement all over it.

THE CROW ATTACK

The attack by the crows on the schoolchildren was a very complicated sequence that had been partially filmed on location in Bodega and Bodega Bay. Ray Berwick had trained 24 crows to land on the jungle gym bars that had been erected outside the school house. Back in the studio, Ray tirelessly trained another 125 crows to roost on a duplicate jungle gym. Just before the crows take off to attack the children, a slight jump cut was necessary in the editing as two eager birds flew off ahead of the flock, so 15 feet of film had to removed from the sequence.

To get the full effect of the crow attack, Hitchcock recreated the scene of the children running in the studio for ten days between 20 and 29 June. As Veronica Cartwright recalls, 'When we got back into the set at Universal, a treadmill was brought in and the kids and I ran on this treadmill. Boy, we had a workout. Generally speaking, a lot of the close shots I believe were shot on the stage in front of the sodium screen.'

Bird puppets on wires would swoop down on the children running on the treadmill. The crew released these bizarre-looking creatures that were like model airplanes with motorised wings that moved up and down. 'They had big mobiles with all sorts of birds hanging on that would swoop down on us,' remembers Veronica. 'And some of the kids had mechanical birds which looked like they were pecking.' For close-up shots, hand puppets were used for biting the children.

Real crows were then brought in with their trainers to simulate the attack. The 30 crows were trained to fly from one perch to another in the studio against the sodium vapour screen, inside a wind tunnel. Trainers encouraged the crows to fly in front of the camera, but the smart birds got accustomed to the commands so that they started to anticipate them and flew before the cameras started rolling. So the bird trainers ended up not giving them any verbal commands at all, because the crows were so clever. Some of the birds were trained to land on the necks and shoulders of the children, which were used for foreground shots.

The footage was then blown up and superimposed on the original film of the schoolchildren running down the street on location and on the treadmill. As Robert Boyle described it, 'We had the actual movement down the hill. That was the background. We had several shots, a side shot, a back shot.' A lot of footage was needed for these kinds of scenes, so that the editing could be fast and exciting, and in the end the crow attack would have 67 cuts.

'During the treadmill sequence, Hitchcock showed a sadistic side to him,' Veronica laughs. 'He kept speeding the treadmill up and there was a huge mattress on the other end, so you are desperately trying to stay in the front, because you knew that if one person went down, it would be like a bowling pin, and you would be wiped out. You'd be flying off the end, all these bodies.'

Shari Lee Bernath was one of the kids who got wiped out on the treadmill, and she remembers running and falling off the back. 'And my mouth was bleeding because I cut my lip falling off. Hitchcock looked at me and said, "You could have spat it (the blood) out and we would have used it in the film." I looked at him as if to say, "Are you nuts?" But he was very nice to me. He sat with me when the nurse came.' She remembers that Hitchcock had a very droll, dry sense of humour. 'I think he was a loner in the industry because he was a visionary,' Shari says. 'So he didn't participate with the others. He gave me the time to do my scenes, and I knew to follow directions and not to mess around when I was on the set with him. My mother and I wanted for nothing and he was also very nice to my mother.'

One person who is noticeably absent during the crow attack in the studio filming is Suzanne Pleshette. Because of delays in the production, Suzanne's contract ended in mid May and she was obliged to go on to her next film. But, from the storyboards, it is evident that her character was supposed to be part of the treadmill filming (Figure 23).

FIRST BIRD ATTACK

Just as with the crow sequence, the first bird attack on Melanie by the seagull while she is in the outboard boat was achieved using a combination of location and studio filming. Hitchcock had decided early on that the gull should hit the top of Melanie's head. In a memo dated 28 October 1961, he wrote, 'I think it would be better if we had Melanie's wound on the top of her head in the hair and showed the blood trickling down her temple and cheek. If we don't do this and we have the wound below the hairline we'll have to show it for the rest of the picture, whereas if the wound is on the top of the head the hair can be combed over it.'

Howard Smit applied Tippi's preliminary makeup in the Santa Rosa motel and later touched it up on the set after the gull has hit her. Tippi rehearsed her reaction shot in the boat on location in Bodega Bay. Back in the studio, on 3 July, the film crew put up a bright-blue background to later print in rear projection of the bay. Up in the rafters they had a wire on a slope and, at the top, a dummy seagull. The wire went from the rafters down to almost over Tippi's head.

Bobby Bone, the prop man, was on standby with a tube and a plunger full of fake blood. The tube ran up through Tippi's dress and hair. 'And then Virginia Darcy, my hairdresser, did the French roll and the whole thing and she hairsprayed my hair. It was almost like a wig, I mean, a real solid helmet, except for one little lock of hair that was loose.' This is where the tube ended. Then the prop man let the dummy bird go down the wire. He had the plunger ready and, when the bird got to the right place just above Tippi's head, he pressed the plunger, and the bird went over, and the lock of hair went forward with the blast of air.

Bob Burks, the cinematographer, later synchronised the dummy gull with footage of a real gull shot at the San Francisco garbage dump, so that, when they let go of the dummy bird to swoop down at Tippi, it looked as if the gull had actually hit her. At the same time, a trickle of blood was released to create the illusion that she had been cut. 'I thought it was very clever,' remembered Tippi. Hitchcock said of the scene, 'That was called a double printing job. The girl was in a boat with a tube of compressed air run up her back and into her hair. At a crucial point, a jet of air was blown which blew her hair. On a separate film we took a picture of a gull that was trained to swoop down. And we put the film together.'[51]

The first unit production for *The Birds* ended on Tuesday 10 July 1962 with the filming of Melanie dropping off the lovebirds at Mitch's apartment in San Francisco, only to discover that he has gone 60 miles up the coast to Bodega Bay. Character actor Richard Deacon, most famous for playing Mel Cooley on *The Dick Van Dyke Show*, was cast as Mitch's neighbour, who indiscreetly informs Melanie of Mitch's whereabouts.

After five months of location and studio filming, the first unit's work was complete, but the special-effects team and the bird trainers continued working until the end of August to get footage of the birds for the attacks. Bob Boyle's work came to an end on 27 August 1962, and he went on to work on the new Doris Day film, *The Thrill of it All*, for Ross Hunter at Universal. Ray Berwick's contract came to an end on 28 November 1962, but he was brought back for two weeks in early February 1963 to work with Hitchcock on the film's trailer and also the publicity. Between them all, they had orchestrated the seemingly impossible. Now it was up to the postproduction team to turn the footage into realistic and chilling bird attacks.

NOTES

1   Tippi Hedren, BBC *Omnibus*, Hitchcock documentary, 1986
2   Albert Whitlock, 'Roundtable on *The Birds*', *Cahiers du Cinema*, 1982
3   Harrison Carroll, 'It's for *The Birds*', Harrison Carroll, *LA Herald Examiner*, 22 April 1962, p. 1
4   Peter Bogdanovich, *All About The Birds*, Universal DVD, 2000
5   Harold Michelson, 'Roundtable on *The Birds*',*Cahiers du Cinema*, 1982
6   Hitchcock to Truffaut, August 1962
7   'On Style', *Hitchcock on Hitchcock*, University of California Press, 1995, p. 296
8   Hitchcock to Truffaut, August 1962
9   Hitchcock to Truffaut, August 1962
10 Hitchcock to Truffaut, August 1962
11 'On Style', *Hitchcock on Hitchcock*, University of California Press, 1995, p. 301
12 Hitchcock to Truffaut, August 1962
13 Kyle Counts, 'The Making of Alfred Hitchcock's *The Birds*', *Cinefantastique*, Vol 10, 1980, p. 30
14 'On Style', *Hitchcock on Hitchcock*, University of California Press, 1995, p. 290
15 Hitchcock to Truffaut, August 1962

16 Interview with Veronica Cartwright, 29 November 2012, Los Angeles

17 Hitchcock to Truffaut, August 1962

18 Hitchcock to Peter Bogdanovich, 14 February 1962

19 Hitchcock to Truffaut, August 1962

20 Rod Taylor in *All About The Birds*, DVD, 2000

21 Rod Taylor in *All About The Birds*, DVD, 2000

22 Leon Worden, 'SVC Newsmaker of the week: Tippi Hedren', *Signal Multimedia*, 6 March 2005

23 Erskine Johnson, 'Latest Hitchcock Picture Not For But By The Birds,' *Oscala Star Banner*, 27 May 1962

24 Kyle Counts, 'The Making of Alfred Hitchcock's *The Birds*', Vol. 10, *Cinefantastique*, p. 32

25 Erskine Johnson, 'Latest Hitchcock Picture Not For But By The Birds', *Oscala Star Banner*, 27 May 1962

26 Kyle Counts, 'The Making of Alfred Hitchcock's The Birds', *Cinefantastique*, p. 33

27 Camille Paglia, *The Birds*, BFI Publishing, p. 17

28 Interview with Tamara Mellett, 14 July 2012, Escondido, California

29 Susan Stewart, 'Tippi Hedren from birds to cats', *Bangor Daily News*, 16 August 1985

30 Evan Hunter, *Me and Hitch*, Faber and Faber, 1997, p. 68

31 Evan Hunter, *All About The Birds*, Universal DVD, 2000

32 Hitchcock to Peter Bogdanovich, 14 February 1963

33 Albert Whitlock, 'Roundtable on *The Birds*', 1982

34 Albert Whitlock, 'Roundtable on *The Birds*', 1982

35 Evan Hunter, *All about The Birds*, Universal DVD, 2000

36 Charles L P Silet, 'Writing with Hitch: An interview with Ed McBain', Mystery Net, 1995

37 Hitchcock to Truffaut, August 1962

38 Hitchcock to Truffaut, August 1962

39 Hitchcock to George R Isaacs, 24 June 1963, Alfred Hitchcock Collection, Margaret Herrick Library

40 Evan Hunter, *Me and Hitch*, Faber and Faber, 1997, p. 65

41 Hitchcock to Bogdanovich, 14 February 1963

42 Bob Boyle, 'Roundtable on *The Birds*', *Cahiers du Cinema*, 1982

43 Evan Hunter, *Me and Hitch*, Faber and Faber, p. 68–69

44 Hitchcock to Pritchett, 9 April 1962, Alfred Hitchcock Collection, Margaret Herrick Library

45 Evan Hunter, *Me and Hitch*, Faber and Faber, 1997, p. 70

46 Tony Lee Moral, *Hitchcock and the Making of Marnie*, Scarecrow Press, 2005

47 Transcript between Hitchcock and Hedren, 24 February 1962, Margaret Herrick Library

48 Hitchcock to Bogdanovich, 14 February 1963

49 Hitchcock to Truffaut, August 1962

50 Hitchcock to Truffaut, August 1962

51 Hitchcock to Dick Cavett, *The Dick Cavett Show*, 8 June 1972

ELECTRONIC SOUND

'*With this new system, I'm going to not only indicate the sound we want, but the style and nature of the sound*' – Alfred Hitchcock

One of the most unique aspects of *The Birds* is that the film does not have a musical score of any kind. Early on in production Hitchcock decided that the film would have no conventional music. As Evan Hunter said, 'We had a long discussion about music and a score. Using a score, you know? And I felt that it would really, uh, make the movie almost unbearable if we had music in it and, you know, underscoring the terror and adding to the screaming of the birds. I think the audience would have jumped out of their seats. And he said no, he felt it would be more effective the other way.'

Hitchcock wanted a more indirect and arty approach to the soundtrack. 'Conventional music usually serves either as a counterpoint or a comment on whatever scene is being played. I decided to use a more abstract approach,' Hitchcock said. 'After all, when you put music to film, it's really sound, it isn't music per se.'

While Hitchcock was filming in the studio in April, Peggy Robertson received a letter from a German composer of electronic music named Remi Gassmann who was writing at the suggestion of Saul Bass, the graphic designer who had designed the opening titles for *Vertigo*, *North by Northwest* and *Psycho*.[1] Electronic music was gaining ground on the new music concert scene but was still rare in film. Remi had been born to Russian-German parents on 30 December 1908, beginning musical studies at the age of five at St Mary's Academy in Kansas. At Berlin's college of music, Remi met another German composer named Oskar Sala, and together they composed a special 20-minute ballet called *Electronics*, choreographed by George Balanchine and performed at the Berlin State Opera and the New York City Centre. The ballet was hailed by the *New York Times* as 'definitely works of art...' and the London *Times* announced, quoting composer Aaron Copland, that 'the future is here... we are going to have a new kind of music.'

Remi also collaborated with choreographer Tatjana Gsovsky and premiered *Paean* (1960), one of the first ballets set to electronic music, establishing him at the forefront of the avant-garde. It was the first time a full symphonic score had been played without the use of any musical instruments. The device that was used to create the electronic sound was called a trautonium, and it was used by the New York City ballet and unveiled with considerable fanfare.

The trautonium was a unique electronic sound instrument invented in Berlin in the 1930s, and named after its inventor Dr Frederick Trautwein. Hitchcock first heard the instrument while working in Germany. It was basically the forerunner of many modern keyboard instruments in that the player was able to take commonplace, ordinary sounds and manipulate them by playing the instrument.

By 1961, Remi was lecturing on electronic sound at the University of California, Los Angeles and at Stanford University. He was also acting as an agent for Oskar Sala and the trautonium in the United States. Remi was staying in Laguna Beach at the time and, on 18 April 1962, he wrote to Hitchcock at Revue Studios: 'The recent matter I asked to have brought to your attention, at the suggestion of Mr Saul Bass, concerns a new and, in many respects, very startling development in the creation and application of sound for film soundtracks. We felt this was so important an extension of existing sound resources for film use, it warranted asking you to take a moment in your present busy production schedule to become acquainted with it.'

Remi continued by pointing out that, 'For the first time, we have at our disposal, through electronic generation, what has aptly been called the totality of the acoustical.' In other words, both familiar sounds and unfamiliar could now be produced electronically for film, and the result was much like a new dimension in film production. The letter from Remi included a short demo film and tapes, and mentioned the ballet *Electronics* as the first major attempt at purely musical utilisation. It would allow Hitchcock to manipulate sounds in a way that could be very musical in effect. He also went on to explain that sounds 'from common noise to music and esoteric effects' could now be used electronically using the trautonium.

Peggy Robertson replied in a letter on 24 April that Hitchcock was busy filming *The Birds*, but was interested and that Remi's letter had been passed on to Waldon Watson, nicknamed 'Watty', head of sound at Revue Studios. It was also brought to the attention of Bernard Herrmann, Hitchcock's regular composer.

William Russell, sound director at Revue Studios, was intrigued and called Remi, inviting him to come in. As Hitchcock recalled in an interview, 'I was sitting in my office minding my own business, when Russell burst into Miss Gauthier's office next to mine and demanded to see me. He was too agitated to be sent back. She let him in. The first thing he said was, "Hitch, we've got our sound." I was sure he had cracked up at long last.'[2]

Russell had just listened to a tape taken of the trautonium that Remi had brought over for a demonstration. Remi also showed him photographs of the sound machine and gave him a detailed and professional description of its operation, which convinced Russell that Remi knew more about sound than he did. Russell was in fact so convinced that, only three weeks after writing to Hitchcock, on 9 May, a contract was sent to Remi, acting on behalf of Oskar Sala. The agreement was to create a separate soundtrack made up of sound effects and various other sounds synchronised with the action of 750 feet of film from a sequence of *The Birds*. The payment for this would be $3,000. The sequence that Hitchcock chose to send was a reel containing the climactic attack on the Brenner house – the only sequence where the attackers are heard and not seen. This gave Remi and Oskar Sala a chance to demonstrate the new technology by adding electronically created bird sounds.

Hitchcock wanted to use this revolutionary electronic sound composition for his most avant-garde film to date. He was still pushing the boundaries of what was possible, just as he had done with the optical effects and taking on an unknown actress in the lead role. But he received caution from Waldon

Watson, who said it could be disastrous to commit to a new and untested piece of technology in the middle of postproducing a film that was already behind schedule because of the numerous special effects. But Hitchcock, ever the technical innovator, ignored Watson's warnings and pressed on.

As filming progressed and was completed by July, Hitchcock turned his attentions to the postproduction. On 7 August, Peggy wrote to Paul Donnelly, the production manager at Revue Studios, with the following questions from Hitchcock:

1) Will this electronic system do traffic sounds, etc, or do we do our own?

2) Can we blend the electronic sounds with our ordinary sounds? We have natural bird sounds behind our dialogue in the bird shop and, in this particular scene, the question of using electronic sounds does not arise.

When he was nearing completion of a film, Hitchcock would dictate a new script to himself, which was a fairly intense sound script, and he kept running every reel and every sound in detail. 'In those particular cases I was asking for natural sound, don't forget a motor horn here. There should be a silence here, I'm not going to indicate the sound but the style and nature of the sound.'

ELECTRONIC SOUNDS & NATURAL SOUNDS

By 23 October, Hitchcock had written background sound notes for *The Birds* and flagged up that there would be two kinds of sounds. It was the intention to record the natural sounds in the studio and leave the electronic sounds to be done in Germany. After hearing the results, Hitchcock decided that the soundtrack should consist of both electronic and natural sound, and he proceeded to write a list that also dictated the style and nature of the sounds he wanted, reproduced below:

Electronic Sounds

Electronic – title backgrounds as will be seen behind the titles, we have silhouetted flying birds. These will vary in size, start in very close. In fact so close that they almost take on abstract forms. For the electronic sounds we could try just wing noises only with a variation of volume and a variation in the wing expression of it in terms of rhythm.

The birthday party – the electronic sounds should start with the attack by the gulls. It will be very necessary to watch that the screams of the children and the screams of the gulls do not sound the same.

The sparrow attack – the overall sounds in this sequence should have a quality of shrill anger as though the birds in their own particular way were invading the room and almost screaming at the occupants.

The crow attack – in the long shot we see the crows coming over the top of the school house and for the first time we hear the distant massing electronic sounds of growing anger as they descend upon the children.

The attack on the Tides – before the mass of gulls appear in this high shot we should begin to hear them out of shot, faint but the volume growing. It should start to mount as we see the gulls appear in the foreground of our high shot and then increase as their number increase.

The death of Annie – in this sequence we should have only the faintest brooding and natural sounds of the crows that have paused between their attacks. This sound should be quite subdued so that it does not detract from the silence of death, which should surround the cottage of Annie.

The attic sequence – it is very essential in this final attack by the birds in the attic that we give the sound a quality that gives this volume but is not of such a serious quality as to cause the people downstairs to be awakened by it.

Final sequence – if it is at all feasible, what we would like to have electronically is the equivalent of a brooding silence. Naturally, to achieve some effect like this will necessitate some experimentation.

Natural Sounds

Opening – this sequence calls for San Francisco street sounds including that of the cable car and general passerby sounds.

The bird shop – the existing background sounds of birds singing, twittering should remain.

Melanie's journey to Bodega Bay

The journey to and from the Brenner house

Fawcett's farm – After Mrs Brenner has entered the house, we should be in silence so that we can hear the choking sounds of Mrs Brenner when she dashes out and just the simple sounds of the roaring truck as she dashes back to her home.

The boarding-up sequence – we should have complete silence except for the radio announcement and even the birds that are moving to Santa Rosa should pass by in silence.

Six copies of Hitchcock's background sound notes were sent to Waldon Watson in the sound department, two copies to editor George Tomasini, and one to Bernard Herrmann. By 26 October, contracts had been sent to Oskar Sala in Germany and Remi Gassmann who was now back in New York. The agreement was to send a black-and-white print of the film so that the German composers could create a separate soundtrack made up of various sounds synchronised with the action. The soundtrack was to be delivered by the week of 3 December 1962 and Remi was to be paid $25,000, with a reimbursement of $3,000 for his trip to West Berlin.

With only six weeks to the delivery date, Remi set to work in Berlin on a rigid 9am to 10pm schedule, including Sundays, just to complete the soundtrack in time. However, Remi's progress was hampered by the delay in receiving the film reels from Hitchcock's office. On 14 November, he wrote to Hitchcock from the Berlin Hilton saying that he had received nine reels of *The Birds* but was missing reels 1, 4, 6, 7, 8 and 14. The general attack of the birds on the Brenner house, which was prepared the previous summer (reel 12), had now been completely re-worked, and he hoped he would find its effectiveness improved. Remi warned that, since they had not yet received the missing sequences, they couldn't guarantee to be prepared for Hitchcock's visit in December, and the projected delivery date.

He also wrote to Paul Donnelly, production manager at Revue Studios, saying that reels 1, 4, 6 and 7 were still missing, which contained the biggest and most time-consuming scenes for electronic sound, namely the opening titles, the children's party, the attack of the sparrows, the crow sequence and the final sequence.

On 16 November, Peggy wrote back to Remi in Germany saying that they were sending reels 4, 8 and 14, along with the main titles. Reel 10 – the attack on the Tides restaurant, which included the telephone booth – and reel 13 – the attack on Melanie in the attic – Remi should already have. Peggy also wrote that 'we were rather disappointed in your letter concerning the delay' and hoped that matters were progressing in accordance with the last two conversations Remi had had with Hitchcock and Tomasini. And 'please do not look for any further special-effects shots, but use your imagination in the sequence of the attacking birds as you discussed with Mr Hitchcock.'

In private, Remi was disappointed with Hitchcock's office who he thought were unfairly blaming him for the lack of progress. On 22 November, Remi wrote to George Shapitric, a counsellor at law in LA, confiding that he had finished everything that had been sent so far to Berlin, but was worried because the reels which had not yet arrived comprised about half of the work to be executed electronically. Among the scenes he had scored electronically was Annie's death, which had gained by 'a very economical use of crow mutterings before and after the actual death scene, which remains silent, except for a murderous crow cry from the roof to justify Mitch's wanting to throw a stone'.

Remi had also just received a cable from Peggy requesting that Hitchcock arrive on Saturday 15 December, with editor George Tomasini a week earlier. Remi confided in Shapitric that he would not answer until the remaining reels were in his hands 'since, so far, they have not shown themselves to be too reasonable about such matters'. But if the reels arrived before the weekend, he was certain he could finish in time for their arrival.

On 23 November, the missing shipment of reels finally arrived on Air France and were being processed through customs. Remi felt that he was now able to cable Peggy and say he would do everything possible to meet Hitchcock's proposed schedule, but that they would need every available moment between now and Hitchcock's arrival, including weekends. He also enquired whether a projection theatre and projectionist should be engaged the weekend Hitchcock was in Berlin.

Peggy wrote back to Remi on 28 November saying it had been decided that George Tomasini should arrive in Berlin as soon as possible, and would therefore depart LA on Monday 3 December, and that a projection theatre and projectionist would indeed be necessary for the weekend work when Hitchcock arrived. By 2 December, Remi had received the final shipment of *The Birds* and was now waiting for George Tomasini whose flight was delayed by fog.

HITCHCOCK'S TRIP TO BERLIN

Bernard Herrmann, who had scored many memorable films for Hitchcock, including *The Man Who Knew Too Much*, *Vertigo*, *North by Northwest* and *Psycho*, was hired as a sound consultant on *The Birds* with a contract starting on 9 October 1962 (Figure 29). One might think that Bernard Herrmann would be angry that he wasn't writing the music for the film himself, but Herrmann, always an innovator, was intrigued by electronic sound and its application on *The Birds*.

As Hitchcock said to Truffaut, 'I hope to make a deal with Bernard Herrmann, who has done music before – of course he's a very temperamental fellow, you know, very temperamental – to supervise the sound of the whole picture, because you often hear musicians when they compose and orchestrate. They talk of making sounds which is what they do.'[3]

By 12 December, Hitchcock's itinerary was in place. That Friday, 14 December, he and Herrmann were to fly from LA to Copenhagen and then transfer to Hamburg. On arrival in Hamburg the next day, Hitchcock had lunch with Mr and Mrs Max Schmeling, the latter aka Anny Ondra, star of Hitchcock's first talking picture *Blackmail* (1929). Ondra had been living in Germany for many years having married the boxer Schmeling, with whom she had appeared in the film *Knockout* (1935).

That same afternoon, Hitchcock and Herrmann took a flight to Berlin and stayed at the Hilton hotel until Thursday 20 December. It was a very happy trip, and later Herrmann regarded it as one of the most pleasant times he ever spent with Hitchcock.[4]

THE ATTIC ATTACK

Hitchcock was also experimenting with silence, particularly in the attic attack, where he said that he wanted to create 'a silent murder'. In the shower sequence in *Psycho*, he originally wanted to have just the sound of the water running, Janet Leigh's screams and the sounds of the knife. Hitchcock and Herrmann ultimately decided music would be more effective. But in *The Birds* Hitchcock creates a very sinister sound of flapping bird wings and creates one of the most intense sequences of violence, but without any music.

'When the girl is locked in the attic, there are a lot of natural wing sounds – but when we stylise there should be waves of menace rather than one level, an assimilation of wing sound,' said Hitchcock. 'I'm going to take the dramatic licence of not having the birds scream. I'm going to say to this person, now we've got you where we want you, and here we come, we don't have to scream with triumph or anger, this is going to be a silent murder, this is what the birds are saying.'[5]

For the final sequence in the film, when Mitch opens the door of the house and sees the vast amount of birds covering the area, Hitchcock asked for an electronic silence, a sound that might suggest the birds' thoughts as they rest before preparing to attack again. 'There should be a monotony "like the distant roar of the sea". But it should be strange, it should say "we're not ready to start yet, we're getting ready, we're like an engine that is purring, but we haven't started off yet". Not the cooing of birds, it should be so low that you don't know whether you can hear anything or not.'[6]

Hitchcock wanted to communicate a sense of what the birds were thinking at the end of the movie when everybody is leaving the Brenner house. They created this tremendously unsettling effect that is very quiet but does give the birds much more of a personality, a far more sinister quality. Secondly, he creates a final note by increasing the sound of those birds under the final shot, and it's very ambiguous as to whether they're on the verge of another major attack.

The trautonium and the experimental sound it produced turned out to be very successful, and Herrmann and Hitchcock were both very pleased with the results. Hitchcock knew the importance of music in cinema and, in particular, the importance of music in his own films, but for him a film score wasn't music per se but another element of the overall sound design.

Herrmann was very happy about the score for *The Birds*, but he never spoke of it as his own music. He later said to his third wife, Norma Shepherd, 'Do you know that anything I can do with a synthesiser, I can do with an orchestra, if I have the right talent and the right instruments.'[7] And, over the years, there has been more and more electronic music. In the year that *The Birds* was released, Herrmann started work on another Hitchcock project, but this time for the small screen. From 1963 to 1965 he scored 17 episodes of *The Alfred Hitchcock Hour*, a total of about five hours of music.

Hitchcock would later say about his trip to Berlin, 'All I did then is to listen and to offer a few changes. It took me all of four days... upon which I retired to St Moritz to contemplate.'[8] On 20 December 1962, Hitchcock sent a cable to Peggy: 'Work in Berlin completed to my satisfaction, Hitch.'

Hitchcock was instrumental in not only a visual-effects revolution for the next couple of decades, but a sound revolution too. He then went to Paris and St Moritz for a Christmas holiday with his family, staying at the Palace Hotel. On 6 January 1963, he arrived back in New York and then returned to LA on 8 January to continue with the film's complicated postproduction.

After *The Birds* was released, many efforts were expended by Remi Gassmann to launch Oskar Sala's work in the US, and it was certainly not to be anticipated that a contract with a major studio and a major producer such as Hitchcock would be achieved so quickly. In March 1963, Remi held two very important demonstrations for the heads of two of the major Hollywood studios, MGM and Warner Brothers. One notable rejection letter, dated 2 January 1964, involves the audition of electronic sound compositions for Walt Disney and exhibitions for the World's Fair. But the success of the trautonium lived on in *The Birds*.

NOTES

1 Letter from Remi Gassmann to Hitchcock, 18 June 1962, Alfred Hitchcock Collection, Margaret Herrick Library
2 Hitchcock interview, BFI, *Screen*, 15 February 1963
3 Hitchcock to Truffaut, 1962 interview
4 Interview with Norma Shepherd, 27 June 2012, Brighton
5 Hitchcock to Bogdanovich, 13 February 1963
6 Hitchcock to Truffaut, August 1962
7 Interview with Norma Shepherd, 27 June 2012, Brighton
8 Hitchcock to *Screen* magazine, 15 February 1963

POSTPRODUCTION AND EDITING

'I've always regarded the long or short of a scene by the preoccupation of the audience' – Alfred Hitchcock

The complicated process of editing *The Birds* began on Tuesday 11 July, the very day after principal photography had ended, and continued until early 1963. As Albert Whitlock remembered, 'The postproduction period was quite extended. I was on it for 13 months. There were a lot of matte shots. And Hitchcock used to say, "I don't know if we're ever going to get this thing finished."'

In the early spring of 1962, Hitchcock had moved his offices from Paramount to Universal. The biggest and best bungalow was set aside for him on the Universal lot, and there were also separate offices for Peggy Robertson and Suzanne Gauthier, as well as his design staff. The bungalow had two levels and there was a screening room, a dining room, adjoining rooms with editing equipment, a kitchen, cocktail lounge and a bathroom attached to Hitchcock's spacious private office.[1] In Evan Hunter's words, 'The office was standard Universal issue. Sort of pseudo English manor house. To call it a bungalow is to understate the case a bit.'

It was intended that *The Birds* should have a release date of Thanksgiving 1962, but this was pushed back to the spring of 1963. Universal executives then moved the date forward to 28 March 1963, as they were keen to get the film finished by 3 March, the property tax date in California, which meant that Technicolor had to make all the prints and get them out of the state by that date.

Universal was also hoping that a lucrative Easter box office would offset the expense of the film, which by now had escalated to $3.2 million. In addition, the 412 planned optical-effects shots would take more time than originally anticipated.

George Tomasini was Hitchcock's editor on a number of films beginning with *Rear Window* (1954). A large jovial man, he was immensely liked by everyone. As Harold Michelson remembered, 'Just prior to *Psycho*, Paramount was going out of business, ran out of money and was starting to disintegrate. Hitchcock brought Tomasini over to where he was making *Psycho* so George got in at just the right time. He was a lovely man who came to work in a suit and tie every day. There was a dress code we followed and there was this aura of class.'[2] 'George fit in personality wise with Hitchcock,' agrees Marshall Schlom, the script supervisor on *Psycho*. 'Maybe it was something as simple as he wore a suit every day. He was low key, he and Hitchcock were on the same wavelength and he understood Hitchcock and how his films went together.'

Hitchcock would come in to the edit suite every day at 11 o'clock and work with Tomasini editing sequences together, and he would put together things that he wanted to do first. The film was edited in the stop and go rooms, which was like a projection room, with a projection booth so the film could be wound backwards and forwards. George assembled a sequence to what he thought it should be and then Hitchcock would come in and supervise the final editing.

By 6 June 1962, George had cut 16 sequences, including Melanie at the Post Office, Melanie meets Annie, Lydia in Tides, Annie's House - Melanie Rents Room, Melanie to Brenner House for Dinner, Annie and Melanie Drink Brandy, Kids Party, Birds Down fireplace, Al Malone, Fawcett Farm, Melanie's Bedroom, School Crows, Mrs Bundy in Tides, Dead Annie, Mitch Boards Windows, and the 'Drum Roll' sequence, all of which amounted to 97 ½ pages, 6,812 feet, or 1 hour 14 minutes of film.

George was making good progress and a week later, on 15 June, he had cut four more sequences: Melanie Rents a Boat, Melanie and Mitch Argue at the Car, Annie, Dune and Kids Party, and Mitch and Melanie into the Tides, which took the total running time to 1 hour 35 minutes. On 9 August, a rough cut of *The Birds* was screened with Alma Hitchcock, Pat

Hitchcock, Taft Schreiber, Herman Citron, Arthur Park, Jerry Adler, Vince Dee, Bernard Herrmann, Bill Blowitz, George Thomas, Joan Harrison and Norman Lloyd all present.

As Alma was an editor, her experience dictated the shape of some of the key scenes in the film. She was more involved with looking at a scene if it had been edited. But if someone had given a good performance that day, she would go in the next day and look at the dailies. Hitchcock listened very closely to what she said and Alma suggested the following:

1. Sharpen Mrs MacGruder at the opening of the pet shop.
2. Trim the beginning of the Russian River shot where Melanie's car comes downhill.
3. Can the approach to the Tides' parking lot be shortened? (Discussed this with Mr Hitchcock. He has requested George Tomasini to eliminate the writing on the card 'To Cathy' and Melanie's walk around the car and approach down the street at the stop sign to the Tide's parking lot. We now pick Melanie's car up pulling into the parking space.)
4. Interior Tides – too many close-ups of Lydia. We remain in the two shot until the end of the scene.
5. Clarify Mitch's line: 'The chickens won't eat.'
6. Interior Tides: Take out Sam the chef's short line: 'What?'
7. Examine the first close-up of Melanie struggling on the couch.

THE CROW ATTACK

The Birds has some of the finest examples of Hitchcock's use of suspense, montage and counterpoint, with outstanding set pieces including the crows gathering on the jungle gym behind Melanie. Hitchcock wrote eight pages of handwritten notes about how the crow sequence should be assembled in the editing room.[3] They clearly indicate the closer shots of Melanie outlined to Bob Boyle during pre-production and illustrated by Harold Michelson in his storyboards. Shot 11 of the notes suggests, 'Head and shoulders of Melanie. Hold for 20 or 30 feet. She looks up,' and sees the crow. This is followed by a 'big head' of a horrified Melanie.

Hitchcock explained in a later interview how the footage of the crow attack filmed against the sodium screen was assembled in the editing:

'We photographed in colour against a yellow background. This sodium light, as it is called, is a colour that is the narrowest band on the spectrum of light and comes out black. It's the only colour that doesn't photograph. So now you have your coloured image and black background. At the same time there is a prism – a lens which makes two images. One goes through in colour and the other is reflected through a red filter on to an ordinary black-and-white film, so that you make your silhouette at the same time as you're making your scene.'

The two images photographed were put together, so there is a negative of the children running down the street and the silhouette of the birds printed first and then the real birds afterwards, and these are overlayed. Hitchcock used quick intercutting to ensure that the scene wasn't held for very long, just for a flash. 'Then you got a close-up of one of the children and you throw a live trained bird onto the shoulder of the child,' said Hitchcock. 'It's the intercutting, the quick intercutting that gives you the illusion of the scene in close-up and in distance and so forth.'[4]

THE ATTIC ATTACK

The quick cutting of the crow attack would be replicated in many of the other bird attacks, most notably in the attic attack. An 8 November memo from Bob Burks to Bud Hoffman, the assistant editor, outlined the number of shots in the different bird sequences: crow attack 67, attic attack 77, phone booth 50, kids party 43, fireplace 20, miscellaneous 65. The attic attack, with 77 cuts, rivalled the shower sequence in *Psycho*. As Bob Boyle said, 'This was a system of fast editing that Hitchcock had been involved with for a long time in many other films, but that type of editing was at its height in *Psycho* in the shower scene. He did the same thing in *The Birds* with fast cuts, so that you had an impression of more – almost more than was really happening.'

As Harold Michelson remembered, 'We sat in the screening room, [Hitchcock] would say, "Two feet, twenty-eight frames. Three frames." He would just knock them off like he was timing it in his head. And this was amazing to me, because I'd never been involved with that kind of, uh, knowledge before, or sense of film. So he really pre-edited, he knew the craft, the timings.'[5]

On 14 December, when George Tomasini was with Hitchcock in Berlin supervising the sound, Bud Hoffman wrote to him to say that the attack sequence had been changed in the following manner: it had been decided to drop frame the four mechanical bird cuts. In order to do this, it was necessary to shorten the four cuts by a total of ten frames. Probably one of the scenes most indicative of George Tomasini and Hitch's editing was when the man throws the match down after the attack on the gas attendant, and everybody screams at him. Hitchcock and Tomasini showed Melanie watching, almost like still photographs, which was incredibly effective.

For the gull attacks, Bud Hoffman and Albert Whitlock spent many hours searching through the bird footage filmed at the San Francisco dump to find the exact action that the sequence required. 'I went through this film a foot at a time and categorised it according to the action it contained,' remembers Bud. 'Single bird flying in from left to right and right to left, birds milling about, two birds flying off, that kind of thing. It took a long time to run through it all, but it was rewarding in the long run because we were able to find a lot of good footage without any land in it, and some with birds looking as if they might be ferocious.'[6]

One of Albert's crucial matte paintings required gulls to drop into the frame. 'I recall that we sat through what seemed to be miles and miles of bird footage to get something we could use,' Albert said. 'Trying to keep awake watching all the footage. Millions of miles of film. It's a very hypnotic image, a lot of birds flying in the air. You'd sit in the theatre and suddenly you'd wake up and you'd find that half an hour was gone. We'd try to find something from the footage that we were going to be superimposing.' Albert also joked that, forever after, when Bud saw him on the Universal lot, he thought, 'Oh, birds,' because the two had had to sit through, literally, miles of film, trying to keep awake to see if they could find that one little vital bit of footage.

THE SPECIAL EFFECTS

An incredible amount of special effects were needed to make the bird attacks chilling and convincing and, because of the looming deadline, some of the work had to be farmed out, with at least five different studio departments working together. After the crow and attic attacks had been assembled by George Tomasini, they were sent to the special-effects department for enhancement. Ub Iwerks at Disney, who was in charge of the sodium vapour process, turned to some of Hollywood's optical experts for assistance: Bob Hoag at MGM, who was in charge of photo effects; Linwood Dunn, founder of Film Effects of Hollywood, was recruited to work on the attic attack; and the head of special effects at 20th Century Fox, L B Abbott, was to work on the opticals for the crow attack on the school.

On 11 December 1962, Bob Burks sent a memo to Edd Henry with an updated list of all the companies doing optical work on *The Birds*. Over at Disney Studio, Ub Iwerks and his team were working on the children's party, Melanie driving to Bodega Bay, Melanie in the car at Annie's house, the boat crossing, the first two cuts of the crow attack and Melanie jumping up in front of the jungle gym. 'We received half of the boat crossing. It was okayed by Mr Hitchcock. We received Melanie in the car at Annie's and Mr Hitchcock asked that it be retaken and diffusion added. The kids' party is about half completed and Disney feel that they will be in good shape on all our work by 7 January 1963.'

At their first meeting, Hitchcock emphasised to Ub Iwerks that he did not want the composite scenes to be obvious as a special effect that would detract the audience from the story. That was the very reason that Ub had perfected the process for the Disney Studio, to produce believable composite scenes in which the audience would not see them as special effects. One of the first major challenges was the sparrow attack down the Brenner Chimney. Using the optical printer, quadruple superimposition of the birds was made of a large group of the tiny birds flying about a glass-enclosed booth, making it possible for him to optically multiply the number of birds in the living room. The majority of the postproduction optical compositing work was done in the Disney Studio's Process Lab on Printer 10, a triple head printer of Iwerks' design and built by the Studio Machine Shop. Some of the work was also accomplished on Iwerks' R&D printer.[7]

Over at MGM Studios, Bob Hoag was orchestrating the photographic effects for the scene where Melanie is trapped in the telephone booth that comes under attack from seagulls. In Hitchcock's cutting notes of 24 September he had instructed, 'Trim all the shots where Melanie is placid. She must always be in movement.' Hoag said that they were 'in the process of manufacturing mattes and perfecting systems that will handle the work required in this sequence. They will be in a better position to estimate a completion date after their systems are perfected, which should be around 17 December.' Hoag and his crew of 30 worked on many of the dissolves, blue backing and sodium matte shots, and assistant editor Bud Hoffman felt this was the best special-effects work done in the film.

At Film Effects of Hollywood, Linwood Dunn was working on the attic attack and seven miscellaneous shots. He was to deliver a rough cut of the entire sequence for Hitchcock to view before he left for Berlin in December. At Fox Studios, Bill Abbott and his team were working on the crow attack, which would take six weeks to assemble. Bill had two crews working 11-hour days as their task was to combine the footage of crows shot in the wind tunnel and optically add them to the footage of the children on the treadmill. The two biggest challenges were perspective and size ratio. They had to optically make the birds appear to be swooping down at the kids by moving them into the frame, while at the same time adding a slight zoom to bring them in closer. This involved experimenting with the size of the birds to make them look in proportion to the children. Then the crows had to be optically multiplied to make the mass appear larger than it was. It was a very time-consuming process, but Abbott was optimistic about completing the sequence by 14 January 1963.

At Universal, Ross Hoffman was working on the Russian River shot of Melanie's car arriving in Bodega, the birds migrating, the POV of the birds in the trees and the overhead shot. Meanwhile, Al Whitlock at Universal was also working on the POV of the town. This was a very complicated matte shot involving animation and many other manipulations. Unfortunately, Disney couldn't complete their end of the town matte shot until Albert had finished his work. This was the most severe problem on the whole picture. Technicolor was contacted and asked to exert every effort to complete tests for Albert faster than they had been doing up to this point.

On 21 December, Bob Burks wrote to Eustace Lycett at the Disney Studios optical labs. Lycett, as head of the optical department, supervised the day-to-day process. He was a protégé of Ub Iwerks, a pioneer of animation and special effects, and himself would go on to win an Oscar for *Mary Poppins* (1964). 'The shot of the girl jumping up came through *sans* diffusion. I would like to remind you that this shot and all of the shots of Melanie in the car are to be shot with diffusion,' said Bob. Those shots were supposed to be day exteriors, shot with natural light. Hitchcock wanted his leading lady to look good and asked for diffusion through the lens.

ROTOSCOPING TECHNIQUES

One of the most famous shots in *The Birds* is when the seagulls descend on the gas station. Hitchcock called it the 'God shot'. 'What we need,' he said, 'is a shot which shows everything all in one [...], so that we reorient the audience.' As Bob Boyle later remembered, 'He was always thinking of the audience. So what we had to do now was to get a high shot. Some people call it the birds' point of view, but I think Hitchcock was right. He called it God's point of view. Because it was an objective shot – so objective that it wouldn't have been anybody's point of view.'[8]

Harold Michelson drew the perspective shot from above the gas station fire (Figure 28). He was a master of architectural and geometric camera perspective, so the whole shot was laid out very carefully for the camera position that was available, which was on the top of a mountain overlooking the Universal parking lot. As Harold recalled, 'We were up there, and we had set up a big glass plate. Albert Whitlock was the matte artist who was in charge of this. And we shot from the top of this mountain down towards the parking lot, and we marked off with white paint areas where people could run, where firemen could run. And he proceeded to paint on the glass the black areas, so all the stuff that went on with the fire and everything we had to keep in certain areas. And he painted in the whole town.'[9]

The live portion and Albert's matte painting were then printed together. The perspective film was taken out, and then put back into the camera with Albert's painting. The birds had to be put in afterwards. The next task was to make it look as if birds were flying down to the gas station and that the camera was looking down on them. First of all, the camera crew needed footage of gulls flying from above. It was Albert who had heard that there were seagulls nesting in high cliffs in the Channel Islands, including Anacapa Island. Every summer, thousands of Western gulls descend upon Anacapa to mate and lay their eggs. 'It occurred to me that if a cameraman were to get above this cliff and throw fish – charm them out of the cliffs – the birds would dive for the fish, which is exactly what happened,' said Albert.[10]

So a camera crew was dispatched to Anacapa Island, and a camera with a wide-angle lens was set up on the cliff looking down at the water. The crew would throw food out for the seagulls, which would dive towards the food, and that's how they got the movement of the birds seemingly flying down to the gas station.

Back at the studio, the film of the flying seagulls had to be rotoscoped – a method of tracing the outline of an object that you want to isolate from its background. An artist named Millie Weinbrenner painstakingly rotoscoped each of the birds frame by frame, allowing them to be lifted off the film, whilst extraneous background, such as sea and cliffs, was eliminated. The birds were then placed on another matte, which was blacked-out film with clear areas representing the gulls. Eventually, the matte of the birds was placed over Albert's matte painting of the gas station. Millie and another woman took the film frame by frame, only 15 feet in all, but it took them three months to complete the transfer by painting each individual bird on to a plain background. 'We get a down shot on the birds, and then rotoscope – that is, make a hand-painted matte – for all these birds for each frame that they're in. And then the birds were printed in,' said Bob Boyle.

Ross Hoffman was confident Millie would finish rotoscoping the shot by 21 December and that the entire shot should be completed by 7 January 1963. For all the time invested in it, it only lasts ten seconds onscreen.

THE ENDING:
'THE MOST DIFFICULT SHOT I'VE EVER DONE'

If the birds' point of view of the gas station on fire was complicated to assemble, the final image of the film would prove to be even more so, as it would require hundreds of birds to give the impression that they had taken over. Hitchcock said he used 371 trick shots in the film, with the last as 'the most difficult shot I've ever done'. The final shot of the car driving away through a landscape dominated by birds again took three months to complete, and was composed of 32 separate images. It was George Tomasini's task to seamlessly assemble the parts of the film that made up the composite ending.

The shot was initially broken into three panels, using several pieces of film and matte paintings. 'That's 32 pieces of film. First of all, we had a limited number of gulls allowed. Therefore, the foreground was shot in three-panel sections left to right, up to the birds on the rail,' explained Hitchcock. 'The few gulls we had were in the first third, and we reshot it for the middle third, same gulls, and the right-hand third, gulls again. Then, just above the heads of the crows, was a long, slender middle section where the gulls were spread again. Then the car going down the driveway, the car only, with the birds each side of it was another piece of film. Then there was the sky, and that was another piece of film. There was the barn on the left.'[11]

As only 30 gulls were allowed for the film's quota, they were used in the foreground and replicated as Hitchcock explained. Birds, however, were still needed for the far distance, so it was Harold Michelson's idea to use ducks to substitute for the gulls. 'I said to Bob, what we'd better do is get ducks. We'll never see what birds they are,' remembered Harold. 'They'll obviously look like birds, but we don't want them to take off. So we got ducks, and we penned them in, you see, with chicken wire, and made a zigzag from the car going down, the birds, of course, parting as the car went down, and there's one touch in there that I'm kind of pleased with.' The ducks had been purchased from a local slaughterhouse, and were dyed to mask their natural colour. Approximately one third of the birds in the shot were dummies, mostly used in the background and on the barn roof for atmosphere.

Albert Whitlock then painted a matte of the sky, which served as a background and, in contrast to most of the film's dark skies, the blue skies and rays of dawn light here offer a sign of hope. Here Albert may have derived inspiration from another Constable painting 'Hampstead Heath', where morning rays of light emerge from dark clouds to illuminate the land below. The matte painting was then combined with optically composite birds and live-action shots of the car and front of the Brenner porch. Over at Disney, Ub Iwerks had made a trip to London to supervise the sodium travelling matte shooting on the Disney film *The Three Lives of Thomasina* (1963). He came back to LA to work on the final sequence, putting the birds on the porch and on the rail in front of the matte shot.

DELETED SCENES

While Hitchcock was editing the picture, both he and his editor were aware of a dichotomy between the interpersonal story of the characters and the bird attacks. As Albert acknowledged, 'I always thought that the very involved relationships in the picture were a sort of backup so that he could cut back on the birds if it didn't come up. But then you felt that, as he was cutting the picture, he was adding more of the birds because he could get more in the bolder idea. That happened, I know, because George Tomasini used to talk about it all the time, putting more of the bird stuff in, and not taking the people out but playing it down some.'[12]

Some scenes in the interpersonal story were not only downplayed during the editing, they were eliminated altogether, including one love scene between Mitch and Melanie. For Evan Hunter, this missing scene was crucial in explaining possible motivations for the bird attacks: 'In the screenplay, on the morning after the finch attack, Mrs Brenner yells to Mitch that she's going over to Dan Fawcett's farm, and Melanie, in her nightgown, looks through the window and sees Mitch burning the finches in the backyard,' Evan explained. 'She throws on a mink over the nightgown, a humorous poor-little-rich-girl touch, and goes down to talk to him. They begin speculating on the cause of the attacks, making jokes about a bird leader egging the other birds to rebel, and then suddenly they realise that the finches came down that chimney in fury. There is nothing funny about this; the birds are attacking in hatred. Like frightened children, they cling to each other – and they kiss.'

Hitchcock, however, despite having filmed this scene, decided to drop it in postproduction. His reasoning was that, 'I felt that a prolonged love scene at this point might have irritated the public.'[13] Again he was thinking about the audience, which he assumed would be anxious to get on with the horror story of the birds. But Evan felt that the absence of this scene was sorely felt, and that what followed didn't make sense. Without this scene, no one in the film ever really questions why the birds are attacking, and Evan thought that, if the leading characters weren't even looking for answers, then the audience would demand them. The scene also added some substance to the love story between Mitch and Melanie. When Mitch goes off to check things out at the Fawcett farm, he and Melanie are exchanging 'darlings' to each other and embracing. Without the previous scene, however, it doesn't make sense that they should be behaving this way towards each other.

The scene as Evan wrote it is light-hearted at first, echoing the screwball comedy that had opened the story. Melanie comically proposes that the bird attacks must have started with a malcontent sparrow in the hills preaching revolution, attracting other sparrows to his cause, inciting them to unite, his followers growing larger in number until, now, they are a force to contend with. They both laugh at this absurd notion, and then fall silent. What's interesting about their description of the bearded malcontent sparrow is that he bears many similarities to Fidel Castro proclaiming revolution in Cuba, like a bearded Marxist. This was written against the backdrop of the Cuban Missile Crisis and it's no coincidence that, on Sunday 10 June 1962, the tension was at its height, as Soviet nuclear missiles in Cuba were approved by the Soviet Union. Under the plan, 24 medium-range nuclear missiles and 16 intermediate-range missiles would be placed in Cuba.

Mitch goes on to offer some serious reasons why the birds might be attacking. Perhaps the birds are hungry, as it's been a fruitless summer. Everything is deathly still. They realise it is the same lull that occurred the previous day, before the finches attacked. They try to joke about the attacks again, but now the humour falls flat and there is the chill of horror behind Melanie's words when she says that the finches came down the chimney in fury – as if they wanted everyone in the house dead.

RETAKES

The process for retakes had already begun by 24 March 1962, towards the end of the location filming. Scenes 51 through 56–16 were retaken with loops and wildtracks for Melanie. A memo on 26 September requested that Tippi, Veronica, Suzanne and Rod Taylor all be looped for various scenes, with Hitchcock present at all these sessions to give the line readings during the first week of October. On Tuesday 30 October it was requested that the close-ups of Tippi sitting at the piano in the Brenner living room be retaken to cover script scenes 180 through 188. This would be a head close-up using a 75mm lens; and, on Wednesday 15 November, an additional shot of a little boy being hit by a gull was filmed to cut into the children's party against grass matting.

Even after all the independent special effects work had been submitted, the work was far from over. In December 1962, Bob Burks and Budd Hoffman submitted the footage for printing to a variety of optical houses but, as Burks was a perfectionist who had started in the special effects lab at Warner Brothers, he rejected much of the work for not looking real enough. This demanding perfectionism prompted Bud to remark, 'In my opinion, this picture could never have been made without Bob. It was his persistence in doing these shots over and over that made *The Birds* the classic it is today.' Bob Burks finally finished his work on *The Birds* on Friday 1 February 1963, having spent over a year working on the film.

TITLES & CREDITS

For the opening titles of *The Birds* Hitchcock originally wanted to use 'very light, simple Chinese paintings of birds – delicate little drawings'. Instead, he said, he compromised by making the opening titles more ominous. 'I felt people might get impatient, having seen the advertising campaign, and ask, "When are the birds coming on?" That's why I give them a sock now and again. I felt that they might get impatient, not that they would be displeased with the personal story, women I think would feel reasonably interested. When are the birds coming, we've seen all the ads, we've seen the posters, so that's why I give them the sock now and again.'[14]

This 'sock' would be established from the very beginning of the film in the portentous opening titles of shadowy crows flying against a stark white background, all to the eerie cries of the electronic score getting louder and louder, finally reaching a cacophony at the end of the sequence. Hitchcock then cuts to complacent, everyday San Francisco life.

On 14 September, Peggy Robertson sent a memo to Paul Donnelly at Revue Studios saying that, 'Mr Hitchcock wishes to use the services of National Screen Service Corporation for the main titles of *The Birds*. Mr Hitchcock has already had discussions with James Pollak of NSS who has submitted tests.' The main title billing order for *The Birds* was partly based on contractual obligations and on the form of the credits for *Psycho*. Rod Taylor's billing, as per his contract, was to be no less than first co-star billing, at least in the size and density of type of all the other performers. Suzanne Pleshette's co-star billing was to be no less than fourth position of the entire cast, and in type not less than 75 per cent of the type used to display the name of the first star.

Hitchcock approved the second revisions of credits on 17 September, with the following amendments: Jessica Tandy's name should come above Suzanne Pleshette's; Doreen Lang's should be slightly larger than the other names on the card and preceded with the word 'and';

Edith Head was telephoned on 9 August and told by Peggy Robertson that Hitchcock was giving her a screen credit on a separate card, which would read 'Miss Hedren's costumes designed by Edith Head'. Edith was absolutely delighted saying, 'That's just perfect.' On 17 December it was requested that David Lipton in Universal's publicity department use single quotes around 'Tippi' whenever her name was used. This was all part of Hitchcock's plan to build up Tippi as a lady of distinction and aura.

Because the screenplay of *The Birds* was so different to Daphne du Maurier's source story, the Writers Guild of America believed that Evan Hunter should receive sole credit on a separate title card. Writing credits were submitted on 8 August 1962 by James Weinberg to Robert Winokur, highlighting some of the problems:

1. We propose a single writing credit, 'Screenplay by Evan Hunter', to appear on a separate card, immediately preceding Hitchcock's 'Directed by' credit. This position is required by the WGA Agreement.

2. In addition, Hitchcock proposes a source material credit for Daphne Du Maurier on the same card with the title of the photoplay in the form '*The Birds* by Daphne du Maurier'.

3. The problem which most concerns me is the credit by Daphne du Maurier and whether it is in accordance with the facts or the agreements... the picture contains an entirely different storyline from the du Maurier story, played against the same background of birds attacking humans.

4. The proposed credit for Evan Hunter is 'Screenplay by'. He may claim that he is entitled to additional credit for his contribution to the screen story. This problem can be faced if and when he protests, in which event we would be obliged to follow whatever WGA decides.

In the end, Evan received sole credit for the screenplay, but Daphne du Maurier received her own credit at the beginning of the film. James Weinberg wrote on 27 August, 'We now intend that the form of the du Maurier credit will be "From the story by Daphne du Maurier".' But, after an early screening of the film with Hitchcock, Evan recalls an offer to increase his credit from 50 per cent of the title size to 75 per cent. A memo on 27 November from Peggy to James Pollak affirms this: 'Would you please remake Card 15 which reads "Screenplay by Evan Hunter". "Screenplay by" is to remain at 50% but "Evan Hunter" is to be increased to 75%.'

Not only would Evan's credit increase in size, Daphne's would too. Some time later, after the film was released in the US, on 30 April 1963, Peggy wrote yet another memo to James Pollak saying, 'Would you please re-make a new card which reads as follows: "From the Story by Daphne du Maurier". This card should be re-made increasing the words Daphne du Maurier to 60 per cent.' Hitchcock's request may have been for the UK prints as the film was to be released there later in the year.

Aside from the writing credits, the biggest changes were to be made to the end title card. The gloom, the tentativeness, the lack of a resolution all indicates that Hitchcock wanted *The Birds* to appeal to a cultural elite. Instead of ending the picture with the words 'The End', Hitchcock requested to dissolve to 'A Universal Release', imitating the style of European art-house films. A memo on 28 November 1962 from Peggy to James Pollak confirms this: 'At the end of the picture, as you know, we are not having the words, "The End". Instead we dissolve to a card with the words "A Universal Release".'

'I changed that title card three times,' Hitchcock said to Peter Bogdanovich. 'I kept the words "A Universal Release" to as small as I possibly could. I kept it as small and quiet as possible. I would have preferred a medallion, a whirl or something just to show that it was a seal at the end.'[15]

On 11 January 1963, Peggy wrote to James Pollak: 'This is to confirm our telephone conversation of yesterday when I informed you that Mr Hitchcock wished you to remake the End Title Card. The globe, which should be the same as the one behind the Universal Card in the Main Titles, is to be put in behind the wording on the End title. The correct name and punctuation of our company is: Alfred J Hitchcock Productions, Inc.'

Hitchcock favoured a low-key, unresolved ending, just as in European art films. But when the film was previewed to test audiences in the US, they were puzzled and reacted negatively to the open ending, which shows the car driving away through the bird-dominated landscape. In fact, some of the audience misinterpreted the fade to black ending as a break in the reel, thinking that a technical mishap had occurred. So, to avoid any confusion, the 'Universal Release' title card with the globe was added to the end.[16]

Universal Pictures, at one time seen onscreen as 'A Universal Picture', eventually gave way to a name change as 'Universal-International'. Then, in 1962, the studio reverted back to their original name of Universal Pictures, so *The Birds* was the first film to display the new logo onscreen.

CENSORS

Hitchcock had long battled with the censors and his nemesis was Geoffrey Shurlock of the Hays Production Code, which regulated the movie industry. The bird attacks and depictions of animal cruelty during filming were the main points of concern. On 21 November 1961, Shurlock wrote to Peggy Robertson: 'We are seriously concerned, however, with one aspect of this unusual story – the gruesome details of the several attacks by the birds on the human beings. Page 65: It is unacceptable to show Melanie only in a bra and a skirt. She should be wearing a slip.'

After amendments to the script had been made, Shurlock wrote again on 8 February 1962: 'We have read the final script dated 26 January for your proposed production *The Birds* and are pleased to tell you that the basic story seems acceptable under the provisions of the Production Code. In accordance with the code requirements, please consult with Mr James Jack of the American Humane Association as to all scenes in which animals are used.'

The American Humane Association wrote a letter on 2 May 1962: 'Page 172, scene 641, showing Mitch stepping between the dead birds, should be supervised and dummy birds utilised. As you realise, our representative has been present during the complete filming to date and finds that handling, feeding and care of the birds has been very good.' Harold Melniker of the Humane Association also approved a screening on 28 January 1963, as did Rutherford Phillips, the executive director: 'There have been a few people who complained about the use of birds in this picture in its various locations. Such reports were based on rumour or misinformation; it is certainly an unusual picture but there was no harm or mistreatment of the birds used in this film.'

The complicated and lengthy postproduction was finally finished. For some, like Albert Whitlock, it had lasted over a year. All their hard work now depended upon how the film was marketed and accepted by the public.

NOTES

1 Interview with Norman Lloyd, 30 November 2012, Los Angeles

2 Harold Michelson, 'Roundtable on *The Birds*', *Cahiers du Cinema*, 1982

3 Alfred Hitchcock's handwritten notes for the crow sequence: order of shots for the final sequence, 1 March1962, Margaret Herrick Library

4 Alfred Hitchcock, 'It's a bird, it's a plane, it's *The Birds*', *Hitchcock on Hitchcock*, Faber and Faber, 1995, p. 317

5 Interview with Harold Michelson, 5 October 2000, Los Angeles

6 Kyle Counts, 'The Making of Alfred Hitchcock's *The Birds*', *Cinefantastique*, Vol 10, p. 24

7 Disney Archives memo from 7 November 1962 from Dick Pfhaler, the Studio Manager to Bill Anderson, Studio VP in charge of production

8 Bob Boyle, 'Roundtable on *The Birds*', *Cahiers du Cinema*, 1982

9 Harold Michelson, 'Roundtable on *The Birds*', *Cahiers du Cinema*, 1982

10 Albert Whitlock, 'Roundtable on *The Birds*', *Cahiers du Cinema*, 1982

11 Hitchcock to Bogdanovich, 14 February 1963

12 Albert Whitlock, 'Roundtable on *The Birds*', *Cahiers du Cinema*, 1982

13 Hitchcock to Truffaut, *Hitchcock*, 1985, p. 292

14 Hitchcock to Bogdanovich, 14 February 1963

15 Hitchcock to Bogdanovich, 14 February 1963

16 Kyle Counts, 'The Making of Alfred Hitchcock's *The Birds*', *Cinefantastique*, p. 33

THE *BIRDS* IS COMING!

'*Don't you mean the birds are coming, sir?*'
– Universal Executive to Hitchcock

Hitchcock was the maestro of marketing – not just in his films, but in his persona and image as well, as he insisted on his name above the titles, as well as a cameo in each of his movies. With *The Birds*, he embarked upon his most expensive, ambitious and prestigious publicity campaign, with plans to premiere the film at the Museum of Modern Art (MOMA) in New York and at the 1963 Cannes Film Festival.[1] Universal's backing ensured that *The Birds* would have an expensive and far-reaching media campaign focusing on Hitchcock himself as the star, as had been the case with *Psycho*. But Hitchcock also wanted *The Birds* to establish him as a film artist, and not just a popular director.

MARKETING A SLOGAN

It was February 1963, six weeks before *The Birds* was due to have its world premiere in the US. Evan Hunter remembers being in LA when Hitchcock planned to unveil the advertising slogan to all of Universal's marketing execs.

'Gentlemen,' Hitchcock said with his typical showman's flourish, 'here's how we'll announce the movie. Are you ready?' A moment of suspenseful silence ensued and then Hitchcock spread his hands wide in the air and said, '*The Birds* is coming!'

As Evan said, 'It was pure genius, a seemingly ungrammatical catch-phrase that combined humour and suspense.' More amusingly, one of Universal's young advertising execs said, 'Excuse me, Mr Hitchcock, sir?' Hitch turned to him. 'Don't you mean "The birds are coming", sir?' In an age before Facebook and Twitter, Hitchcock had already generated a catchy phrase to ensure that substantial word of mouth would promote his new film.[2]

A couple of weeks later, on 27 February, Evan wrote to Peggy saying, 'A friend of mine at Revue sent me two yellow car stickers proclaiming "*The Birds* is Coming". I have promptly stuck one on my car and one on Anita's, but since my friends in New York are legion, can you send me a dozen more so that I can have them plastered on to additional cars? When is *The Birds* coming?' Peggy wrote back on 1 March 1963, saying, 'We are at this very moment air mailing to you one dozen "*The Birds* is Coming" stickers to be plastered on to your personal fleet of automobiles. Also, at this very moment, Hitch is telephoning you with the details of when the birds is coming.' The date was to be 28 March and *The Birds* was to have its world premiere in New York City.

PHILIPPE HALSMAN PHOTOGRAPHS

Six months before the marketing slogan for the campaign had been devised, during the summer and fall of 1962, publicity for *The Birds* had already begun. Hitchcock invited the famed photographer Philippe Halsman to take a series of photographs to promote the film and capitalise on the director himself as star of the picture. Halsman had already taken photographs of the François Truffaut and Hitchcock meetings, when the French director interviewed Hitchcock in August 1962 for his forthcoming book with Helen Scott as translator.

Hitchcock and Halsman had first met in 1945 while Halsman was at the Black Star photo agency in New York. As his daughter, Irene Halsman, recalled in 2012, 'My father and Hitchcock were friends and corresponded together. Hitchcock had a huge wine collection that he shared with his guests, including my father. On one occasion, Hitch sent him some rare wine goblets.' They had a wonderful rapport and shared humour.

Born in Latvia in 1906, Halsman was famous for the *joie de vivre* of his celebrity portraits. He had originally set up as a photographer in Paris, but, in 1940, had to flee the Nazis, and it was Albert Einstein who helped him enter the US. In New York, Halsman worked mostly for *Life* magazine and became closely identified with the look of the publication. Between 1942 and his death in 1979, he took 101 *Life* cover pictures, including iconic images of Marilyn Monroe, Groucho Marx, Frank Sinatra and Alfred Hitchcock, the latter of which can be seen on the cover of this book.

The *Life* magazine cover photograph mimics both Hitchcock's artifice and humour. The sky is dark and exaggeratedly stormy, evoking Albert Whitlock's matte paintings in *The Birds*, and Halsman's picture makes a nod towards them in a knowing and humorous way. Quite obviously, it's a photographed backdrop, announcing its artificiality in the same manner as Hitchcock's back projection and conspicuous painted backdrops, evident in both *The Birds* and *Marnie*.

Life magazine went on to commission a set of photographs of Hitchcock and Tippi Hedren, which would be published in the early spring of 1963 to coincide with the release of *The Birds*. These included candid shots of Hitchcock having his hair cut while talking to Tippi on the set. Some of the pictures are very funny and one of Irene's favourite's is of Hitchcock eating chicken on a small plate with Tippi in the foreground being attacked by a bird. As she says, 'I really liked [Halsman's] visual sense of humour, which you don't see so often in today's photographs.'[3]

Vogue magazine also commissioned a 14-page spread of photographs from Halsman, including the famous shot of Hitchcock with a bird on the end of his cigar. The photo illustrates the special collaboration between two visual artists who have their roots in surrealism. Having Hitchcock tilt his big head back whilst puffing on a cigar inflates his ruddy cheeks. Hitchcock always saw the marketing potential of his rotundness and was quick to capitalise on it, drawing his famous signature profile on a chalkboard, for example, and making fun of his portly physique in his quick cameos. With the stuffed bird attached to the end of the cigar, Hitchcock and Halsman are acknowledging the artificial style of *The Birds* and the use of mechanical birds in the film.

But the bird is not just a reference to *The Birds*. In *Psycho*, Norman Bates stuffs birds for a hobby and Hitchcock's favourite writer was Edgar Allan Poe, the author of *The Raven*. With this visual joke, Hitchcock may be proclaiming himself to be the successor to America's great writer of the macabre, but with typical Hitchcockian humour. That cigar has a blatantly phallic dimension but is undermined by the bird perched cheekily on it – a joke that's pure Hitchcock. Today, Halsman's contemporary equivalent is Annie Leibowitz – American celebrities' portrait photographer of choice.

PUBLICITY CAMPAIGN

A film as big and prestigious as *The Birds* required an expert publicity campaign and a campaign manager so William Blowitz, head of a public relations firm in New York, was given the task.

Hitchcock was by now a national icon; riding high, both from the publicity and success of *Psycho* and from his television show *Alfred Hitchcock Presents*. With *The Birds*, William Blowitz sent out a memo announcing, 'The star of this picture, as with *Psycho*, is Alfred Hitchcock. Therefore a pivotal element in publicity and advertising will be Hitchcock... Everything that is done in connection with *The Birds* must lead to the eventual merchandising of the finished film. We are not talking about a nit-picking campaign, with fragments of stories seeping out during production. In essence, what we are talking about is the *Psycho* campaign, yet done in such a fashion that no one will say, "They're doing a good job of copying the *Psycho* campaign." But, rather, "Hitchcock is doing for *The Birds* in merchandising what he did with *Psycho*, but different."'

In the production notes on the magazine campaign, the trailer and the ads all duly emphasised Hitchcock as the star (Figure 31). The point of the campaign was to sell tickets to *The Birds* and the aspect of the campaign focusing on 'Tippi' was to be handled in such a way that she would become a desirable story.

To publicise *The Birds*, Hitchcock, Alma and Tippi went to New York and Washington to begin an advance promotional tour on 10 March 1963. Seventeen outfits were especially designed by Edith Head for Tippi to wear on the New York trip, and a black mist mink coat from Frank Somper, the *haute couture* designer of fur fashions, was rented for $250 a week. The grand total for Tippi's wardrobe came to $16,931.64 for the publicity trip.

The group was joined by Ray Berwick who was hired for three weeks to take part in the campaign along with his trained birds. On 13 March they all took part in a one-hour segment of the *Today* show entirely devoted to *The Birds*. It was while watching the show 18 months earlier that Hitchcock had first seen Tippi in a commercial. Hitchcock also addressed a large crowd of top Washington journalists at a luncheon meeting of the National Press Club on 18 March, where he described his movie with characteristic good humour: 'I have only recently completed work on my latest picture, the title is quite short, just two words, there were three, but we cut the first word 'For' and called it quite simply *The Birds*. Naturally, most of the actors in *The Birds* are [for the birds], in fact I have employed more feathered performers than has been seen since *Femme* dancing went out of style.'[4]

To launch the film, Hitchcock planned a number of events aimed at the general public. There was a coast-to-coast pigeon race, with prizes awarded to the first pigeon arriving in New York, where the movie was scheduled to open 28 March at the RKO Palace. As well as the *Today* show, there were plugs on popular television programmes such as the Perry Como and Art Linkletter shows. Ray Berwick was also heavily involved in promoting the film with Hitchcock, travelling with several of his trained crows to theatres set to open the film. A standee cardboard cut out of Hitchcock was also available for cinema managers to place in their foyers.

MOMA SCREENING, NEW YORK

A major promotional coup for the publicity campaign of *The Birds* was that the film would receive its world premiere at the Museum of Modern Art in New York, which would also launch a major retrospective of the director's work. Universal and their publicity department had pushed for this opportunity, fronting the costs of the exhibition and a special 48-page monograph on the director written by Peter Bogdanovich.

Bogdanovich had already arranged two successful directorial retrospectives at MOMA, one on Orson Welles in 1961 and the other on Howard Hawks in 1962 to coincide with the release of Hawks's film *Hatari*. The Hitchcock retrospective was to be the third in a row, and it was deemed a good idea for *The Birds* to launch it. Bogdanovich first interviewed Hitchcock in 1961 and remembers, 'I did a big piece in *Esquire* magazine on Hitch, and had a long, long conversation with him. Then I took my idea to MOMA and they went with it.'[5]

Originally, Bogdanovich proposed a similar idea to the New York repertory theatre, a revival house specialising in movie classics, but the idea was rejected because the cost of a Hitchcock series was too expensive. Bodganovich then met Hitchcock a second time over the course of three days from 12 to 14 February 1961. There was no money for publishing unless some outside source would pay for it, and the films for a retrospective exhibition had to be mostly lent by the company, so the premiere of a new film like *The Birds* was the perfect occasion for something like this.

Bodganovich's ideas were presented to and accepted by curator Richard Griffith who was head of MOMA's film programme at the time. A large man with a barrel chest, he was even bigger in girth than Hitchcock. He was also an alcoholic and neurotic, but had a keen intelligence, though he lacked a young person's point of view. Griffith was influenced by British documentary filmmaker Paul Rotha who had written *The Film Till Now: A Survey of the Cinema* in 1935. An additional section for the revised and enlarged edition, published in 1949, had been added by Griffith, dealing with the classic cinema. Griffith's view of Hitchcock may have come from this work which saw the British director, especially after his move to America, as a popular entertainer rather than a serious artist.

Jim Watters was Richard Griffith's secretary at the time. He had started as an intern in 1961 after graduating with a Master's degree from Columbia. When Griffith's secretary Suzanne Franklin resigned, Watters was offered the job. 'I was thrown into a little department where people didn't know a lot about film,' recalled Watters in 2012. 'I remember, once, Iris Barry, founder of the film department at MOMA, was in Richard Griffith's office screaming at him, "You're not only not cooking with gas here, you're just not cooking!"'[6]

Hitchcock was an old friend of the Film Library (as it was called then), and a friend of Iris Barry from her days in England, and his films were among the first ones she acquired for the collection. In his excellent book *Hitchcock and the Making of a Reputation*, Robert Kapsis suggested that Griffith shunned Hitchcock's films in favour of films with a social realist content.[7] However, Eileen Bowser, Griffith's assistant, disagrees: 'Griffith liked and collected a wide range of films, from the most esoteric to the most popular commercial Hollywood film.'[8]

Why, then, did Griffith allow himself to be persuaded by Bogdanovich to hold a Hitchcock retrospective, especially when it seems he may not exactly have been a fan of Hitchcock's films, and convince the MOMA's board of trustees to go along with it? As Jim Watters remembers, 'Hitchcock was riding high for two reasons: the success of *Psycho* and also his very popular television series. Nelson Rockefeller (former president and on the board of trustees at MOMA) was keen to get in commercial films at MOMA, and the Hitchcock retrospective fit the bill.' Watters also credits Peter Bogdanovich as being revolutionary in taking films seriously at MOMA: 'It was what the museum needed when Peter Bogdanovich came in.'

MOMA at the time had a very rigid pecking order and staff didn't tend to speak to anyone above or below their status. 'The museum then was very conservative and set in its ways,' remembers Jo-Ann Ordano, an assistant at MOMA who supervised the theatres and the acquisition of prints. Ordano was fresh out of college and attained the job because she knew the difference between 16 and 35mm prints. 'I think that Peter Bogdanovich even then was considered very arty, and wore a long flowing cloak.'[9]

Griffith in the past had persuaded the MOMA board to pay a tribute to the actress Marlene Dietrich. Some of the board had been against this, 'Because they thought that Dietrich shouldn't be honoured at the Museum alongside Picassos and Matisses,' remembers Watters. The first task for the Hitchcock retrospective, to be called, simply, *The Films of Alfred Hitchcock*, was securing all of the existing Hitchcock films. MOMA only owned four of them, so Griffith had to borrow prints from other institutions including the National Film Archive, David O Selznick, the British Film Institute, Universal, Paramount, RKO, Warner Brothers, MGM and Twentieth Century Fox.

Peter Bodganovich was intending to have his writing completed in time for publication at the opening of the retrospective in May. But then Hitchcock's publicity team, who were paying for the show, offered a gala premiere of *The Birds* on 27 March 1963 and said that they wanted to distribute copies of the monograph to the audience that night. Which meant that Bodganovich needed to finish the manuscript by then to give to the audience.

It was understood that William Blowitz's office had agreed to pay the costs of the exhibition including 'the writing, designing and printing of a monograph to accompany [it].' On 11 February, Richard Griffith wrote a memo to Philip Gerard at Universal Pictures in New York, saying, 'I find that the cost of the evening preview of Alfred Hitchcock's *The Birds* on Wednesday 27 March will be approximately $1,500.'[10] The memorandum was agreed and signed by Gerard and returned a week later. There was to be a small dinner party prior to the preview and a reception to follow. The only person to be invited to the dinner party from Universal would be Milton Rackmill, president of the company.

On 7 March there was concern following Universal's failure to send a cheque to defray the expenses of the Hitchcock show. 'The cheque was for $5,000, $1,000 of which is to cover the film transport and contingencies for the remainder,' wrote Richard Griffith. 'The New York office of Universal says that the cheque was mailed from Hollywood on Tuesday and, if it doesn't arrive by the afternoon mail of 7 March, I will call Universal and say we must suspend all operations on the show until it does come.'[11] By 12 March the missing cheque had arrived.

Invitations had been sent out to noted actors living in New York including Tallulah Bankhead, Tony Perkins, Teresa Wright, Jessica Tandy, Hume Cronyn, Henry Fonda, Judith Evelyn, Suzanne Pleshette, Rod Taylor, Barbara Bel Geddes, Joseph Cotten, Eva Marie Saint, Mildred Natwick, Farley Granger, John Dall, Cedric Hardwick, Marion Lorne, Montgomery Clift, Dolly Haas, Sylvia Sidney, Margaret Leighton, Robert Montgomery and Martin Balsam.

Philip Gerard wrote back on 13 March, saying he had some concerns, particularly with the slow response to the invitations. 'Everything about the campaign on *The Birds* to date has been on such a high level, and we are looking forward to the Museum gala as the climax to this long-range plan. I know that you are doing everything that you can to assure great success – we can afford nothing less.'[12]

Wednesday 27 March was to be the night of the invitational preview screening for Hitchcock's party. A buffet reception, attended by special guests, was to be held at the guest house of the museum prior to the showing of the film. Both Griffith and Gerard agreed that the reception should be private and that the guests would consist of the president of the museum and its most important trustees, Hitchcock's personal invitees, and the top echelon of Universal. By all accounts, it was going to be a very prestigious affair.

Following the screening, which was scheduled for 8.30pm, there was to be a reception held in the lobby of the museum in honour of Hitchcock.

The Universal City guest list included Edd Henry, Charles Miller, Herbert Rosenthal, Morris Schrier, Jules Stein, Lew Wasserman, David Werblin, Milton Rackmill, Henry Martin and Amerigo Aboaf. On Hitchcock's personal invitee list were Arthur Hornblow, Gerald Murphy, Leland Hayward, Gerry Gordon, Dr Tom Reese, Bennett Cerf, Marlene Dietrich, Anita Colby and escort, Evan Hunter and his wife, Anita, Richard Rogers and Tippi Hedren.

Hitchcock himself arrived at the MOMA offices during his promotional tour of New York to publicise *The Birds* in mid March, with entourage in tow. On 13 March, after taping the Today show at NBC in Rockefeller Plaza, which was just a few blocks away from MOMA on 53rd Street, Hitchcock made an impromptu visit to see Richard Griffith.

As Jim Watters remembers, 'There was a big to do when Hitchcock was coming to the office. He showed up with a small entourage, including the trainer with the raven making quite a noise in the corridors. And they marched down the hall. I remember that the meeting with Griffith took place in the screening room and not in his office.' Accompanying Hitchcock was Philip Gerard from Universal and William Blowitz.

Although Griffith was non-confrontational, he could, according to Watters, still be as temperamental as Hitchcock. A tall man, he towered over Hitchcock and had a barrel-shaped chest. Watters also remembers that, during the meeting with Hitchcock, Griffith wore his overcoat indoors and never took it off, which, to Watters, seemed very strange. 'I do remember that Hitchcock and Griffith chatted for about 15 minutes and they talked about Constance Smith stabbing Paul Rotha,' says Watters. Smith was an Irish film actress and contract player at 20th Century Fox who, in 1962, was sentenced to three months in prison for stabbing her boyfriend, filmmaker and historian Paul Rotha. There was no antagonism during Hitchcock's conversation with Griffith and everything was apparently pleasant and cordial.

'But nothing came out of that meeting,' reflected Watters. 'Hitch was doing his number, saying funny things. I was there to take memos, but there were no notes to be taken. I said to Richard Griffith afterwards, "What do you want me to write up about this?" And Griffith said, "Nothing, forget it."' Watters described the MOMA board at the time 'as a nest of vipers'. 'Everything was so proper in those days. We tried to get Eleanor Roosevelt to watch *La Dolce Vita* but she called it pornography. They were a snooty, holier-than-thou board, made of old New York money.'

Hitchcock also requested that the dinner at MOMA's guesthouse be cancelled and asked for the reception to be catered by '21', one of New York's famous restaurants.[13] This is the caterer Grace Kelly hires to bring a lobster dinner for the wheelchair-bound James Stewart in *Rear Window* (1954). In the words of former MOMA employee Jo-Ann Ordano, 'The museum catering was notoriously dreadful, very cheap liquor and food. If Hitchcock insisted on using something else, for very good reason, it was making him seem too temperamental for the museum.'

Everything seemed to be in place. The guest list had been approved; the invitations had been sent; Hitchcock's preferred catering had been organised. But then, on 21 March, a night letter was sent out to all the invitees: 'The Film Library regrets that the gala preview of Alfred Hitchcock's *The Birds* on Wednesday 27 March, to be followed by a reception for Mr Hitchcock, has had to be cancelled due to prior commitments. *The Birds* will be included in the retrospective of Mr Hitchcock's films, which will begin at the Museum of Modern Art on 5 May. We regret any inconvenience this may cause you.'[14] The word 'prior' was crossed out and replaced by 'conflicting' in the final draft.

Why, at the eleventh hour, with invitations already sent out, was the premiere of *The Birds* cancelled? Clues can be found in the MOMA archives and personal testimony from those working at the museum at the time. A month later, on 20 April 1963, Philip Gerard wrote a letter to Richard Griffith saying, 'I'm sorry about the contretemps involving the museum gala of *The Birds*. It has all worked out, but perhaps some lessons can be drawn from this experience. We can discuss it when we next see each other.'[15] And, according to Richard Griffith in another memo sent several months later, the scheduled preview had to be cancelled because 'the Master' insisted upon turning the preview evening into an Alfred Hitchcock Production.[16]

From the evidence and interviews with MOMA's former employees, it seems that Hitchcock was keen on a Hollywood-style premiere. He was a notorious gourmand, and the museum catering, in the words of one previous MOMA employee, was 'simply awful' and certainly not up to the standard expected by Hitchcock for his A-list guests. Hitchcock wanted spotlights blazing outside of MOMA, red carpets and first-class catering befitting a Hollywood premiere.[17] As Jo-Ann Ordano said, 'I tend to agree with the theory that the museum was not wishing to be exploited as the venue for a Hollywood-type premiere. Even though the museum and the film library had been around for some time, there was still an element of trying to establish or legitimise cinema as an art form, and maybe the notion of a splashy premiere clashed with the museum's perception of itself.'[18]

Hitchcock may have been offended by something someone said during his trip to MOMA. Furthermore, Richard Griffith wasn't a fan of big, glitzy film openings. The MOMA administration may have balked at such undignified proceedings and, when Hitchcock was told that he could not do what he wanted, he cancelled the premiere. Instead he arranged a private dinner at Le Pavillon, a top New York City restaurant that defined French food on East 55th Street, across the street from the St Regis hotel. The Kennedy family were regular visitors there.

The Hitchcock party then went on to the Four Seasons private room for a screening of *The Birds* and cocktails afterwards. As one of the guests wrote after the event, 'I want to thank you so much for a wonderful evening last night, Your picture is fascinating and, if the general public enjoy it as much as I did, I know it will be a colossal success.' Another of Hitchcock's friends remarked, 'The dinner at the Pavillon was just superb and *The Birds* a particular thrill with the advent of your star, Tippi. We are so happy for her and, after seeing your film, so happy for you.'

But not everyone was happy with the film. Evan Hunter was at the preview screening and it was the first time he had seen the film and its unresolved ending. For Evan, the changes meant a movie he could no longer call his own. As he later said, 'I saw the film at an invitational screening at the Four Seasons in New York. That very hip and sophisticated theatrical audience was, to say the least, somewhat glacially polite in its reception.'[19]

Evan was surprised when some scenes were not in the film. 'But when I saw the ending I was shocked, because the way I had the film end, uh, they come out of the house and they get in the car and they start driving away from the house. And we see them coming through town, now, and we see the havoc that has been wreaked in the town, so it becomes not just a personal thing that's directed against Melanie, that, wherever she is, the birds are attacking.'

The next day, on Thursday 28 March 1963, *The Birds* opened to the public. The film was shown at the Palace Theatre on Broadway, where Hitchcock and Tippi Hedren released 1,000 homing pigeons into Times Square. The owner of the winning racing pigeon would get a trophy and a two-week vacation in Florida.

That same evening, MOMA held an evening press screening during which it was announced that the museum would host a major retrospective of Hitchcock's work. Jim Watters remembers being at the screening: 'I didn't like *The Birds* then; I still don't like it now.' Afterwards he wrote a private memo to Griffith: 'Last night I attended the press screening of *The Birds*. This film is a humourless and contrived tale, based on a gimmick, with a weak, unresolved ending. The audience hissed at the conclusion of the showing. No matter how well conceived and executed, the special effects are obvious and thus destroy the illusion of reality and negate the terror. Not since the films of the 1940s have I seen so much process photography... This is minor Hitchcock, for the emphasis is on design details for production value with a complete disregard for developing depth in character and atmosphere, and for doing anything with an ineffectual and undeveloped plot line.' Griffith wrote on the memo: 'Wow! Lucky miss.'[20]

As Albert Whitlock later recalled, 'The resident critic at the Museum of Modern Art didn't like *The Birds* and said, "I'm not going to make a critique of this film because it isn't a movie." I mean, he dismissed it totally. Not only did he say "Hitchcock has lost his marbles" but that "He didn't make a movie".'[21] Griffith himself continued to express dissatisfaction with the film. On 15 April, Philip Gerard wrote to him, 'I should love to see you for lunch, and I hope it will be soon so that we can get caught up and review the fiasco of *The Birds* at the Museum. Incidentally, the picture is a huge success.'[22] Griffith wrote back three days later, detailing some costs for preliminary preparations and for evening invitations: 'I am sorry to charge you anything for this fiasco, but we have no money to meet these charges. They shouldn't come to much. I attribute the success of *The Birds* to your campaign for it. To that and nothing else!'[23]

Despite the fiasco of the failed premiere of *The Birds* at MOMA, the Alfred Hitchcock retrospective was a success, along with Peter Bogdanovich's accompanying monograph. A letter from William Blowitz, the publicity and PR firm in New York handling *The Birds*, to Richard Griffith said: 'The Hitchcock monograph is a magnificent job and I feel sure the retrospective will be most successful.' On 23 April, a press release was issued by MOMA: '*The Cinema of Alfred Hitchcock* by Peter Bogdanovich has been published by the Film Library of the Museum of Modern Art, New York, and will be available in book stores throughout the country in May. The 48-page, paper-bound book, illustrated with

47 photographs, is issued in conjunction with the Museum's current Hitchcock film series.'[24]

CANNES FILM FESTIVAL 1963

Hitchcock was to have more luck overseas, with *The Birds* due to premiere at the Cannes Film Festival, out of competition. On 27 February 1963, Hitchcock wrote to Monsieur Cape Devielle, General Manager of the Carlton Hotel in Cannes, requesting two rooms, 'one for Mrs Hitchcock and myself, and the other for the star of this new picture, *The Birds*, who is Miss Tippi Hedren. She is my newest leading lady and is taking the place (so the magazines and newspapers say) of Grace Kelly, my ex-leading lady.' Cape Devielle wrote back on 4 March saying he was delighted that there was a strong possibility of the Hitchcocks attending and that he had reserved the rooms for them.

On 7 March, a cable was sent from Robert Favre Le Bret, director of the Cannes Film Festival, to Hitchcock: 'I consider this film a masterpiece in every sense of the word. I am honoured and happy to be able to present this film at the festival inauguration. I am counting on your presence and that of Tippi Hedren.' That same day, Hitchcock wrote back stating that the Cannes visit was indeed a certainty. 'Therefore I would like to confirm the reservation for two suites, commencing 6 May until the following Sunday.' Hitchcock considerately sent another note on 8 March, saying, 'I hope Miss Hedren's single room will be a fairly good-sized room.' The cost was charged to David Lipton, head of publicity and exploitation for *The Birds* at Universal Studios.

A press release issued on 27 March officially announced that 'Alfred Hitchcock's *The Birds* will inaugurate the 1963 Cannes Film Festival with a gala showing on the night of 9 May, the opening date of the festival.' Hitchcock, his wife, Alma, and Tippi were scheduled to arrive in Cannes on 6 May for a one-week stay. A record turnout of celebrities was also expected to attend the Cannes showing of *The Birds*. Hitchcock had long been regarded in European art cinema circles as America's leading filmmaker and was known in France as the 'father of the French new wave', with disciples such as François Truffaut and Claude Chabrol.

The Hitchcocks, along with Tippi, flew on Air France from LA to New York on 5 May, staying at the St Regis hotel. The following day they flew to Paris and checked into the Plaza Athénée. It was whilst in Paris that Hitchcock recorded the voiceover for the Spanish and Portuguese trailers for *The Birds*. On his return, he would finish the looping of the French and German trailers. Universal publicity in France advised the Hitchcock party to remain incognito whilst in Paris in order not to diminish the effect of their arrival and presence in Cannes. Also, famous hairdresser, Alexandre of Paris, came on 7 May, spending from noon until 2pm working on Alma and on artistic creations for Tippi, with a top assistant to be available for them all the time in Paris and Cannes.

On Thursday 9 May, the Hitchcocks and Tippi flew from Paris to Nice and undertook the 45-minute journey to Cannes for the start of the film festival. They were met by Giulio Ascarelli, the publicity officer for Universal in Europe, and checked into the Carlton Hotel. A large outdoor billboard was on display near the festival palace, and along the promenade were specially erected poles on which were displayed double-faced posters for all the pictures shown at the festival. There were six posters for *The Birds* in size approximately 48 x 64 inches, and plastered over the promenade were stickers with the slogan '*The Birds* is Coming!' in both French and English. Two trade papers in France, *Le Film Français* and *La Cinématographie Française*, had a full page announcing the showing of *The Birds* at the festival, and the French film publication, *Cahiers du Cinéma*, had Hitchcock as their front cover. Over in the US, *Dr No* had just opened in theatres on 8 May starring Sean Connery, Tippi's future co-star in *Marnie*.

A cocktail party was held in honour of the Hitchcocks and Tippi that evening at the ballroom of Les Ambassadeurs, and 1,000 guests were invited. These included French government officials, French movie industry officials, and Cannes festival management. After the cocktail party they were to change into black tie for the showing of *The Birds* at 9.30pm, and, after the showing of the film, there was a formal dinner at the Carlton Hotel for 300 to 350 guests.

The next day a press conference was held at the festival palace and attended by newspaper journalists of all nationalities. Interviews were scheduled with magazine, radio and television reporters from England, France, Italy, Germany and Belgium. Then Hitchcock and Tippi crossed the Croisette to participate in the most publicised event in Cannes in connection with *The Birds* – the release of 400 pigeons into the air.

Tippi's parents, Dorothea and Bernard Hedren, excited to see their daughter at an international premiere in her first film, were also at the Cannes festival. Afterwards, Dorothea Hedren wrote a letter to Sue Gauthier to say thank you for the itinerary, and that at least they could sort of 'arm chain' follow them. On 13 May, the Hitchcock party flew back to Paris, where Hitchcock was taken to the dubbing studios to prepare the foreign trailers for the film. They arrived back in LA on 16 May.

By all accounts, the Cannes Film Festival was a success for Alfred Hitchcock and *The Birds*. Allen Rivkin from the Hollywood Guilds festival committee wrote to David Lipton on 18 June 1963: 'Your man, Giulio Ascarelli, did a monumental job during the Cannes Film Festival. His arrangements for birds and mockingbirds covered every possible area of getting the most mileage from the hundreds of journalists and photographers present from all over the world.'

The tremendous press interest surrounding *The Birds* in France was also brought to the attention of French poet and playwright Jean Cocteau. In the spring of 1963, Cocteau was 73 years old and dying. Peggy Robertson wrote to Edd Henry on 27 May: 'Mr Hitchcock would also like M Jean Cocteau to see *The Birds* as soon as possible. M Cocteau also should see this picture whenever he wishes – not necessarily at Universal Pictures. For your own information, we have learned that M Cocteau is now dying and one of his final wishes, according to his friends in Paris, is to see *The Birds*.' This he did before he died on 11 October 1963.

REVIEWS OF *THE BIRDS*

When *The Birds* was released in New York at the end of March 1963, many of the newspapers and magazines picked up on Hitchcock's unresolved ending and reacted negatively. *Time* magazine wrote, 'The Master has traded in his uncomplicated tenets of terror for a new outlook that is vaguely *nouvelle vague*,' a comment that was not meant as a compliment.[25]

Variety weighed in with their opinion on 1 April: 'Beneath all of this elaborate feather bedlam lies a Hitch cock-and-bull story that's essentially a fowl ball. The premise is fascinating. The idea of billions of birdbrains refusing to eat crow any longer and adopting the hunt-and-peck system, with *homo sapiens* as their ornithological target, is fraught with potential.

Cinematically, Hitchcock & Co have done a masterful job of meeting this formidable challenge. But, dramatically, *The Birds* is little more than a shocker for shock's sake.'[26]

Evan Hunter was very upset about this review, especially the fact that the story had been called the weakest aspect in the picture. Hitchcock later mentioned that Evan came up to him for guidance: 'You have to help me through this.' But with the exception of a few reviews from such noted critics as Andrew Sarris and Vincent Canby, the press gave the film an indifferent reception. Judith Christ called the film 'dull and plotless' and Pauline Kael described it as 'incomprehensible'. Some of the critics didn't take to Tippi Hedren as Hitchcock's newest discovery. Brendan Gill in the *New Yorker* wrote that 'Miss Hedren is so new a newcomer that Universal has boasted in print of her having no previous acting experience whatsoever. Not everything about this is hard to believe.'

Andrew Sarris of the *Village Voice* was one of those who liked the film: '*The Birds* finds Hitchcock at the summit of his artistic powers.' And Bosley Crowther wrote in the *New York Times*, 'Mr Hitchcock and his associates have constructed a horror film that should raise the hackles on the most courageous and put goose-pimples on the toughest hide.'[27] Peter Bogdanovich would write in the spring edition of *Film Culture*: '*The Birds* should place [Hitchcock] securely among the giants of the cinema.'

EUROPEAN EXPLOITATION TRIP

The Birds was to open in Europe at the end of August and, in order to keep the publicity machine going on the film, and to build up Tippi as a star, a tour of Europe was planned. Hitchcock was busy preparing *Marnie* and was working with his new screenwriter Jay Presson Allen. Jay had replaced Evan after he had failed to reach an agreement with Hitchcock over a crucial scene. With *Marnie* scheduled for a fall filming schedule, there was no opportunity for Hitchcock to embark on a lavish promotional tour as he had done with Tippi in Cannes, so, instead, he sent along his girl Friday Peggy Robertson to take his place.

The Rank Organisation, which was responsible for distributing *The Birds* in the United Kingdom, wrote to Hitchcock 31 July: 'We would like Miss Hedren to arrive in London on Friday 23 August and stay until

Saturday 31 August, to begin interviews on Monday.' Hitchcock wanted Tippi to receive the same build up as she had in Cannes, and that meant a careful control of her public appearances, looks and hairstyles. He asked for Gwendolyne, Alexandre of Paris's assistant, who had been at the Cannes Film Festival, to come to London to do Tippi's hair at all times. Photographs of her hairstyles taken in Cannes were first approved by Hitchcock, before being sent to London to copy.

As for the New York trip, a personal wardrobe of 17 outfits had been designed by Edith Head for Tippi to take with her to Europe. Each outfit was named after a bird, with tags such as swift, pigeon, dove, willow, corvus, golden thrush, cockatoo, magpie, chaffinch, swallow and canary. Also, a mink stole was rented for Tippi to wear.

On 15 August, Hitchcock sent a further memo to Alexandre of Paris instructing that 'Miss Hedren's hairstyles should be kept simple, as they were at the Cannes Film Festival. In other words, I do not want Miss Hedren's hair to be overdone or to be worn in any exaggerated styles'. This was all part of his careful build up of Tippi as a star, and a woman of some elegance. Hitchcock also selected imitation jewellery for her to wear, including one single strand of pearls, one pair of single-pearl earrings, one pair of solitaire earrings, and one paste-diamond bracelet.

Peggy Robertson and Tippi arrived in London on Wednesday 21 August, where a chauffeur met them and drove them to Claridges, Hitchcock's favourite London hotel. When they arrived in their suites, they found that Hitchcock had sent them flowers. After a day's rest, the publicity campaign for *The Birds* in the UK began in earnest. A memo instructed Tippi to conduct her interviews in her hotel suite in Claridges as much as possible, in order to generate a star aura around her. On Friday 23 August, Tippi had lunch with showbiz journalist Donald Zec of the *Daily Mirror* in her hotel suite, and that evening she had dinner with Peter Evans from the *Daily Express*.

The next day, Tippi, dressed in riding clothes, appeared in a photo shoot for the publication *Rotten Row*, to promote both *The Birds* and her forthcoming film *Marnie*. Hitchcock had stipulated that Tippi was to appear in riding boots and britches, not jodhpurs. This was followed by photocalls that would take place in Trafalgar Square with the pigeons, and in Hyde Park, the Tower of London with the ravens, and by the aviary at London Zoo. In Hyde Park, Tippi was interviewed by an ITN news crew and, when asked if Alfred Hitchcock was a difficult man to work with, she replied, 'No, not at all. I've never heard him raise his voice and he has no great show of temperament whatsoever. He's wonderful to work with.'[28]

After a day of rest on Sunday, more interviews were scheduled for Monday 24 August with the *Evening Standard*, *Today* magazine, *Evening News*, as well as dinner with the *News of the World*. The day of the premiere, Thursday 29 August, was fast approaching and special photographs of Tippi appeared in the West End, with her posing on a London bus behind the huge poster sites for *The Birds*. When the film opened at the Odeon Leicester Square it broke all records, making £11,076 in the first seven days, but not everyone was pleased with the film.

Daphne du Maurier, who was living in Cornwall, didn't go to the premiere, but her son Kits Browning did. He was in the film business at the time and enjoyed going to the movies. 'I thought it was a great film,' remembers Kits, 'but when my mother saw it she was very disappointed that the whole thing had been changed. She was slightly old fashioned about the commercialisation of films and the changes of location made it totally different. And, forever after, whenever there's a bird attack in Cornwall, every single newspaper says it's "Hitchcock's *The Birds*", it's not it's "Daphne du Maurier's *The Birds*".'

After the premiere, Peggy sent a letter from Claridges on 30 August to Sue Gauthier in LA saying that 'everything is going fabulously, premiere in London had best reception of all'. But, like their American counterparts, the British press wasn't overly enamoured about the film. That same day, Ian Wright wrote in the *Guardian*: 'But something is lacking. The actors appear to be very closely directed – particularly Tippi Hedren, whose acting does not give the impression of any great range.'

Back in Hollywood, Tippi's appearances in Europe were being carefully watched by Hitchcock, who was monitoring all the press coverage. A memo to Peggy Robertson was sent on 14 September with the following directions for Tippi:[29]

1) For arrival at London airport, wear hair in French roll
2) No one liked the hairstyle at Chasens last night 9/13/63
3) Stay out of sun
4) Get yellow out of hair
5) Take to London photograph in the Cine Monde page 10 as example of good hairstyle

These detailed notes show just how much control Hitchcock wanted to exert over his new star, dictating her style, appearance and hairstyles. 'I know, towards the end of *The Birds*, Tippi was getting tired of the "hot-house system" where everything was carefully controlled,' remembers Rita Riggs. 'Everything was so carefully manipulated with Peggy Robertson and Suzie Gauthier. It was a whole system and we all recognised it and followed it. I'm surprised he went ahead with *Marnie*, because it was an undertaking, more of an acting challenge, and I think he felt he could get things out of people as a director and he believed in himself as a director.'[30]

But carry on with Tippi he did, and the disastrous falling out between Hitchcock and Hedren is detailed in the revised edition of the author's book, *Hitchcock and the Making of Marnie*.

This was just the beginning of the European exploitation tour, and Tippi and Peggy Robertson continued with whirlwind visits to other key cities, starting with Paris on 5 September, Frankfurt on 9 September, Berlin on 11 September, Stockholm on 13 September, Brussels and Antwerp on the 17 and 18 September, and Copenhagen on 19 September. They were due to return to LA from Copenhagen on 20 September. The Rome premiere was scheduled for 20 October. Guilio Ascarelli from Universal Pictures in Rome, who had masterminded and received praise for his excellent press coverage during the Cannes Film Festival, accompanied Peggy and Tippi on their European tour. Ascarelli later wrote to Peggy, on 18 October 1963, saying, '*The Birds* is doing very well in Sweden and is still playing at the Rex-Normandie-Rotonde in Paris. It will open in Italy at the end of the month and there is great expectancy for it.'

When Tippi and Peggy finally returned to their homes in Sherman Oaks on 20 September, after being a month away, they were greeted by a heatwave of 112 degrees Fahrenheit in the Valley.

THE 1963 OSCARS

The Birds went on to enjoy a respectable, but not overwhelming, box office. In a survey by *Variety*, it grossed $5.1 million upon its release, recouping its costs, but by no means matching *Psycho*'s earnings of $14 million in the first year. By 1972, *The Birds* had earned some $11 million. According to theatre managers, many patrons expressed the opinion that they had been misled by the advertising campaign and that the picture had been oversold to them, leading them to believe it was another *Psycho*. In that respect, *The Birds* was a disappointment.

The film was also in contention for its only Academy Award, Best Special Effects, in 1963. The Academy was often dismissive of horror and thriller films, which didn't often win awards. Even though *The Birds* was a commercial success, the decisions by Academy voters generally favoured films that featured bravura performances.

'A very important thing about *The Birds*: I never raised the point, "Can it be done?"' said Hitchcock. 'Because then it would never have been made. Any technician would have said "impossible". So I didn't even bring that up. I simply said, "Here's what we're going to do." No one realised that, had the pioneering technical work on it not been attempted, the film would not have been made.'

But *The Birds* lost out in the end to *Cleopatra* (1963), Joseph Mankiewicz's historical spectacle starring Elizabeth Taylor. Later, Hitchcock would dismiss *Cleopatra* as 'just quantities of people and scenery'.[31] He was particularly proud of the special effects in his own film and what had been achieved with live birds: 'Just what the bird trainer has done is phenomenal. Look at the way the crows chase the children down the street, dive all around them, and land on their backs. It took days to organise those birds on the hood of the car and to make them fly away at the right time. *The Birds* could easily have cost $5 million if Bob Burks and the rest of us hadn't been technicians ourselves.'[32]

Ray Berwick was particularly disappointed that *The Birds* didn't win for 1963 special effects. 'He was so irate,' remembers his daughter Tamara, 'as he felt he had given so much of himself for the movie.' After filming was complete, he released all the birds back into the wild, save one or two intelligent crows and ravens.

PUBLIC RECEPTION: WHAT DO THE BIRDS MEAN?

When *The Birds* was released in the spring of 1963, it received a lukewarm reception from audiences which were baffled by the film's meaning and its ambiguous ending. Do the birds signify nuclear war? Cold war spies? Or the hostility between the characters? There was much speculation about the love triangle and a possessive mother's love. No attempt was made to explain why the birds attacked, and Hitchcock rejected alternative endings to leave the film open and ambiguous. Perhaps it's an extreme example of what he liked to refer to as 'the ice box syndrome'. When a couple returned home after the movies, they would reach into the ice box and discuss the film. 'That's why it's a mystery,' he would often say in response to unresolved plots in his films.

Hitchcock himself said that the film was about complacency: 'Generally speaking, that people are too complacent. The girl represents complacency. But I believe, when people rise to it, they are all right, they don't panic. The mother is not strong; it's a façade. The son is substituting for the husband. She is the weak character in the story. The girl represents that people face up to it, can be strong. Like the people in America at the time of Cuba – well, if it's going to come, it's going to come. When they have Missouri floods and so forth, people aren't panicking, they are helping people, each other. It's like air raids, London during the war. The girl was strong enough to face those birds and try and beat them off. They were the victims of Judgement Day.'[33] The recent hurricanes, earthquakes and tsunamis the world over, just show how prescient Hitchcock was 50 years ago.

In an arresting analogy, the novelist Salman Rushdie recently compared the crows gathering on the jungle gym behind Melanie to the West's ongoing struggle with radical Islam.[34] The first crow represented the relatively small appearance of danger, which by the time of the 9/11 terrorist attacks had exploded into full-blown catastrophe. *The Birds* also has contemporary relevance as a post-9/11 film about people being in the wrong place at the wrong time.

Many critics thought that *The Birds* suffered because of the conflict between the personal story and the central dramatic event, namely the coming of the birds. 'One tended in *The Birds* to try and make the personal story not too consequential,' Hitchcock said. 'The central figure of the girl was a nothing; she was a flighty daughter of a rich man in San Francisco. No depth to her at all. An occasional glimpse about her upbringing, but nothing very much. In other words, you were saying that all these inconsequential people, their lives are going on in a very humdrum way. The mother is a bit upset about her son and so forth, but all of a sudden come the birds, and now their comparative equanimity is disturbed.'

But eminent Hitchcock scholar Robin Wood believed that the characters and their relationships in *The Birds* were 'too slight ever to adequately represent humanity and human potential' and, as a result, felt that the film was seriously flawed because of the split between levels.[35] Interestingly, Hitchcock said in an interview only three years after the film was released that, if he was to make *The Birds* over again, 'I would feel inclined to make the personal story more amusing, and that will more or less epitomise the fripperies of people, the lightness with which they live, the inconsequential, not bothering about the fact that nature can turn on them. If I had any second thoughts about it, it would be a light comedy to start with.'[36]

What interested Hitchcock was that we all take things for granted, and we take birds for granted. But what if they suddenly turned on us? Complacency is a theme that runs through many Hitchcock films, people going through their lives unthinkingly. And then something happens, and they have to join together. Hitchcock firmly believed in humanity and human potential, and that, at the end of the day, people are all right, with mankind worth preserving.

NOTES

1 For a detailed review see Robert Kapsis, *Hitchcock: The Making of a Reputation*, University of Chicago Press, 1992

2 Evan Hunter, *Me and Hitch*, p. 77

3 Interview with Irene Halsman, 27 June 2012, New York

4 Hitchcock to National Press Club, Washington DC, 18 March 1963

5 Interview with Peter Bogdanovich, 17 July 2012, Los Angeles

6 Interview with Jim Watters, 13 November 2012, London

7 Robert Kapsis, *Hitchcock: The Making of a Reputation*, University of Chicago Press, 1992, p. 85

8 Interview with Eileen Bowser, 30 July 2012, New York

9 Interview with Jo-Ann Ordano, 24 September 2012, Half Moon Bay, California

10 11 February 1962 memo from Richard Griffith to Philip Gerard, Universal Pictures. Film, 136. MoMA Archives, NY

11 7 March 1963 letter from Richard Griffith to Universal. Film, 136. MoMA Archives, NY

12 13 March 1963 letter from Gerard to Richard Griffith. Film, 136. MoMA Archives, NY

13 Letter from Hitchcock's office to Miss Rubenstein and Richard Griffith. Film, 136. MoMA Archives, NY

14 21 March letter from Richard Griffith about premiere cancellation. Film, 136. MoMA Archives, NY

15 20 April letter from Gerard to Richard Griffith. Film, 136. MoMA Archives, NY

16 Richard Griffith letter to the National Archives 1963. Film 136, MOMA Archives, NY

17 Interviews with Eileen Bowser and Joanne Koch, July 2012, New York

18 Interview with Jo-Ann Ordano, 25 September 2012, Half Moon Bay, California

19 Evan Hunter, *Me and Hitch*, p. 66

20 28 March memo from Watters to Richard Griffith about the press screening. Film, 136. MoMA Archives, NY

21 Allbert Whitlock, 'Roundtable on *The Birds*', *Cahiers du Cinema*, 1982

22 15 April letter from Gerard to Richard Griffith. Film, 136. MoMA Archives, NY

23 15 April letter from Richard Griffith to Gerard. Film, 136. MoMA Archives, NY

24 23 April 1963 Press Release, Department of Film Exhibition Files, 136. The Museum of Modern Art Archives, New York.

25 *Time* Magazine review of *The Birds*, 5 April 1963

26 *Variety* review of *The Birds*, 1 April 1963

27 Bosley Crowther, review of *The Birds*, *New York Times*, 1 April 1963

28 Tippi Hedren, ITN news interview, 24 August 1963

29 *The Birds* publicity folder: European Exploitation Tour, Margaret Herrick Library

30 Interview with Rita Riggs, 5 September 2012, Los Angeles

31 Hitchcock to Bogdanovich, 14 February 1963

32 Hitchcock to Bogdanovich, 14 February 1963

33 Hitchcock to Bogdanovich, 14 February 1963

34 Salman Rushdie, *Joseph Anton*, Random House, 2012, p. 4

35 Robin Wood, *Hitchcock's Films Revisited*, 1992, p. 222

36 Hitchcock to Bogdanovich, 16 August 1966

AFTERWORD

This 50th anniversary celebration of the making of *The Birds* was written in memory of the talented men and women who worked on the film. Of the crew and cast members, George Tomasini died in 1964, Bob Burks in 1968, Bernard Herrmann in 1975, Alfred Hitchcock in 1980, his wife Alma in 1982, Edith Head in 1981, secretary Suzanne Gauthier in 1988, Ray Berwick, the bird trainer, in 1990, Jessica Tandy in 1994, story editor Peggy Robertson in 1998, matte artist Albert Whitlock in 1999, screenwriter Evan Hunter in 2005, storyboard artist Harold Michelson in 2007, Suzanne Pleshette in 2008, makeup artist Howard Smit in 2009, assistant director Jim Brown and production designer Robert Boyle (who lived to the age of 100) in 2010. As of 2013, Rod Taylor, Tippi Hedren, Veronica Cartwright, Shari Lee Bernath, Rita Riggs, Ted Parvin, John 'Bud' Cardos and Virginia Darcy are all alive and well.

For many of the crew members, making *The Birds* was a very rich, rewarding and collaborative experience, and you often couldn't differentiate one person's contribution from another's, as everyone was working together to interpret what Hitchcock wanted. As Bob Boyle said, 'It was a wonderful experience and a real, I hate to say it, team effort. It sounds like football, but it's true. We were together, and I think we were also bound by another thing, not only the respect we had for Hitchcock, but an actual love. With all of the things we might say about, for and against Hitchcock, one thing that came right through everything was a real love for the man. At least, I felt that... I look back at the film and it had many imperfections, but that doesn't matter. The imperfections were part of the film process. If you made it today, it would be absolutely perfect. There would be millions of birds and there would be nothing left to the imagination.'[1]

'We knew it was going to be difficult to put real birds into the situations suggested by the story because of certain problems involving travelling mattes,' Bob continued. 'While I think that a space opera like *Star Wars* is an extraordinary technical achievement, it had access to means that were not available to us in the early 1960s. Working around model ships is one thing, but in *The Birds* we were faced with superimposing living, moving things around our characters.'

Albert Whitlock agreed: 'We were stretching the known systems to the limit, I would say. Putting birds over all those scenes we were doing. But I don't think there was anything revolutionary about it. Nobody could say, "That goes back to *The Birds*." I mean, what went back to *The Birds* went further back.' Albert recalled that Hitch was one of the few directors who could accurately explain the type of special effects he wanted in his pictures. 'His understanding of these techniques was really much more profound than that of most moviemakers.'[2]

The Birds is an outstanding example of how far the filmmaking process can go using real birds, live action and sodium screen elements. Even today, it's a modern and frightening movie, beautifully executed. 'I felt a sense of great satisfaction at the end of *The Birds*,' said Jim Brown, the assistant director. 'And that we had created something special.'[3] '*The Birds* does have the craft of film,' acknowledges costume supervisor Rita Riggs. 'It's amazing that it has lasted and doesn't seem to be as dated, even though it was 50 years ago. We who started in the 1950s were rebelling against much of (that craft) in the 1960s and 1970s, and now film has become so digital and instantaneous, maybe we are going back to the craft, and Mr Hitchcock was a supreme craftsman.'[4]

'I was privileged to work with Hitchcock and privileged to be close to him,' says Virginia Darcy. 'He had a drive inside him and he was good to a lot of people. Yes, he went over the side sometimes, but I don't know anyone who doesn't.'

EVAN HUNTER

Evan Hunter's working relationship with Hitchcock was as complex at times as the director's was with Tippi Hedren. He was courted – as was his wife, Anita – manipulated, controlled and monopolised by Hitchcock. Long after the release of the film, Evan continued to feel a sense of disappointment about *The Birds*, but he went on to work with the director on *Marnie* because he wanted to continue the relationship. Unfortunately, the misunderstandings, the lack of communication during the writing of the screenplay, and the differing viewpoints that were prevalent during *The Birds*, would reach a crisis point on *Marnie*. For an account on how Evan fared, see the author's book *Hitchcock and the Making of Marnie*.

'I don't think Hitchcock was fair to my script,' Evan said. 'He juggled scenes and cut scenes and even added one scene – the writer of which still remains unknown to me.' Hitchcock put Evan's complaints down to the fact that he was suffering from a bad story notice saying, 'He came up to me the night we showed the film in New York and said he'd read that *Variety* had called the story the weakest thing in the picture. He said to me, "You'll have to help me through this."'

When asked, 'Why was Evan Hunter the ideal writer for this project?' Hitchcock admitted, 'Hunter wasn't the ideal screenwriter. You look around, you pick a writer, hoping for the best.' But Evan felt the blame for the film's shortcomings should be shared by Hitchcock and what he perceived to be a lack of chemistry between the lead actors, and not placed solely on him. 'If there were weaknesses in my screenplay,' Hunter said, 'they should have been pointed out to me before shooting began, and they would have been corrected. I feel the weaknesses were manifold, but only some of them were in the script. The concept of the film was to turn a light love story into a story of blind, unreasoning hatred.'

Perhaps Evan, being a novelist, wasn't as accustomed to the close collaboration that was demanded during the making of a Hitchcock film. He had been given the freedom to write away from the office, which he preferred, whereas Hitchcock, who relished the writing process, boasted that he was with Ernest Lehman for almost a year during *North by Northwest*: 'I was with him on every shot.'[5] Inevitably, the transference of collaboration from screenwriter to production team took place, as

Hitchcock turned to the artistic experience of Bob Boyle, Bob Burks, Albert Whitlock and Harold Michelson to get the film made. However, he did make Evan feel welcome during those times he visited the set, as Evan himself acknowledged in a letter: 'In the meantime, I want to thank you for your graciousness in making me feel so very much at home on the set. I sincerely appreciate it.'[6]

In time, Evan, who had reservations about the script, later came to appreciate it. 'The last time I saw it was on television, with the script in my lap. I felt a little better after that.' In 1971 he wrote a short story called *The Sardinia Incident*, which appeared in *Playboy* magazine. In the story a director is being interviewed, and, in the course of the interview, some accidents occur, brought about by the director because of his jealousy of the leading man. The figure of the director was modelled after Hitchcock, and the leading lady bears some resemblance to a Hitchcock blonde.

THE ACTORS

While feeling that he was handcuffed during the making of *The Birds*, Rod Taylor acknowledges that Hitchcock was a great craftsman. 'It's my number one commercially most important film,' says Rod. 'And I'm stopped more for *The Birds* and *The Time Machine* than any other, but I'm more fond of my other films, such as *Young Cassidy*.' 'It's a really good scary movie,' says Veronica Cartwright. 'I thought the special effects were terrific.' When *The Birds* premiered on network television in the US, on NBC in January 1968, it became the highest-rated movie of all time. It also ran a second time in February 1969 and its record was only shattered four years later by *Love Story* in October 1972.

Tippi Hedren's experience and memories of *The Birds* have been mixed and fluctuating. While she recognises Hitchcock's genius as a filmmaker, in 2012 she publicly complained about the man, accusing him of becoming obsessed with her, which she described as a form of sexual harassment. Hitchcock was intent on making her a star and tried to control her professional and personal life in attempting to achieve his goal.

In his interviews with Peter Bogdanovich in February 1963, Hitchcock talked about his problems in creating stars. 'There's a whole rhythm. It's like this girl, Hedren. Until I have launched them, they belong to me, and they better face that fact. You can't run around with men, you can't start having babies, one thing at a time, get the career going and then start to have the babies.'[7]

Hitchcock's own words clearly indicate what he really thought about the contract system of his stars, and his belief that he owned them. He felt that he was halfway through with Tippi Hedren, and that, with *Marnie*, he would launch her, 'bring her out' and make her a star.[8] Hitchcock felt that performers had to be handled carefully if they were to become box-office stars. 'There isn't enough care taken in the molding of performers into top box-office attractions,' he said, and 'this is a serious matter for the industry. A star used to be made on a series of first-class pictures but we're not making as many pictures these days.'[9] Hitchcock's intention of making a star out of Tippi, leading him to be exacting in his demands about her clothes, hairstyles and publicity build up, may have been interpreted as obsessive behaviour.

'He thought he owned me, but he didn't,' Tippi would say years later.[10] She accompanied Hitchcock on almost all of his personal appearances on behalf of *The Birds* and was the subject of as much publicity as the film itself. During the production of the film, Tippi was dating her agent, Noel Marshall, who she married shortly after the completion of *Marnie* in 1964. This displeased Hitchcock who thought that actors shouldn't marry but remain committed to their craft. After Hitchcock's death in 1980, Tippi confided in biographer Donald Spoto for his book *The Dark Side of Genius*, talking for the first time about Hitchcock's controlling side. 'With Spoto I felt I had found a writer that I could trust,' she said.[11] In 1985, she reunited with crew members from *The Birds* for a viewing of her screen test at the Academy of Motion Pictures (Figure 32). And then, in 2012, to publicise a BBC/HBO television dramatisation about the making of *The Birds* and *Marnie*, Tippi appeared as a guest speaker at the British Film Institute's 'The Genius of Hitchcock' retrospective in London, requesting that Spoto be her interviewer. During the talk, she was very candid in her remarks about Hitchcock, saying she felt he had stalked and sexually harassed her.[12]

The international media basked in Tippi's interviews and labelled Hitchcock a misogynist, sadist and an ogre. However, many of Hitchcock's co-workers on *The Birds* spoke out against such a portrayal in the popular press. Nora Brown, Jim Brown's widow, said to the *Daily Telegraph*, 'From my conversations with my husband, Jim Brown, I doubt that he would have endorsed any of the sexual allegations against Alfred Hitchcock. He had nothing but admiration and respect for Hitch, understood his clever cockney sense of humour, and thought the man a genius. If he was here today, I doubt that he would have any negative comments and would be saddened by the image portrayed of his friend and mentor.'[13] When Jim Brown was interviewed by this author he said, 'I loved Hitchcock as a father, and he treated me like a son. Some of the things that are expressed about him are highly over exaggerated. I think Hitch became upset because he thought Tippi wasn't fulfilling the star quality that he thought she had or was looking for.'[14]

'I don't know what his relationship to Tippi was,' says Veronica Cartwright in response to the media frenzy following the BBC/HBO film. 'I think the story has got a little more exaggerated over the years. You watch that movie, who is fabulous is Jessica Tandy, unbelievable. Some of the looks she gives, the jealousy that comes up, she's the stand out. I thought Hitchcock was fabulous. Maybe Tippi didn't understand his sense of humour. I mean, British sense of humour is a lot different to the American sense of humour. Sometimes I think things are hysterical and other people don't understand it.'

'I never saw nor heard anything about Hitchcock's supposed obsession with Ms Hedren at the time and Evan would have mentioned it if he knew about it,' says Anita Hunter. When Evan was asked in 1998, his response was, 'I don't know what Hitchcock thought about Tippi, he only ever referred to her as "The Girl".'

Only Tippi knows of the private dialogue that took place between Hitchcock and herself. We only know that, when they were alone together, whatever transpired, none of the crew witnessed it. He was indeed possessive of her, as co-star Rod Taylor affirms, not wanting other male cast and crew to ride in the same car with her. But the call sheets testify that most of the time, on location, Tippi rode in the cast car with Peggy Robertson and Suzanne Pleshette, while Rod rode with Ted Parvin and the male crew members. Such segregation between male and female stars was routine during the era of the studio system. The portrayal of sexual harassment and intentional sadistic physical abuse as depicted in the BBC/HBO television dramatisation during the making of *The Birds*, especially the phone booth and attic scenes, was not endorsed by many of the crew members who worked on the film, including Virginia Darcy, Rita Riggs,

Norman Lloyd and Jim Brown, all of whom were willing to be recorded on tape. Neither are some key events portrayed in the television drama supported by the historical archive held at the Margaret Herrick Library, which attests to the value of preserving production reports that are often more reliable than 50-year-old memories.

Aside from its controversy, *The Birds* has had a lasting legacy in film and popular culture. Theatrical trailers, short, punchy radio commercials and lobby spots aimed at cinemagoers, together with a clever marketing campaign, all fuelled the public's interest. 'If you have ever eaten a turkey drumstick, caged a canary or gone duck hunting, *The Birds* will give you something to think about,' Hitchcock said in one radio spot. 'If you are the type of person who goes to a bull fight and roots for the bull, you'll love *The Birds*.'

When *The Birds* debuted, it swiftly became known as a precursor to the modern horror movies. Others that followed in the next few decades included *The Fog* (1980) and *The Mist* (2007). Hitchcock knew that suspense grew from the fear of the unknown, and in allowing the audience to use their imaginations. This use of suggestion, and not visually showing the menace during the attack on the Brenner house, was to become an important influence for many directors in their films. As Roger Corman said, 'Hitchcock's importance to me, personally, is exemplified by the way he reveals his monsters. Whether they be birds or a man dressed as his mother, Hitchcock never lets the audience see the entirety of the monster until the end of the film.' This would be most evident in later monster movies, such as *Jaws* (1975) and *Predator* (1987) where a full sighting of the actual beast is not allowed until near the end of the picture. To reveal the monster too early would be cheating the audience and depriving them of the pleasure of seeing it in all it's glory later on.

The Man versus Monster film would also take the form of Man versus Alien in films such as *Alien* (1980), *The Thing* (1981) and *Close Encounters of the Third Kind* (1983). In *Alien*, Ridley Scott similarly holds back the first full sighting of the alien. '[Hitchcock] was a forbearer for a lot of people in the business now in the way he approached things,' says Veronica Cartwright who was one of the co-stars of *Alien*. 'When that one bird that flies and everyone looks at it. He would tease you and I think that was so interesting. Even when we did *Alien* you didn't see the monster whole in the beginning, you saw little snatches of it so your imagination is what made the whole alien. Because you were tantalised and that's what Hitchcock would do.'

The Birds also started the man-versus-nature cycle. It's of interest to note, that during the film's production in the summer of 1962, *The New Yorker* published excerpts from Rachel Carson's *Silent Spring*, which is credited with launching the environmental movement.[15] Man-versus-nature films that followed *The Birds* include *Jaws* (1975), *The Swarm* (1978), *Arachnophobia* (1997), and the more recent *The Grey* (2012). *The Birds* also influenced the wave of disaster films that defined the 1970s, such as *The Poseidon Adventure* (1972), *Earthquake* (1974) and the genre's revival with films like *Dante's Inferno* (1997) and *Armageddon* (1998).

In the 50 years since its release, *The Birds* has had a tremendous impact on science fiction and popular culture. No other Hitchcock film, apart from *Psycho*, has achieved such long lasting influence and notoriety. With birds a part of our everyday lives, Hitchcock's film is likely to remain in our consciousness for the next 50 years.

NOTES

1 Robert Boyle, 'Roundtable discussion on *The Birds*', 1982
2 Albert Whitlock, 'Roundtable discussion on *The Birds*', 1982
3 Interview with Jim Brown, 1 September 2000, Angels Camp
4 Interview with Rita Riggs, 5 September 2012, Los Angeles
5 Hitchcock to Bogdanovich, 14 February 1962
6 Letter from Evan Hunter to Hitchcock at the Fairmont, 23 March 1962
7 Hitchcock to Bogdanovich, 14 February 1962
8 Hitchcock to Bogdanovich, 14 February 1962
9 Alfred Hitchcock, 'Market Slump for Average Release & New Stars', Wednesday 3 April, 1963
10 Tippi Hedren at the BFI, 'Genius of Hitchcock', 16 August 2012
11 Tippi Hedren interview, 19 June 1999
12 Tippi Hedren at the BFI, 'Genius of Hitchcock', 16 August 2012
13 Anita Singh, 'Alfred Hitchcock Drama *The Girl* Sparks Angry Backlash', *Daily Telegraph*, 22 October 2012
14 Interview with Jim Brown, 1 September 2000, Angels Camp, California
15 Rachel Carson, 'Reporter at Large: Silent Spring', *The New Yorker*, 16 June 1962

Timeline of Events

5 MARCH 1953
The Birds short story is published in the US in 'The Apple Tree'

25 JUNE 1961
Hitchcock acquires *The Birds* story rights from Daphne du Maurier

18 AUGUST 1961
Seagulls smash into Santa Cruz causing damage

18 SEPTEMBER 1961
Evan Hunter begins scriptwriting on *The Birds*

25 SEPTEMBER 1961
Bob Boyle scouts Bodega Bay

13 OCTOBER 1961
Hitchcock spots Tippi Hedren in a television commercial

18 OCTOBER 1961
Tippi signs a seven-year contract with Alfred J Hitchcock Productions

6 NOVEMBER 1961
The Bel Air fire

8 NOVEMBER 1961
Tippi Hedren's screen test

28 NOVEMBER 1961
Hitchcock offers Tippi the lead role in *The Birds*

22 FEBRUARY 1962
Location filming begins in Bodega Bay

31 MARCH 1962
Location filming ends

2 APRIL 1962
Studio filming begins

10 JULY 1962
Studio filming ends

11 JULY 1962
Postproduction begins

14 DECEMBER 1962
Hitchcock and Herrmann travel to Berlin for sound work

27 MARCH 1963
Cancelled preview of *The Birds* at MOMA, NY

28 MARCH 1963
Premiere of *The Birds* in New York

9 APRIL 1963
The Birds opens the Cannes Film Festival in France

31 AUGUST 1963
Premiere of *The Birds* in London

28 MARCH 2013
50th anniversary of *The Birds*

Production Credits

CAST

Mitch Brenner – Rod Taylor
Lydia Brenner – Jessica Tandy
Annie Hayworth – Suzanne Pleshette
Melanie Daniels – 'Tippi' Hedren
Cathy Brenner – Veronica Cartwright
Michelle – Shari Lee Bernath
Mrs Bundy – Ethel Griffies
Sebastian Sholes – Charles McGraw
Mrs MacGruder – Ruth McDevitt
Deke Carter – Lonny Chapman
Deputy Al Malone – Malcolm Atterbury
Mitch's neighbour – Richard Deacon
Helen Carter – Elizabeth Wilson
Hysterical Mother – Doreen Lang

CREW

Producer/Director – Alfred Hitchcock
Screenwriter – Evan Hunter
Assistant to Mr Hitchcock – Peggy Robertson

Assistant Director – James H Brown
Editor – George Tomasini
Director of Photography – Robert Burks
Special Photographic Advisor – Ub Iwerks
Special Effects – Lawrence Hampton
Production Manager – Norman Deming
Production Designer – Robert Boyle
Pictorial Design – Albert Whitlock
Storyboard Illustrator – Harold Michelson
Set Decorator – George Milo
Wardrobe Supervisor – Rita Riggs
Costume Designer – Edith Head
Makeup – Howard Smit
Hairstylist – Virgina Darcy
Titles – James S Pollak
Electronic Sound Production – Remi Gassmann, Oskar Sala
Sound Consultant – Bernard Herrmann
Sound Recording – Waldon Watson, William Russell
Bird Trainer – Ray Berwick
Bird Handler – John 'Bud' Cardos

Select Bibliography

Bogdanovich, Peter, *The Cinema of Alfred Hitchcock* (New York: The Museum of Modern Art Film Library, 1963)

Bogdanovich, Peter, *Who the Devil Made it? Conversations with Legendary Filmmakers* (Knopf, 1997)

Counts, Kyle B, 'The Making of Alfred Hitchcock's *The Birds*', *Cinefantastique* (Volume 10, Number 2, 1980)

du Maurier, Daphne, *The Birds and Other Stories* (Penguin 1963)

Gottlieb, Sidney (ed), *Hitchcock on Hitchcock: Selected Writings and Interviews* (Berkeley: University of California Press, 1995)

Hunter, Evan, *Me and Hitch* (London: Faber and Faber, 1997)

Krohn, Bill, *Hitchcock At Work* (Phaidon Press, 2003)

Moral, Tony Lee, *Hitchcock and the Making of Marnie*, Revised Edition (Maryland: Scarecrow Press, 2013)

Moral, Tony Lee, *Alfred Hitchcock's Movie Making Masterclass* (Michael Wiese Productions, 2013)

Truffaut, François, *Hitchcock*, Revised Edition (Simon & Schuster, 1985)

DVDS

Universal Home Studios, *All About The Birds*, 2000

Raim, Daniel, *Something's Gonna Live*, 2010

Index